1,000
QUESTIONS
& ANSWERS
FACTFILE

1,000
QUESTIONS
& ANSWERS
FACTFILE

KINGFISHER
BOSTON

KINGFISHER

a Houghton Mifflin Company imprint
222 Berkeley Street
Boston, Massachusetts 02116
www.houghtonmifflinbooks.com

First published in 2002
First published in this format in 2006
10 9 8 7 6 5 4 3 2 1

1TR/0406/C&C/UNI/128MA/C

LIBRARY OF CONGRESS CATALOGING-IN-PUBLICATION DATA
has been applied for.

ISBN-13: 978-07534-5947-8
ISBN-10: 0-7534-5947-7

Printed in China

Authors: **Robin Kerrod, Wendy Madgwick,
Sarah Reed, Fergus Collins, Philip Brooks**

Artwork archivists: Wendy Allison and Steve Robinson

Illustrations:
GD Achille, Jonathan Adams, Susanna Addario, Graham Allen, Marion Appleton, Norman Arlott, Julian Baker,
Sue Barclay, Andrew Beckett, Owain Bell, Gary Bines, Simone Boni, Richard Bonson, Peter Bull, J. Burgess,
John Butler, Vanessa Card, Robin Carter, Jim Channel, Kuo Kang Chen, Dan Cole, Stephen Conlin, David Cook,
Peter Dennis, Francis D'Ohani, Francesca D'Ottavi, Sandra Doyle, R. Draper, Lee Edwards, Angelika Elsebach,
James Field, Wayne Ford, Chris Forsey, Terry Gaby, Luigi Galante, Lee Gibbons, Peter Goodfellow, Jeremy Gower,
Ruby Green, Peter Gregory, Ray Grinaway, Alan Hardcastle, Martin Hargreaves, David Harley, Alan Harris, Nick
Harris, Nicholas Hewitson, Steve Homes, Tim Hayward, Adam Hook, Christian Hook, Biz Hull, David Hurrel,
Mark Iley, Ian Jackson, John James, Roger Kent, Martin Knowlden, Eddy Krähenbühl, Stuart Lafford, Terence
Lambert, Ruth Lindsay, Bernard Long, Mike Loates, Steiner Lund, Chris Lyons, David McAllister, Angus McBride,
Doreen McGuinness, Brian Mcintyre, Kevin Maddison, Shirley Mallinson, Janos Marffy, John Marshall, Josephine
Martin, Robert Morton, William Oliver, Nicki Palin, Alex Pang, Roger Payne, Bruce Pearson, Mark Pepe,
Melvyn Pickering, Sebastian Quigley, John Rignall, Andrew Robinson, Bernard Robinson, Eric Robson, Michael
Roffe, Mike Saunders, Chris Shields, Nick Shrewring, Tim Slade, Guy Smith, Tom Smith, Mark Stacey, Roger
Stewart, Mike Taylor, George Thompson, Ian Thompson, Shirley Tourret, Kevin Toy, Rose Walton, Wendy Webb,
Andrea Wheatcroft, Sohraya Willis, Ann Winterbotham, Dan Wright, David Wright

Picture credits
p.94 tl courtesy of the Department Library Services, American Museum of Natural History, Neg. no.410 764,
Shackelford 1925; p.204 tr Nokia; p.207 br Science Photo Library; p.209 c Science Photo Library/Mehau Kulyk;
p.227 cl Nokia; p.229 bl Mary Evans Picture Library; p.249 br Science Picture Library; p.263 b Princess Cruises

Contents

Dinosaurs

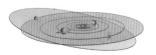

Ancient Civilizations

Knights and Castles

Inventions

Transportation

1,000
QUESTIONS
& ANSWERS
FACTFILE

STARS AND
PLANETS

Contents

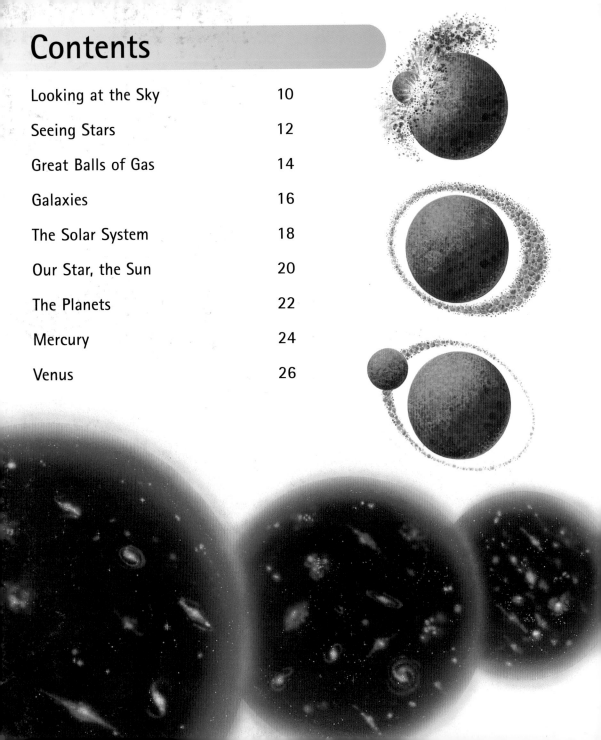

Looking at the Sky

The night sky is one of the most beautiful sights in nature. Stars beyond number shine out of a velvety blackness, bright planets wander among the stars, and long-tailed comets come and go. Astronomy, the study of the night sky, is one of the most ancient sciences.

What can we see?

We can see many things in the night sky with just our eyes, but we can see much more through binoculars or a telescope. To the naked eye, the moon looks small, and we see few features. With binoculars or a telescope, it looks larger, and we can see craters on its surface.

When did people first study the stars?

People must have been stargazing for millions of years. But they probably began studying the night sky seriously about 5,000 years ago. Early civilizations in the Middle East left records of their observations. The Babylonians were skilled observers, and we know the Egyptians were too, because they lined up their pyramids with certain constellations, or star patterns. In England, around 2800 B.C., Stonehenge was built, possibly as a kind of observatory. Stones were lined up with the positions of the sun and moon in different seasons. Ancient Chinese and Mayan astronomers left accurate records of their observations.

Stonehenge

Constellations

Shafts   Pyramid

Mayan astronomer

Ancient Egyptian astronomer-priests

Ancient Chinese star map

Aerial telescope

Who first used telescopes?

The first telescope was built in the Netherlands in about 1608, but it was Galileo, an Italian, who first used one to study the night sky. He made his first observations in the winter of 1609–1610. He saw the moons of Jupiter, craters on Earth's moon, and spots on the sun. Galileo's telescope was quite small. Later devices, known as aerial telescopes, were around 165 feet long.

Sunspots

Moon craters

Jupiter   Galileo's telescope

How do radio telescopes work?

Stars give off radio waves as well as light waves. Astronomers have built telescopes to pick up these radio waves. Radio telescopes are not like light telescopes. Most are huge, metal dishes that can be tilted and turned to any part of the sky. The dishes pick up radio waves, or signals, and focus them onto an antenna. The signals are sent to a receiver and then to a computer, which changes them into images.

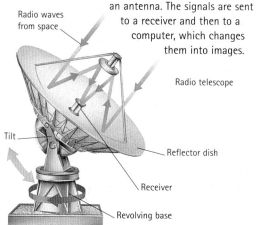

Radio waves from space

Radio telescope

Tilt

Reflector dish

Receiver

Revolving base

Quick-fire Quiz

1. What is the study of stars called?
a) Astronautics
b) Astronomy
c) Aerobics

2. Who first studied the stars using a telescope?
a) The Britons
b) The Mayans
c) Galileo

3. How long were some of the early aerial telescopes?
a) 6 feet
b) 65 feet
c) 165 feet

4. Where are modern observatories built?
a) On the moon
b) On mountains
c) In valleys

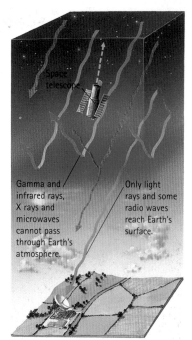

Space telescope

Gamma and infrared rays, X rays and microwaves cannot pass through Earth's atmosphere.

Only light rays and some radio waves reach Earth's surface.

Where do astronomers work?

Astronomers look at, or observe, the stars from observatories. The great domes on these observatories house big telescopes that use curved mirrors to collect the light from the stars. Some mirrors are as big as 33 feet across. Modern-day astronomers do not often look through these telescopes. Instead they use them as giant cameras and take pictures with them. Most observatories today are built on mountains, above the thickest part of the atmosphere, where the air is cleaner and clearer.

What is special about space telescopes?

Some of the most outstanding discoveries of recent years have been made by space telescopes. In space, telescopes can get a much clearer view of the night sky than they can from Earth. Also, space telescopes can pick up invisible rays, such as X rays, which cannot pass through the atmosphere.

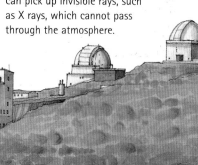

Seeing Stars

Using just your eyes, you can see thousands of stars in the night sky. If you look closely, you will see that some are brighter than others. The bright stars make patterns that you can recognize every time you go stargazing. We call them constellations.

Northern Hemisphere
Ursa Minor
Celestial sphere
Earth's axis
Plane of equator
Equator
Plane of eclipse (path of the sun)
Southern Hemisphere
Southern Cross

The signs of the zodiac

Can we all see the same stars?

Because Earth is round and rotates on its north-south axis, we only see the stars above the hemisphere in which we live. Earth seems to be in the middle of a great, dark ball, which we call the celestial sphere. People in the far north can always see the Ursa Minor (Little Bear), but never the Southern Cross, which is seen in the far south. In the far south, no one ever sees the Ursa Minor. People near the equator can see almost all the stars at some time of the year.

What are star signs?

During the year, the sun appears to move through the stars of the celestial sphere. It seems to pass through 12 main constellations, called the constellations of the zodiac, or star signs. They are important in astrology because astrologers believe that human lives are affected by the stars.

Leo the Lion

Scorpio the Scorpion

The night sky in the
Southern Hemisphere

Some of the major constellations

Northern Hemisphere	Southern Hemisphere
1. Pegasus	1. Aquarius (The Water-bearer)
2. Perseus	2. Orion (The Hunter)
3. North Star	3. Scorpio (The Scorpion)
4. Ursa Minor (Little Bear)	4. Southern Cross
5. Ursa Major	5. Hydra (Water Snake)
6. Leo (The Lion)	6. Libra (Scales)

Quick-fire Quiz

1. What is a pattern of bright stars called?
a) Congregation
b) Constellation
c) Configuration

2. From where can you see Ursa Minor?
a) Everywhere
b) The south
c) The north

3. Which way do the stars seem to travel overhead?
a) North to south
b) East to west
c) West to east

4. How many star signs are there?
a) 10
b) 12
c) 20

Why do the stars move across the sky?

If you go stargazing at night, you will notice that the constellations gradually move across the sky from east to west, as the sun does during the day. Ancient astronomers thought that the stars were fixed on the inside of the celestial sphere and that this sphere was spinning around Earth, which stood still. We now know that the opposite is true. It is Earth that is moving and the stars that are standing still. Earth spins around in space, moving from west to east. This makes the stars appear to travel in the opposite direction.

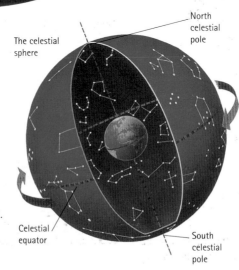

The celestial sphere

North celestial pole

Celestial equator

South celestial pole

Great Balls of Gas

Stars might look like tiny, bright specks in the night sky, but they are not tiny at all. They are actually huge balls of searing hot gas. They only look small because they are many millions of miles away. If you could get closer to the stars, they would look more like our sun— because the sun is a star too.

Do stars last forever?

No. Stars are born, grow older, and eventually die. The diagram below shows two different ways in which stars can die. After shining steadily for some time stars swell up into red giants. If a star has about the same mass as the sun, it shrinks to become a white dwarf, then a black dwarf star. Larger stars swell up from a red giant into a supergiant before exploding as a supernova.

Outer layers break away

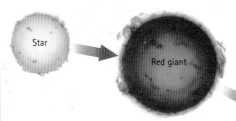

Star

Red giant

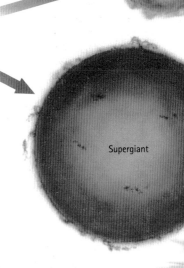

Supergiant

Quick-fire Quiz

1. What is an exploding star called?
a) Supergiant
b) Supernova
c) Superstar

2. What will our sun be one day?
a) Supernova
b) Black dwarf
c) Black hole

3. Which is the hottest?
a) The sun
b) Red giant
c) Blue-white star

4. Which is the smallest?
a) The sun
b) Supergiant
c) Pulsar

How big are stars?

We can measure the size of one star directly, because it is so close. This is our own star, the sun. The sun measures about 865,000 miles across. Astronomers can figure out the size of other stars too. They have discovered that there are many stars smaller than the sun, and also many much larger. Astronomers call the sun a dwarf star. They know of red giant stars that are many times bigger, and supergiant stars that are bigger still. Some supergiants measure 250 million miles across.

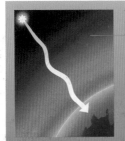

Why do stars twinkle?

When we look up at the sky, we can see thousands of stars shining down, but they do not give off a steady light. They seem to twinkle, or change brightness all the time. In fact, they do shine steadily, but air currents in Earth's atmosphere make the light bend. Some of the light gets into our eyes, and some is bent away. So, to us on Earth, the stars seem to twinkle.

How hot are stars?

Stars are great globes of very hot gas, but their temperatures vary. Astronomers can tell the temperature of a star by the color and brightness of the light it gives off. Yellowish stars like the sun have a temperature of about 10,000°F. Dim red stars are about 5,800°F, but blue-white stars can reach 50,000°F.

White dwarf

Dead black dwarf

Why do some stars explode?

Massive stars explode when they come to the end of their lives. They swell up into huge supergiants. Supergiants are unstable, so they collapse and blast into pieces in an explosion called a supernova. Supernovae are the most intense explosions in the universe, as bright as billions of suns put together.

Star

Black hole

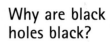

Black hole

Why are black holes black?

After a star explodes as a supernova, what is left of it shrinks rapidly. If the star was very large, it shrinks to almost nothing. All that is left is a tiny area of space that has enormous gravity. The gravity's pull is so great that it will suck in any nearby matter, including other stars. The area is called a "black hole" because the pull it exerts is so powerful that even light cannot escape it.

What is a pulsar?

A smaller star that explodes as a supernova ends its life as a tiny star called a pulsar. It gets this name because it "pulsates," or sends out pulses of energy. Astronomers think that pulsars spin around quickly, sending out narrow beams of energy. On Earth, we see a pulse of energy as light when this beam sweeps past us.

A pulsar passing Earth

Supernova

Pulsar

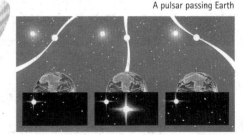

Galaxies

From Earth, space seems to be full of stars. But if you traveled far away from Earth, you would eventually leave the stars behind. Looking back, you would see that the stars form a kind of island in space. In other directions, you would see other star islands, which we call galaxies. The galaxies and the space they occupy make up the universe.

The Local Group

Milky Way

Andromeda

Do all galaxies look alike?

Astronomers can see galaxies of all shapes and sizes through their telescopes. Some are known as barred spiral galaxies. They have curved arms coming from a bar through the center (1). Ordinary spirals do not have the bar. Elliptical galaxies (2) have an oval shape. Galaxies with no particular shape are called irregulars (3).

What is the Local Group of galaxies?

There are thousands of galaxies in space. Many are in groups called clusters. Earth's galaxy is called the Milky Way, which is in a cluster called the Local Group. The Milky Way is the second-largest galaxy in the Local Group. The largest is the Andromeda galaxy.

How do galaxies form?

Galaxies start to form in clouds of dark gas so huge that even light would take hundreds of thousands of years to cross them. Over time, gravity begins to pull the particles of gas together. Gradually, the gas cloud shrinks and becomes more and more dense. Here and there it becomes dense enough for stars to form. At the same time, the gas cloud begins to rotate and flatten out.

1 A huge cloud of gas shrinks and becomes denser. Stars form in the center.

2 The starry cloud spins and flattens into a disk shape.

3 Matter in the disk collects on arms, where more stars form.

How did the universe begin?

Astronomers believe that the universe began about 13 billion years ago with a huge explosion known as the Big Bang. The Big Bang created a hot bubble of space that has been getting bigger and bigger ever since. Astronomers believe the universe is constantly expanding.

Big Bang

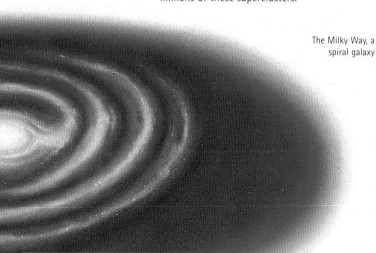

The universe expands after the Big Bang

What makes up the universe?

Simply speaking, the universe is made up of matter and space. The matter is found as planets, moons, and stars. The stars gather together into great galaxies, and the galaxies gather into groups, or clusters. Even the clusters gather together to form gigantic superclusters of galaxies. The universe is made up of millions of these superclusters.

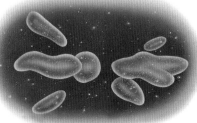
Superclusters

The Milky Way, a spiral galaxy

What are quasars?

Quasars look like stars. But they are so far away that, for us to detect them, they must be brighter than thousands of galaxies put together. Astronomers think quasars get their great power from black holes. As matter is sucked into a black hole, enormous energy is given off as light and other radiation.

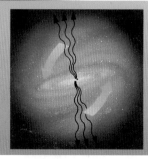

The Solar System

Every day, the sun travels across the sky from east to west. It seems to circle around Earth, but the opposite is true—Earth circles around the sun. Earth is one of nine planets orbiting the sun. Together, the sun and the planets make up the solar system.

How big is the solar system?

Earth is about 93 million miles from the sun. This seems like a huge distance, but it is only a small step in space. The farthest planets are billions of miles away from the sun. The diagram on the right shows the orbits, or paths, of the nine planets around the sun. The distance from one side of Pluto's orbit to the other is over 9 billion miles. It takes Pluto 249 years to orbit the sun.

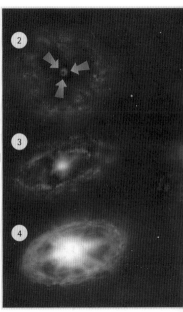

Who first realized that Earth travels around the sun?

Early astronomers thought the sun and other planets circled the Earth. Nicolaus Copernicus (1473–1543) was a Polish priest and astronomer. He came up with the theory that the sun was the center of the universe, and that Earth and the planets moved around it. This was the first real challenge to the idea that Earth was the center of the universe, which ancient astronomers believed. Copernicus published his theory while he lay dying in 1543, but religious leaders opposed his ideas for many years.

What happened at the birth of the solar system?

1 The solar system was born in a great cloud of gas and dust about 5 billion years ago. There are many clouds like this, called nebulae, in the spaces between the stars.

The orbits of the planets around the sun

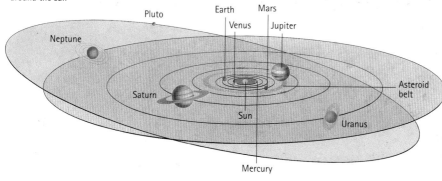

Pluto
Neptune
Earth
Mars
Venus
Jupiter
Saturn
Sun
Mercury
Uranus
Asteroid belt

5

6

7

2 Some parts of the cloud became much denser. Gas and dust in these areas started to stick together due to the pull of their gravity. In time, they formed into a ball-shaped mass.

3 The ball shrank and warmed up. Slowly, it started to glow, forming a "baby" sun by the time it was about 100,000 years old.

4 The baby sun was spinning rapidly, flinging out masses of material into space. At the same time it was shrinking and getting hotter and hotter.

5 In time, the baby sun grew hot enough to set off nuclear reactions. These produced the fantastic energy it needed to shine as a "grown-up" star.

6 The ring of material thrown out earlier by the sun began to clump together. It gradually formed larger and larger lumps at different distances from the sun.

7 The large lumps grew into the planets we know today. Smaller lumps formed the moons of the planets, and even smaller lumps formed the asteroids.

Our Star, the Sun

The sun is our local star. Like other stars, it is a ball of very hot gas. It lies about 93 million miles from Earth and is about 865,000 miles across. The sun pours huge amounts of energy into space. The light and heat that reach Earth make life possible.

Where does the sun get its energy?

The energy that keeps the sun shining is produced in its center, or core. The pressure in the core is enormous, and the temperature reaches 27 million °F. Under these conditions, atoms of hydrogen gas fuse (join together) to form another gas, helium. This process is called nuclear fusion. It produces enormous amounts of energy.

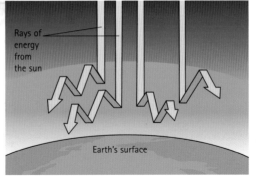

Hydrogen atoms

Helium atom

Energy

What is the sun's surface like?

The sun's surface is a bubbling, boiling mass of very hot gas, constantly in motion, like a stormy sea. Here and there, fountains of flaming gas thousands of miles high shoot out. These fountains, called prominences, eventually curve over and fall back. Violent explosions called flares also often take place, blasting particles into space that can cause magnetic storms on Earth.

Rays of energy from the sun

Earth's surface

What happens when the sun warms Earth?

The sun pours energy onto Earth, warming the land and the water in the oceans. Gases in the air trap the heat and warm the atmosphere. They act like a greenhouse, so the warming process is called the "greenhouse effect." One of the main gases that traps heat is carbon dioxide, produced when fuels burn.

Quick-fire Quiz

1. What is an explosion on the sun called?
a) Prominence
b) Flare
c) Sunspot

2. What produces the sun's energy?
a) Burning coal
b) Burning hydrogen
c) Nuclear fusion

3. Which gas in air traps heat?
a) Nitrogen
b) Carbon dioxide
c) Oxygen

4. How many more years will the sun last?
a) 50 million
b) 500 million
c) 5 billion

Is it safe to look at the sun?

Never look directly at the sun. Its light is so bright that it can damage your eyes and even blind you. Instead, use binoculars or a telescope to throw an image onto paper, and look at that.

What is the sun like inside?

The sun is made up of many layers. In the center is the very hot core, where energy is produced. This energy travels in the form of radiation to the outer layer, called the convection region. There, currents of hot gas carry the energy to the surface (photosphere), where it escapes as light and heat. The temperature of the surface is about 10,000°F. Sunspots are dark patches on the surface. They are about 2,000°F cooler. Some sunspots grow to be bigger than Earth.

Why do eclipses happen?

Occasionally, the moon moves across the face of the sun during the day, blotting out its light and casting a dark shadow on Earth. Day turns suddenly into night. We call this a total eclipse of the sun. Eclipses occur because, from Earth, the moon seems to be almost the same size as the sun and can cover it up. Total eclipses can only be seen over a small part of Earth because the moon casts only a small shadow.

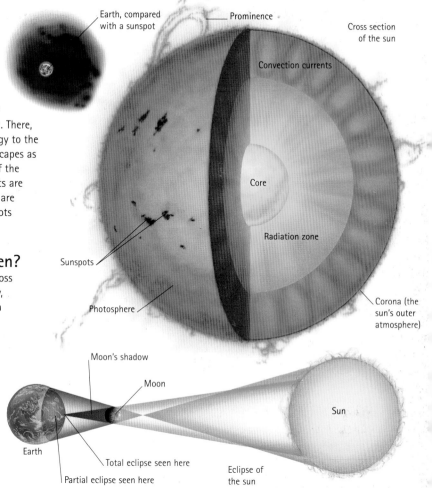

Earth, compared with a sunspot

Prominence

Cross section of the sun

Convection currents

Core

Radiation zone

Corona (the sun's outer atmosphere)

Sunspots

Photosphere

Moon's shadow

Moon

Sun

Earth

Total eclipse seen here

Partial eclipse seen here

Eclipse of the sun

Will the sun always shine?

1 The sun was born, along with the rest of the solar system, about 5 billion years ago. It has been shining steadily ever since.

2 In another 5 billion years, the sun will swell up and get hotter. Earth's oceans will boil away, and all life will die.

3 As the sun gets bigger, hotter, and redder, Earth will be scorched to a cinder. In time, it may be swallowed by the sun's outer layers.

4 The red giant sun will gradually begin to shrink again. Eventually it will become a white dwarf star about the size of Earth, and finally a black dwarf.

The Planets

The nine planets are the most important members of the solar system. In order of distance from the sun, they are Mercury, Venus, Earth, Mars, Jupiter, Saturn, Uranus, Neptune, and Pluto. The first four are small, rocky bodies. The next four are giants, made mainly of gas. Pluto is a tiny ball of rock and ice.

Jupiter

Mercury

Venus

Earth

Mars

How big are the planets?

The pictures on these two pages show the relative sizes of the planets. You might think that Earth is a big place. But look how much bigger some of the other planets are! Even the largest planets, however, are dwarfed by the sun. The sun is nearly ten times bigger across than Jupiter, and it could swallow more than a million Earths. However, Earth is bigger than four of the planets— nearby Venus, Mars, and Mercury, and tiny, distant Pluto.

Sun

Which is the biggest planet?

Jupiter is by far the largest of the planets. It has more mass than all the other planets put together. It measures nearly 89,000 miles across, which is 11 times bigger than Earth. Despite its huge size, it takes less than 10 hours for it to spin around once. This means that its surface is spinning around at a speed of 28,000 miles per hour. This is 30 times faster than Earth spins.

Which planets have rings?

Once it was thought that Saturn was the only planet that had rings around it because they are the only ones that can be seen through a telescope. But close-up photographs taken by the *Voyager* space probes have shown us that the other three gas giants—Jupiter, Uranus, and Neptune—have rings too. The rings around these other planets are much thinner, narrower, and darker than Saturn's.

Why is Uranus sometimes called "new"?

Astronomers have studied the planets for thousands of
years. They have watched the way they move, or "wander,"
across the stationary stars in the night sky. But ancient
astronomers could see only five planets in the night
sky. Not until 1781, when a powerful enough
telescope was built, could we see other planets.
That year, Uranus was the first of three "new"
planets to be discovered. Neptune was discovered
in 1846, and Pluto was discovered in 1930.

Uranus

What is special about Saturn?

Two things are outstanding about Saturn. One is obvious when
you look at the planet through a telescope—the planet is surrounded
by a set of bright, shining rings. Many people think the rings make
Saturn the most beautiful object in the solar system. The other
special thing about Saturn is that it is the lightest (least dense)
of all the planets. It is lighter even than water. This means that
if you could place it in a huge bowl of water, it would float.

Rings

Which planet is
farthest from the sun?

As far as we know, the most distant planet
from the sun is Pluto, the last "new" planet to be
discovered. But Pluto is not always the farthest away.
For 20 years, between 1979 and 1999, Neptune was
farther away because Pluto was
traveling inside Neptune's orbit.
Neptune will become the farthest
planet again in a little over 200 years'
time. Pluto travels more than 4 billion miles
away from the sun and it takes nearly 249 Earth
years for Pluto to orbit the sun once.

Saturn

Pluto

Neptune

Mercury

Mercury

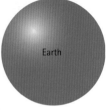
Earth

Mercury is the closest planet to the sun. It is also the fastest-moving planet, whizzing around the sun in just 88 days. Mercury is very hot during the day and very cold at night. Its surface is covered in thousands of craters, much like the moon.

How big is Mercury?
Mercury is the smallest of the rocky, Earthlike planets. With a diameter of only 3,032 miles, it is less than half the size of Earth. But the planet Pluto, a deep-frozen ball of rock and ice, is even smaller.

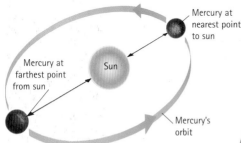

Mercury at nearest point to sun

Mercury at farthest point from sun

Sun

Mercury's orbit

What is strange about Mercury's orbit?
Most planets have a nearly circular orbit, or path, around the sun. Mercury, however, has an oval orbit. At times it travels as far as 43 million miles away from the sun. At others, it gets as close as 29 million miles.

Why does Mercury get so hot?
Because Mercury swings so close to the sun, daytime temperatures on the planet can soar to 800°F—hot enough to melt lead. But when Mercury is farther from the sun, nighttime temperatures can drop as low as -280°F.

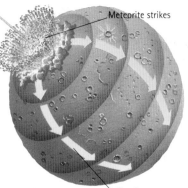

Meteorite strikes

Why does Mercury have craters?

Billions of years ago, all the planets were bombarded by huge meteorites. The impact of these meteorites formed craters. On Earth, most craters were worn away by the weather. Because Mercury has no atmosphere, there is no wind or rain. Its craters still remain, and the planet's surface is covered with them. One huge crater, called the Caloris Basin, was made by a giant meteorite that sent shock waves all around the planet.

Shock waves

Caloris Basin

Craters

What is Mercury made of?

Like Earth and the other rocky planets, Mercury is made up of different layers. Underneath the rocky crust is a rocky mantle, and at the center is a huge, metal core. The shrinking of the core has caused great ridges up to 2 miles high on the surface.

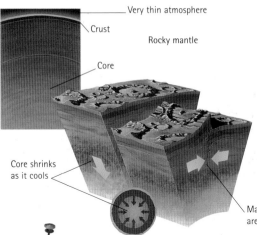

Very thin atmosphere

Crust

Rocky mantle

Core

Core shrinks as it cools

Mantle and crust are squeezed

Have any space probes visited Mercury?

Only one space probe has studied Mercury. Named *Mariner 10*, it flew to the planet in 1974, after visiting Venus. Its pictures revealed for the first time that Mercury looked a lot like some parts of the moon. *Mariner 10* flew past Mercury two more times. The US *Messenger* craft will fly by Mercury in 2008 and 2009 and will begin a year-long orbit of the planet in 2011.

Mariner 10

MERCURY DATA

Diameter at equator: 3032 mi.
Mass: 0.06 times Earth's mass
Average distance from sun: 36 million mi.
Minimum distance from Earth: 57 million mi.
Length of day: 59 Earth days
Length of year: 88 Earth days
Temperature: -280°F to 800°F
Satellites: 0

Venus

Venus's orbit brings it closer to Earth than any of the other planets. It is often seen shining in the western sky after sunset, which is why it is known as the Evening Star. Venus is about the same size as Earth, but it is waterless with a scorching climate.

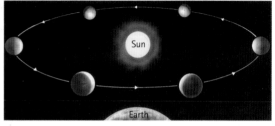
Venus in orbit

Why does Venus change shape?

From Earth, Venus seems to change its shape and size over time. This is because it orbits closer to the sun than Earth. When it is on the far side of the sun, we see it as a small circle. As it moves closer to Earth, it appears bigger, but we only see it as part of a circle. Finally, it is just a thin crescent.

What is the surface of Venus like?

Space probes have shown that great plains cover much of Venus's surface. There are two big highland regions, which we can think of as continents. One, found in the north, is called Ishtar Terra. The other, found near the equator, is called Aphrodite Terra.

Venus landscape

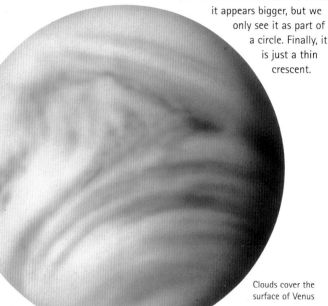
Clouds cover the surface of Venus

Why is Venus so cloudy?

We cannot see Venus's surface from Earth because of thick clouds in its atmosphere. These clouds are not like the clouds on Earth, which are made up of tiny water droplets. Venus's clouds are made up of tiny droplets of sulphuric acid, one of the strongest acids we know. The sulphur was spewed into the atmosphere from the many volcanoes that have erupted on Venus over the years.

How can we see through Venus's clouds?

Space probes can see through Venus's clouds to show us what the planet's surface is like. But they do not "see" ordinary light. They "see" with radar beams, because radar beams can go through clouds. The most successful radar probe, named *Magellan*, mapped the entire planet between 1990 and 1992. A new mission arrives in April 2006.

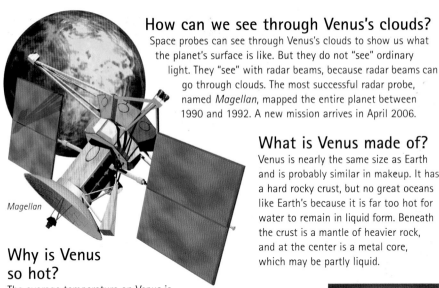

Magellan

What is Venus made of?

Venus is nearly the same size as Earth and is probably similar in makeup. It has a hard rocky crust, but no great oceans like Earth's because it is far too hot for water to remain in liquid form. Beneath the crust is a mantle of heavier rock, and at the center is a metal core, which may be partly liquid.

Why is Venus so hot?

The average temperature on Venus is more than twice as hot as an oven set on "high." This is because its atmosphere contains mainly carbon dioxide, a heavy gas that traps heat. Over the years, it has caused the atmosphere to trap more and more heat, as a greenhouse does. The cloud layers trap heat too, making the temperature reach a scorching 865°F.

Venus's atmosphere

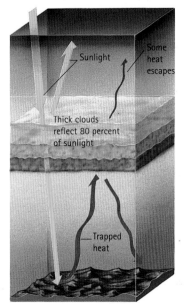

Sunlight

Some heat escapes

Thick clouds reflect 80 percent of sunlight

Trapped heat

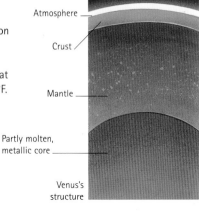

Atmosphere

Crust

Mantle

Partly molten, metallic core

Venus's structure

VENUS DATA

Diameter at equator: *7,521 mi.*
Average distance from sun: *67 million mi.*
Minimum distance from Earth: *26 million mi.*
Length of day: *243 Earth days*
Length of year: *225 Earth days*
Surface temperature: *865°F*
Satellites: *0*

Earth

From space our home planet appears to be mainly blue in color. This is the color of the oceans, which cover over two thirds of Earth's surface. The land areas, or continents, cover less than a third. The layer of air above the surface is thin, but it makes life on Earth possible.

Earth

What causes day and night?

Almost every place on Earth has a time when it is light (day), followed by a time when it is dark (night). Day and night occur because Earth spins around in space, so different parts of its surface face the sun at different times. It is day when a place is on the side of Earth facing the sun. It becomes night when the place is on the side facing away from the sun.

Earth land and seascape

What makes Earth different?

A number of things make Earth different from the other planets. It is covered with great oceans of water, and its atmosphere contains a lot of oxygen. The atmosphere also acts like a blanket, holding in enough of the sun's heat to keep Earth at a comfortable temperature. The water, the oxygen, and the temperature make Earth a suitable place for living things— at least one and a half million different kinds of plants and animals.

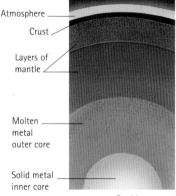

Atmosphere

Crust

Layers of mantle

How has Earth changed?

Earth formed about 4.6 billion years ago when bits of matter in space came together (1). At first, Earth was a great, molten ball (2). It gradually cooled, and the atmosphere and oceans formed (3). In time, it changed into the world we know today (4 and 5), made up of layers of rock with a metal core. Our world is still changing. Currents in the rocks beneath the crust are widening the oceans and driving the continents farther apart (see below).

Molten metal outer core

Solid metal inner core

Earth's structure

Quick-fire Quiz

1. How many years old is Earth?
a) 4.6 million
b) 4.6 billion
c) 46 billion

2. How long does it take Earth to circle the sun?
a) 265.25 days
b) 365.25 days
c) 465.25 days

3. What is Earth?
a) A star
b) A meteorite
c) A planet

4. What causes the seasons?
a) Tilting Earth
b) Tilting sun
c) Tilting moon

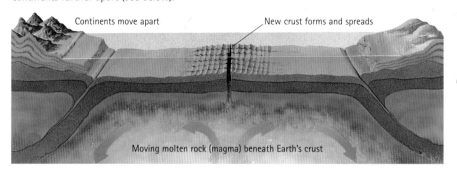

Continents move apart

New crust forms and spreads

Moving molten rock (magma) beneath Earth's crust

What causes the seasons?

The changes in weather that we call the seasons happen because of the way Earth's axis is tilted in space. Because of this tilt, some places lean more toward the sun at some times of the year than at others. It is this that causes the changing seasons. When a place is tilted toward the sun, it is summer. When a place is leaning away, it is winter.

Over thousands of years, Earth's orbit changes from circular to elongated.

EARTH DATA

Diameter at equator: 7,926 mi.
Average distance from sun: 93 million mi.
Length of day: 23 hours, 56 minutes
Year length: 365.25 days
Surface temperature: -129°F to 136°F
Satellites: 1 (the moon)

Northern winter

Fall

Spring

March 21

Sun

June 21, the longest day in the north

Northern summer

Axis

December 21

September 23

Southern summer

Spring

Fall

Southern winter

The Moon

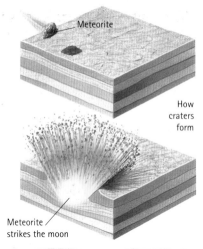

Meteorite

How craters form

Meteorite strikes the moon

Any object that orbits a planet is called a satellite or a moon. Our moon, Earth's nearest neighbor in space, circles Earth once a month. We can see it clearly through telescopes, and astronauts have explored it on foot. It is about one fourth the diameter of Earth. It has no atmosphere, no weather, and no life.

How did the moon form?

Most astronomers think that the moon formed after another large body smashed into Earth billions of years ago (1). Material from Earth and the other body were flung into space. In time, this material came together to form the moon (2). This explains why moon rocks are different from rocks on Earth.

1

2

When did astronauts land on the moon?

The first astronauts landed on the moon on July 20, 1969. They were Edwin Aldrin and Neil Armstrong, the crew of the lunar landing module of the *Apollo 11* spacecraft. Armstrong was the first person to stand on the moon. There were five more lunar landings— one in 1969, two in 1971, and two in 1972.

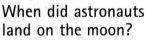

Moon rock

Terraced crater

Concentric crater

Ray crater

Ghost crater

What made the moon's craters?

The surface of the moon is covered with thousands of pits, or craters. They have been made by meteorites raining down from outer space. Most large craters have stepped, or terraced, walls and mountain peaks in the middle. The largest craters are more than 125 miles across. Some recent craters have bright streaks, or rays, coming from them, while only the tips of some old "ghost" craters can be seen.

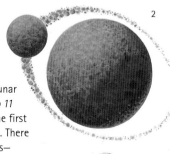

Where are the moon's seas?

Early astronomers thought that the dark areas we see on the moon might be seas. They called them "maria," the Latin word for "seas." We now know that they are vast, dusty plains, but we still call them seas. Most seas are found on the side of the moon that always faces Earth, the near side. There are only one or two small seas on the opposite, or far, side.

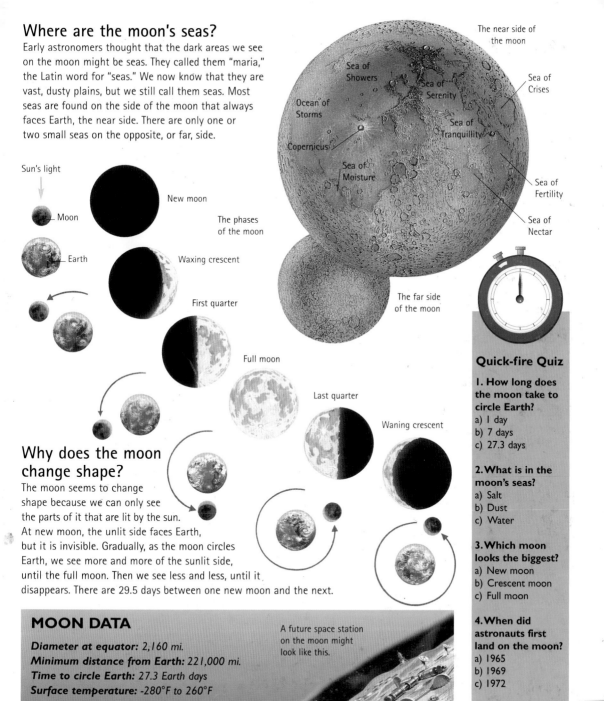

The near side of the moon

Sea of Showers

Ocean of Storms

Sea of Serenity

Sea of Crises

Sea of Tranquillity

Copernicus

Sea of Moisture

Sea of Fertility

Sea of Nectar

The far side of the moon

Sun's light

Moon

Earth

New moon

The phases of the moon

Waxing crescent

First quarter

Full moon

Last quarter

Waning crescent

Why does the moon change shape?

The moon seems to change shape because we can only see the parts of it that are lit by the sun. At new moon, the unlit side faces Earth, but it is invisible. Gradually, as the moon circles Earth, we see more and more of the sunlit side, until the full moon. Then we see less and less, until it disappears. There are 29.5 days between one new moon and the next.

MOON DATA

Diameter at equator: 2,160 mi.
Minimum distance from Earth: 221,000 mi.
Time to circle Earth: 27.3 Earth days
Surface temperature: -280°F to 260°F

A future space station on the moon might look like this.

Quick-fire Quiz

1. How long does the moon take to circle Earth?
a) 1 day
b) 7 days
c) 27.3 days

2. What is in the moon's seas?
a) Salt
b) Dust
c) Water

3. Which moon looks the biggest?
a) New moon
b) Crescent moon
c) Full moon

4. When did astronauts first land on the moon?
a) 1965
b) 1969
c) 1972

Mars

Small and red in color, Mars is more like Earth than any other planet. People once believed that intelligent beings lived on Mars, but space probes have shown that there are no Martians, and no other life on the planet. It is too cold, and the atmosphere is too thin for life to exist.

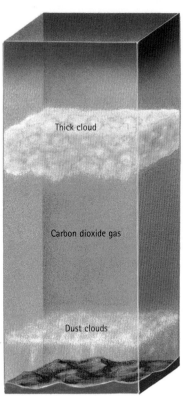

Mars's atmosphere

Thick cloud

Carbon dioxide gas

Dust clouds

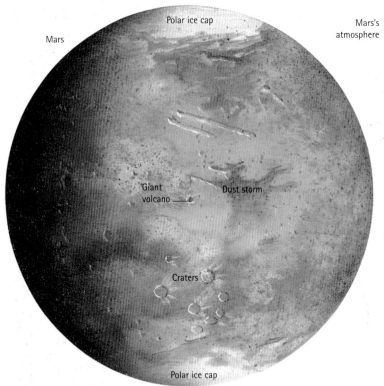

Mars

Polar ice cap

Giant volcano

Dust storm

Craters

Polar ice cap

What is Mars made of?

Mars is a rocky planet, with a makeup similar to Earth's. It has a hard crust, a rocky mantle, and an iron core. Its atmosphere, however, is much thinner than Earth's. The atmospheric pressure on Mars is only about one hundredth of what it is on Earth. The main gas in the Martian atmosphere is carbon dioxide, instead of nitrogen and oxygen, as on Earth. There is very little moisture in the atmosphere, and no oceans, lakes, or rivers. Around the cold poles, the moisture freezes to form the planet's ice caps. Although Mars is similar to Earth in some ways, it is much smaller.

Why is Mars called the "Red Planet"?

Astronomers call Mars the "Red Planet" because of the red-orange color of its surface. This color comes from the rustlike iron minerals in the surface rocks and soil.

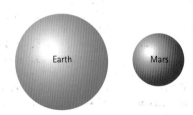

Earth

Mars

MARS DATA

Diameter at equator: *4,223 mi.*
Average distance from sun:
142 million mi.
Minimum distance from Earth:
35 million mi.
Length of day:
24 hours, 37 minutes
Length of year: *687 Earth days*
Surface temperature:
-184°F to 63°F
Satellites: *2*

Viking lander

The *Sojourner* rover

Deimos

Phobos

Does Mars have moons?

Mars has two small moons, Phobos and Deimos. Phobos is larger than Deimos, but it is less than 20 miles across. Astronomers believe they were once asteroids, captured by Mars's gravity.

Which space probes explored Mars?

In 1965, *Mariner 4* flew past Mars and sent back pictures. *Mariner 6* and *7* also flew past, and *Mariner 9* went into orbit around it. Two *Viking* craft dropped landers onto the surface. In 1997, the *Pathfinder* probe landed, carrying a small vehicle named *Sojourner*, which investigated the surrounding rocks. Two larger Mars rovers landed in 2004.

Dust storm

Olympus Mons and the surface of Mars

Mars's structure

Atmosphere

Crust

Mantle

Iron core

What is Mars's surface like?

Mars's surface is dotted with vast deserts, craters, and volcanoes. The highest volcano, Olympus Mons, is nearly 20 miles high. There is also a gash in the surface over 2,500 miles long and 4 miles deep in places. It has been called Mars's Grand Canyon, but its proper name is Mariner Valley. Smaller valleys look as if they have been made by flowing water, so astronomers think that Mars may once have had rivers and seas.

Quick-fire Quiz

1. What color is Mars?
a) Yellow
b) Blue
c) Red

2. What is Mars's atmosphere made of?
a) Oxygen
b) Carbon dioxide
c) Sulphur dioxide

3. What was the name of the Mars rover?
a) *Sojourner*
b) *Surveyor*
c) *Mariner*

4. What were Mars's moons originally?
a) Planets
b) Comets
c) Asteroids

33

Jupiter

Jupiter is the giant among the planets. All the others could fit into it with room to spare, and it could swallow more than 1,300 bodies the size of Earth. Jupiter is a gassy planet, mainly made up of hydrogen. Its stormy atmosphere is full of clouds. Jupiter travels through space with a large family of moons, some as big as planets.

What makes Jupiter so colorful?

The colored "stripes" we see on Jupiter are different kinds of clouds in the thick atmosphere. Because Jupiter spins around quickly, these clouds are drawn out into bands parallel with the equator. The paler bands are called zones, and the darker ones are called belts.

Jupiter's ring

What is Jupiter made of?

Jupiter is a great ball of gas and liquid. Its atmosphere is more than 600 miles deep and is made up mainly of hydrogen gas, with some helium. It is full of clouds of ice, ammonia, and ammonium compounds. At the bottom of the atmosphere, the great pressure turns the hydrogen into a liquid. Deeper down, rapidly increasing pressure turns the hydrogen into liquid metal. At the center, there is a small core of rock.

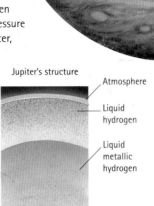

The Great Red Spot

Jupiter's atmosphere

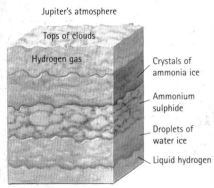

Tops of clouds

Hydrogen gas

Crystals of ammonia ice

Ammonium sulphide

Droplets of water ice

Liquid hydrogen

Jupiter's structure

Atmosphere

Liquid hydrogen

Liquid metallic hydrogen

Rocky core

The Great Red Spot

Europa

Callisto

Io

Ganymede

Surface
of Io

Erupting volcano

Why is Io special?

Io has been nicknamed the "pizza moon" because it is so colorful. It is a very unusual moon because it has active volcanoes on it. These pour out yellow-orange liquid sulphur giving Io its brilliant and varied colors. The *Voyager 1* probe discovered Io's volcanoes when it flew past Jupiter in 1979.

How many moons does Jupiter have?

Jupiter has at least 63 moons. We can see the four largest with binoculars. The Italian astronomer Galileo discovered them in 1610, so they are known as the Galilean moons. In order of distance from Jupiter, they are Io, Europa, Ganymede, and Callisto. With a diameter of 3,262 miles, Ganymede is the largest of Jupiter's moons and, at roughly the same size as the planet Mercury, is the biggest moon in the solar system. The smallest of Jupiter's moons, recently discovered, measure about 0.6 miles across.

What is the Great Red Spot?

The most prominent feature on Jupiter's surface is a large, red, oval region called the Great Red Spot. Astronomers did not know what it was until space probes looked at it closely. We now know that it is a gigantic swirling storm, like a huge hurricane on Earth. It measures about 25,000 miles across—three times the size of Earth.

JUPITER DATA

Diameter at equator: *88,846 mi.*
Average distance from sun: *484 million mi.*
Minimum distance from Earth: *390 million mi.*
Length of day: *9 hours, 50 minutes*
Length of year: *11.9 Earth years*
Temperature at cloud tops: *-250°F*
Satellites: *16 known*

Which probes have visited Jupiter?

Pioneer 10 flew past Jupiter in 1973 and took the first close-up photographs of its colorful atmosphere. *Pioneer 11* followed the next year, then traveled on to Saturn. *Voyagers 1* and *2* flew past in 1979, sending back astounding pictures and information. In 1995, the *Galileo* probe went into orbit around Jupiter after dropping a probe into its atmosphere.

Galileo probe

Quick-fire Quiz

1. What is Jupiter mainly made of?
a) Rock
b) Carbon dioxide
c) Hydrogen

2. What is the Great Red Spot?
a) A storm
b) A sea
c) A sunspot

3. Which is Jupiter's biggest moon?
a) Io
b) Callisto
c) Ganymede

4. What makes Io colorful?
a) Its clouds
b) Its volcanoes
c) Its oceans

Saturn

Saturn is the second largest planet, after Jupiter. Like Jupiter, it is a giant ball of gas. Saturn is probably best known for its shining rings. The rings appear to change shape year by year as the planet makes its way around the sun.

SATURN DATA

Diameter at equator: 74,898 mi.
Diameter of visible rings: 170,000 mi.
Average distance from sun:
 888 million mi.
Minimum distance from Earth:
 763 million mi.
Length of day: 10 hours, 40 minutes
Length of year: 29.5 Earth years
Temperature at cloud tops:
 -288°C
Satellites: 18 known

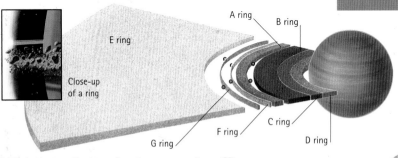

A ring

B ring

E ring

Close-up
of a ring

C ring

D ring

F ring

G ring

What are Saturn's rings made of?

Saturn is surrounded by many rings, but only three can be seen from Earth—the A, B, and C rings. The other rings were discovered by space probes. The rings look like solid sheets, but they are not. They are made up of millions upon millions of pieces of ice, whizzing around the planet at high speed. The pieces vary in size from minute specks to large chunks. In places, the rings are less than 165 feet thick.

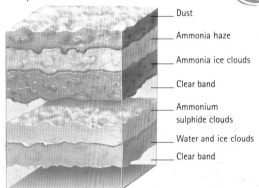

Saturn's
atmosphere

Dust

Ammonia haze

Ammonia ice clouds

Clear band

Ammonium
sulphide clouds

Water and ice clouds

Clear band

Why is Saturn so cloudy?

Saturn is a very cloudy planet. The clouds form into bands parallel to the equator because the planet spins so fast. These bands are not as easy to see as Jupiter's because of the haze that tops the atmosphere. There seem to be three main cloud layers on Saturn, located at different levels, with clear areas in between. The upper layers of clouds are made up of ammonia and ammonium compounds. At the lowest level, the clouds seem to be made up of water and ice particles, like the clouds we have on Earth.

What is Saturn like inside?

Saturn is a gas giant, which means that it is composed mainly of gas and liquid gas. Its cloudy atmosphere is made up almost entirely of hydrogen and helium. Below that lies a vast, deep ocean of liquid hydrogen. Deeper down is a layer of hydrogen in the form of liquid metal. At the center of the planet, there is a small core of rock.

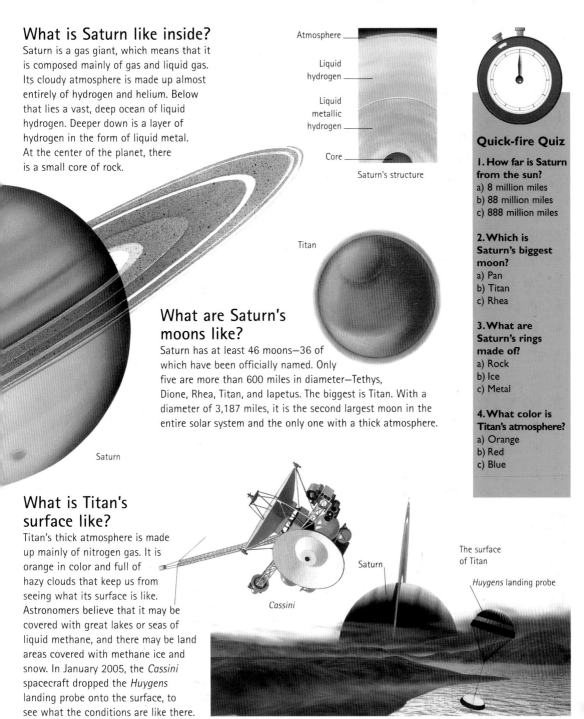

Atmosphere

Liquid hydrogen

Liquid metallic hydrogen

Core

Saturn's structure

Titan

Saturn

What are Saturn's moons like?

Saturn has at least 46 moons—36 of which have been officially named. Only five are more than 600 miles in diameter—Tethys, Dione, Rhea, Titan, and Iapetus. The biggest is Titan. With a diameter of 3,187 miles, it is the second largest moon in the entire solar system and the only one with a thick atmosphere.

Quick-fire Quiz

1. How far is Saturn from the sun?
a) 8 million miles
b) 88 million miles
c) 888 million miles

2. Which is Saturn's biggest moon?
a) Pan
b) Titan
c) Rhea

3. What are Saturn's rings made of?
a) Rock
b) Ice
c) Metal

4. What color is Titan's atmosphere?
a) Orange
b) Red
c) Blue

What is Titan's surface like?

Titan's thick atmosphere is made up mainly of nitrogen gas. It is orange in color and full of hazy clouds that keep us from seeing what its surface is like. Astronomers believe that it may be covered with great lakes or seas of liquid methane, and there may be land areas covered with methane ice and snow. In January 2005, the *Cassini* spacecraft dropped the *Huygens* landing probe onto the surface, to see what the conditions are like there.

Cassini

Saturn

The surface of Titan

Huygens landing probe

Uranus

Uranus, the third largest planet, is four times bigger across than Earth. It is so far from Earth that it is barely visible with the naked eye. This unique planet was discovered in the 1700s, with the help of a telescope.

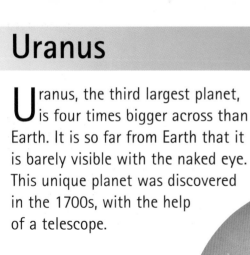

Who discovered Uranus?

In March 1781, an English astronomer named William Herschel was looking at the sky through a telescope. He saw what he thought must be a new comet, but it was actually a new planet. Until then, astronomers knew of only six planets. The new planet, which was later called Uranus, turned out to be twice as far away from the sun as Saturn.

Why is Uranus sometimes called the topsy-turvy planet?

All planets spin as they orbit the sun. We say they spin around their axis (an imaginary line that runs through their north and south poles). In most planets, the axis is nearly upright as the planet spins. But Uranus's axis is at right angles to normal, so it is as if Uranus is lying on its side. This means that, for part of its orbit, Uranus's poles point straight at the sun. At these times the poles become hotter than the rest of the planet, instead of always being colder, as on Earth.

How many rings does Uranus have?

Astronomers used to think that Saturn was the only planet with rings circling it. But in 1977, they discovered that Uranus had rings too. There are about 11 main rings, made up of pieces of rock up to 3 feet across, which whizz around the planet at high speed. The particles in some of the rings are kept in place by tiny "shepherd" moons.

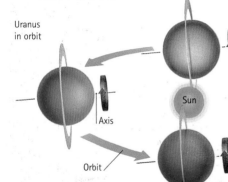

Uranus in orbit

Sun

Axis

Orbit

Direction of Uranus's rotation

Which probe has visited Uranus?

We can find out very little about Uranus through earth-based telescopes because it is so far away. Most of what we know came from the *Voyager 2* spacecraft, which visited Uranus in 1986. *Voyager 2* had already visited Jupiter (1979) and Saturn (1981). It has now gone far beyond the planets and will soon leave the solar system and begin a journey to the stars.

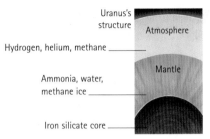
Voyager 2

Uranus's structure

Atmosphere

Hydrogen, helium, methane

Mantle

Ammonia, water, methane ice

Iron silicate core

What is Uranus made of?

Uranus has a thick atmosphere of hydrogen, helium, and methane surrounding a mantle of water, ammonia, and methane ice. At the center there is an iron silicate core.

What are Uranus's moons like?

We can only see the five largest of Uranus's moons from Earth—Miranda, Ariel, Umbriel, Titania, and Oberon. Ten smaller moons were discovered by *Voyager 2*. The Hubble Space Telescope discovered 12 more, bringing the total to 27 moons. Titania is the biggest moon. It is around 992 miles across.

Miranda
Ariel
Titania

URANUS DATA

Diameter at equator: *31,763 mi.*

Average distance from sun: *1.8 billion mi.*

Minimum distance from Earth: *1.6 billion mi.*

Length of day: *17 hours, 14 minutes*

Length of year: *84 Earth years*

Temperature at cloud tops: *-357°F*

Satellites: *15*

Quick-fire Quiz

1. What makes Uranus unique?
a) Its many moons
b) Its large size
c) The tilt of its axis

2. What do shepherd moons keep in place?
a) Space sheep
b) Meteorites
c) Ring particles

3. When was Uranus discovered?
a) 1681
b) 1781
c) 1881

4. Which is Uranus's biggest moon?
a) Miranda
b) Ariel
c) Titania

What is special about Miranda?

Miranda is the smallest moon that can be seen from Earth, with a diameter of only about 355 miles. Close-up photographs show it to be the most interesting moon of all. Its surface is a patchwork of different kinds of landscapes—craters, grooves, cliffs, and valleys. Astronomers think that, ages ago, Miranda shattered into pieces when it collided with another body. Then the pieces came together to create the landscape we see today.

The surface of Miranda

Neptune and Pluto

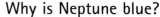

Neptune and Pluto were the last planets to be discovered. They lie billions of miles away from Earth, at the edge of the solar system. Neptune is a gas giant planet, much like Uranus. Pluto is a tiny ice ball, smaller than our own moon.

Why is Neptune blue?

Neptune is a lovely blue color, much like Earth. This color comes from a gas in the atmosphere called methane. Methane absorbs the red colors in sunlight, making the light coming from Neptune's atmosphere appear blue. Dark spots that sometimes appear in Neptune's atmosphere are violent storms.

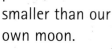

Neptune's structure

Atmosphere of hydrogen and helium

Water, ammonia, and methane

Rocky core

Does Neptune have moons?

Through a telescope, we can see two moons circling around Neptune—Triton and Nereid. When *Voyager 2* visited the planet, it found six more. Using improved earth-based telescopes, astronomers found five more satellites in 2002 and 2003, raising the total to 13. Triton is by far the biggest moon, measuring some 1,674 miles across. It circles the planet in the opposite direction to most moons.

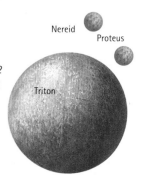

Nereid

Proteus

Triton

What is Neptune like?

Neptune's make-up is similar to that of its twin planet, Uranus. Its atmosphere consists mainly of hydrogen, together with some helium. Beneath this there is a huge, deep, hot ocean of water and liquid gases, including methane. In the center, there is a core of rock, which may be about the same size as Earth.

Voyager 2 over Neptune

When did *Voyager 2* visit Neptune?

Neptune was the last planet *Voyager 2* visited on its 12-year journey. Launched in 1977, *Voyager 2* passed about 3,000 miles above Neptune's cloud tops on August 24, 1989—closer than to any other planet. By then, it was more than 2.5 billion miles from Earth, and its radio signals took more than four hours to get back.

NEPTUNE DATA

Diameter at equator:
30,800 mi.
Average distance from sun:
2.8 billion mi.
Minimum distance from Earth:
2.7 billion mi.
Length of day: 17 hours, 6 minutes
Length of year: 165 Earth years
Temperature at cloud tops:
-353°F
Satellites: 8

PLUTO DATA

Diameter at equator: 1,430 mi.
Average distance from sun:
3.7 billion mi.
Minimum distance from Earth:
2.7 billion mi.
Length of day: 6 Earth days, 9 hours
Length of year: 248½ Earth years
Surface temperature: -380°F
Satellites: 1

Who found Pluto?

Percival
Lowell

United States astronomer
Percival Lowell built his
own observatory and led
a search for a ninth
planet. An astronomer
who worked there, Clyde
Tombaugh, finally
discovered it in 1930.

Charon

Why is Charon special?

Pluto's only moon, Charon, is unique in the solar
system. It is half as big across as Pluto itself. No other
moon is as big compared with its planet. Also, it circles
Pluto in the same time it takes Pluto to spin around
once. This makes Charon appear
fixed in Pluto's sky.

Pluto

What do we know about Pluto?

We do not know much about Pluto because
it is so far away. At its farthest, it travels more
than 4.5 billion miles away from the sun. Even in
powerful telescopes, it looks only like a faint star.
So far, no space probes have visited the planet.
All we know is that Pluto is a deep-frozen ball
of rock and ice. It probably has a covering
of "snow" made of frozen methane gas.

Pluto's structure

Thin atmosphere of
methane and nitrogen _____

Mantle of ice _____

Rocky core _____

What would Charon look like from Pluto?

Because it appears fixed in Pluto's sky, Charon can only be
seen from one side of the planet. From that side, Charon would
appear huge, much bigger than our moon does on Earth.
This is because Charon circles very close
to Pluto, only about 12,400 miles
away. Our moon is 20 times
farther from us.

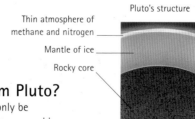

Charon seen from Pluto

Web Addresses

www.bbc.co.uk/science/space
This site provides lots of information on many aspects
of space. You will find space news, chat rooms, space games, and
links to other space-related sites.

www.nasa.gov
This is the official NASA site, which provides news and
information on space research and travel at all levels.

kids.msfc.nasa.gov
This site is devoted to introducing kids to the wonders of space
and space travel. Log on and find out all kinds of fascinating
facts, play games, do projects, join a Kids' Club, write space
stories, and even get your own NASA Kids' e-mail address.

www.enchantedlearning.com/subjects/astronomy
This is an interesting site for all ages. A comprehensive online
site about space and astronomy, with fun activities, quizzes, and
puzzles, as well as more advanced information on all aspects of
the solar system. It also lists many links to space-related sites.

**www.bbc.co.uk/history/discovery/revolutions/
launch_ani_cosmology_01.shtml**
This is a lively animation showing how the theories of
cosmology have changed over the centuries—from Aristotle
to Galileo.

homeschooling.gomilpitas.com/explore/astronomy.htm
This site offers plenty of lessons, interactive activities, and
experiments on all aspects of space. Follow the links to different
web sites offering a huge range of information.

www.seti.org/game/index.html
Play space science adventure games and look up
space words in the glossary at this site put together
by SETI—the organization of Science for Extraterrestrial
Intelligence.

KidsAstronomy.com
This site offers in-depth information on astronomy, current
space topics, and includes interactive games.

www.spacekids.com
This is a fun site for kids, with videos, games, photos,
jokes, news, and homework help.

starchild.gsfc.nasa.gov/docs/StarChild/StarChild.html
This learning center for young astronomers is organized
into different levels. It offers good graphics, articles
with an attached glossary, as well as activities
and plenty of fun facts.

www.thinkquest.org/library/index.html
The ThinkQuest Library is a collection of more than 5,500
educational web sites designed by participants in the
ThinkQuest competitions. To see what they have created
on stars and planets, check out subjects such as stars,
planets, solar system, and universe.

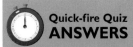

**Quick-fire Quiz
ANSWERS**

Page 11 Looking at the Sky
1. b   2. c   3. b   4. b

Page 13 Seeing Stars
1. b   2. c   3. b   4. b

Page 15 Great Balls of Gas
1. b   2. b   3. c   4. c

Page 17 Galaxies
1. c   2. b   3. c   4. a

Page 19 The Solar System
1. b   2. c   3. b   4. c

Page 21 Our Star, the Sun
1. b   2. c   3. b   4. c

Page 23 The Planets
1. b   2. c   3. b   4. b

Page 25 Mercury
1. b   2. c   3. b   4. a

Page 27 Venus
1. c   2. b   3. c   4. a

Page 29 Earth
1. b   2. b   3. c   4. a

Page 31 The Moon
1. c   2. b   3. c   4. b

Page 33 Mars
1. c   2. b   3. a   4. c

Page 35 Jupiter
1. c   2. a   3. c   4. b

Page 37 Saturn
1. c   2. b   3. b   4. a

Page 39 Uranus
1. c   2. c   3. b   4. c

Page 41 Neptune and Pluto
1. b   2. c   3. b   4. c

1,000
QUESTIONS
& ANSWERS
FACTFILE
PLANET
EARTH

Contents

Earth's Formation

In the vastness of outer space lies a star system, or galaxy, known as the Milky Way. Inside this galaxy is our solar system—a bright star orbited by nine planets. The planet that is third closest to this star, which we call the sun, is a unique, life-supporting planet called Earth.

Why is Earth unique?

Earth is a rocky planet that is more than a million times smaller than the sun. Unlike the other eight planets in the solar system, Earth has water and an atmosphere that contains oxygen. This means that life can exist on Earth.

How did Earth form?

1 The sun was formed when a nebula—a vast cloud of gas and dust—shrank under the pull of gravity. Hot clouds of dust and gases spun around the newly formed sun.

2 When specks of this dust collided, lumps formed. Gravity pulled these lumps together, creating a large, spinning, fiery ball. Heavy elements like iron sank to the center of the molten ball.

3 Lighter metals and rocks rose to the surface of the ball, which cooled enough for a solid, hard shell to form.

4 Gases escaped from the planet and formed an atmosphere with clouds. As rain fell oceans were formed, which contained oxygen-producing plants.

5 Over time the planet became the one we live on today—but planet Earth continues to change.

Who proved that Earth is round?

For thousands of years it was a common belief that Earth was flat. After all, it appears flat to the naked eye. But in 1522 Portuguese explorer Ferdinand Magellan's ship *Victoria* completed a historic journey—it sailed all the way around the world. This proved once and for all that Earth was round.

Who was Copernicus?

Copernicus

Before 1500 most people believed that the sun and the planets revolved around Earth. In 1530 Polish astronomer Nicolaus Copernicus (left) wrote a book showing that Earth spins on an axis and, along with the other planets, journeys around the sun. His ideas outraged many people, and the book was banned until 1830.

How long does Earth take to orbit the sun?

It takes 365.25 days (one year) for Earth to complete its orbit around the sun. At the same time, Earth spins on an axis that runs from the North Pole to the South Pole. It takes 24 hours (one day) for Earth to spin all the way around once on its axis.

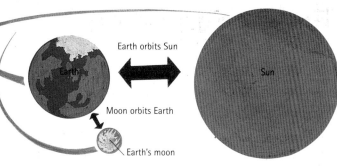

Earth orbits Sun

Earth

Sun

Moon orbits Earth

Earth's moon

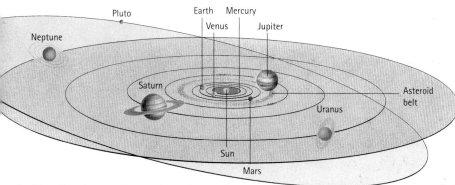

Pluto

Neptune

Earth   Mercury

Venus   Jupiter

Saturn

Asteroid belt

Uranus

Sun

Mars

Is Earth the only rocky planet?

No. The nine planets of our solar system are divided into two groups—rocky planets and gaseous or icy planets. The four planets closest to the sun—Mercury, Venus, Earth, and Mars—are rocky. Jupiter, Saturn, Uranus, Neptune, and Pluto are gaseous or icy planets.

How old is Earth?

Earth formed at the same time as the sun and the other eight planets of our solar system. By studying rocks and fossils, scientists have estimated that this was about 4.6 billion years ago.

Quick-fire Quiz

1. What is a nebula?
a) A cloud of gas and dust
b) A shooting star
c) A big bang

2. How many planets are there in our solar system?
a) Five
b) Eight
c) Nine

3. When did Copernicus write his famous book?
a) 1430
b) 1530
c) 1630

4. How long does it take Earth to spin once on its axis?
a) 24 hours
b) 30 days
c) 365.25 days

5

Crust to Core

Explorers have charted the continents and oceans of Earth's surface, and satellites beam back detailed pictures of our planet from space. But geologists—scientists who study Earth—seek to understand what lies beneath the surface and to discover what Earth is made of.

Ocean

Crust

Mantle

What is Earth made of?

It is about 4,000 miles (6,440km) from the surface of Earth to its center. Earth is made up of different layers of rock and metal. There are three main zones—the outer crust, the mantle below, and the core at the center. The rocky outer crust is divided into two parts—continental crust and oceanic crust. The mantle, which lies beneath the crust, is a layer of molten rock about 1,800 miles (2,800km) thick. Earth's core consists mainly of the metals nickel and iron. It is hot and dense and is divided into two areas—a liquid outer core and a solid inner core.

How do we know what is inside Earth?

Geologists cannot be absolutely certain what the inside of Earth is like, but they can discover a lot from examining the rocks spewed out from volcanoes. They can also use seismic waves from both earthquakes and nuclear bomb tests to build a three-dimensional picture of the planet. Seismic waves move quickly through hard, dense rock and more slowly through soft rock. In the 1960s scientists tried to drill through the oceanic crust to the mantle (left), but failed because the project was too expensive.

Crust

Mantle

Outer core

Inner core

EARTH DATA

Age: 4.6 billion years
Mass: 6.6 sextillion tons
Circumference (distance around Earth at equator): 24,902 miles
Distance from surface to center: 4,000 miles
Temperature at center: 9,000°F

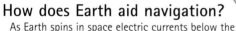

How does Earth aid navigation?

As Earth spins in space electric currents below the surface cause it to act like a magnet. Like a bar magnet, Earth has north and south magnetic poles and a magnetic field. A magnetized needle floating in a bowl of water will align itself with Earth's magnetic poles, creating a simple compass. Some animals, such as pigeons and dolphins, also use Earth's magnetic field to navigate.

Quick-fire Quiz

1. What are scientists who study Earth called?
a) Geographers
b) Geologists
c) Genealogists

2. How thick is Earth's mantle?
a) 180 miles
b) 1,800 miles
c) 18,000 miles

3. What is Earth's core made of?
a) Oxygen and nitrogen
b) Granite and marble
c) Nickel and iron

4. Which layer of the atmosphere do we live in?
a) Troposphere
b) Ozone
c) Stratosphere

Is Earth round?

From space, Earth looks spherical. However, it is not perfectly round. In fact, it is slightly flatter at the top and the bottom—the poles—and it bulges slightly at the middle, around the equator.

How high is the sky?

The sky, or atmosphere, that surrounds Earth contains a mixture of gases that makes life on the planet possible. The atmosphere is made up of several layers and reaches about 1,000 miles (1,600km) into space. The troposphere, the lowest layer, contains enough air for plants and animals to breathe. The air in the stratosphere is much thinner and contains a thin layer of ozone—a type of oxygen gas that warms the atmosphere and absorbs harmful rays from the sun. The other layers in the atmosphere are the mesophere, the ionosphere, and the exosphere.

Exosphere

Ionosphere

Mesosphere

Stratosphere
Troposphere

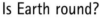
Ozone layer

Water

From space Earth looks blue. This is because 71 percent of the surface of the planet is covered by water. About 97 percent of the planet's water is salty seawater. The remaining water is in rivers, lakes, and glaciers.

Pacific Ocean

In which sea is it easy to float?

Seawater contains common salt and other minerals. On average, the sea is 3.5 percent salt. However, the Dead Sea, an inland sea, is 25 percent salt. High salt content gives water great buoyancy, so it is very easy for swimmers to float in the Dead Sea.

Which is the biggest ocean?

Oceans are huge bodies of salt water. There are four oceans—the Pacific, the Atlantic, the Indian, and the Arctic. The Pacific is the largest and the deepest. It is more than twice as big as the second-largest ocean, the Atlantic. The Pacific is wide enough to fit all the continents and deep enough to swallow Mount Everest, the world's highest mountain.

Water falls as snow in mountainous areas

Water is transferred inland as clouds move with winds

Plants give off water in a process called transpiration

Water evaporates from lakes and rivers as it flows back into oceans

What is the water cycle?

The world's water is constantly being recycled (above). Rain falls on the land and into the oceans. The sun's rays heat Earth, causing water to evaporate back into the atmosphere. As the water in the atmosphere cools it condenses to form rain clouds.

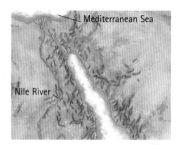
Mediterranean Sea

Nile River

Which is the world's longest river?

The longest river in the world is the Nile in Africa (left). It runs 4,157 miles (6,693km) from its source in Lake Victoria, Burundi, to the Mediterranean Sea. Rivers not only play an important role in shaping the landscape, they are also a vital resource for humans, providing food and water for drinking and irrigation. The Nile is so long that it is even visible from space!

How do lakes form?

Lakes can form in a variety of ways. Oxbow lakes are formed when a loop of a winding, or meandering, river gets cut off from the river. Volcanic lakes form in the natural hollows of old volcanoes. Lakes can also form in rift valleys, which occur when the land between two faults—fractures in Earth's crust—slips away.

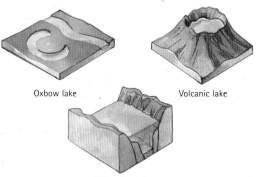
Oxbow lake

Volcanic lake

Rift-valley lake

What causes waves and tides?

As wind blows over the ocean's surface, friction between the air and the water causes wavelets on the surface. These grow bigger, creating waves with high points, or crests, that are separated by low points, or troughs. Tides are caused by Earth's spin and the gravitational pulls of the moon and the sun.

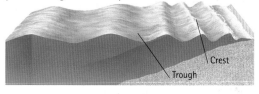
Crest

Trough

What is the difference between seas and oceans?

Water falls as rain on oceans

Water evaporates from oceans

Seas are sections of oceans, but are partly cut off from them by land. The largest sea, the South China Sea, is part of the Pacific Ocean. Most seas and oceans are rich in marine life and mineral resources.

Land

Earth's crust is divided into sections called plates that are moved by the mantle over millions of years. Continental crust—crust that makes up Earth's land—is 19 to 25 miles (30–40km) thick.

The different colors represent the tectonic plates of Earth's crust. The arrows indicate the direction each plate is moving.

What are tectonic plates?

The surface of Earth is made up of about 20 tectonic plates (above) that move slowly over Earth's surface, causing continents to collide and split apart. Areas where plates pull apart from each other are called divergence zones. Areas where plates push against each other are called convergence zones.

How has Earth changed?

1 About 200 million years ago all the continents were joined together in one giant land mass called Pangaea.

Pangaea

2 By about 130 million years ago Pangaea had split into a northern continent called Laurasia and a southern continent called Gondwanaland.

Laurasia

Gondwanaland

3 By about 65 million years ago Gondwanaland had split into Africa and South America, and Laurasia was splitting into North America and Eurasia.

North America

Eurasia

South America

Africa

4 About 65 million years from now it is likely that North America will split from South America to join Asia. It is also likely that Africa will group closely together with Europe.

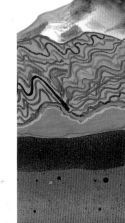

What evidence of plate movement is there?

The shapes of the eastern coast of North and South America and the western coasts of Europe and Africa suggest that they were once joined. Also, scientists have found similarities between rocks, fossils, plants, and animals from different continents—African ostriches and South American rheas probably share an ancestor.

North and South America

Africa

How many continents are there?

There are seven continents—North America, South America, Africa, Asia, Europe, Antarctica, and Australasia. Europe, which is attached to Asia, is the smallest continent, and it is argued that it is really part of Asia. Australasia is made up of Australia, New Zealand, and other Pacific Islands. India is called a subcontinent of Asia because it is so large and distinct.

How else have tectonic plates shaped the world?

Plate movement has not only mapped out our continents, but it has also created many geographical features. Mountains are formed when plates crumple land as they collide, and volcanoes erupt when plates dive under the mantle and melt or split apart (below). Earthquakes occur where tectonic plates move past each other.

Are the continents still moving?

Yes. North America and Europe are estimated to be moving 3 inches (7cm) farther apart every year. This means that the Atlantic Ocean is getting wider and the Pacific Ocean is getting smaller.

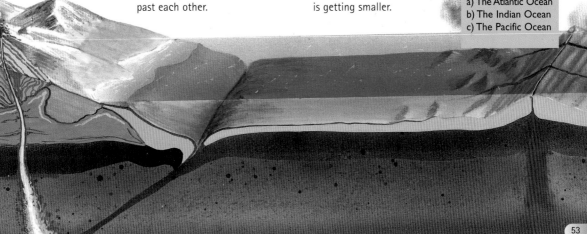

Earthquakes

Epicenter

Focus

Shock waves

Earthquakes can be devastating natural disasters. More than a million earthquakes are detected each year, but only a fraction of them are strong enough to cause damage.

What is a fault line?

When plates of continental and oceanic crust slide and push against each other, they cause rocks to snap, forming a line of weakness called a fault. Earthquakes occur along these fault lines. The San Andreas Fault (right), which runs down the western coast of North America, is one of the biggest fault lines in the world. In 1906 a catastrophic earthquake along this fault caused 500 deaths in San Francisco.

San Andreas Fault

San Francisco

Stars indicate epicenters of past earthquakes

What are shock waves?

Shock waves are waves of energy caused by earthquakes. The source of the waves is called the focus of the quake, and the point on the surface above the focus is referred to as the epicenter. There are two kinds of shock waves. Body waves travel through the rock below the surface, causing it to compress, expand, and move up and down. Surface waves reach Earth's surface and have a rolling motion, just like ocean waves. Usually an earthquake causes the most damage in areas closest to the epicenter.

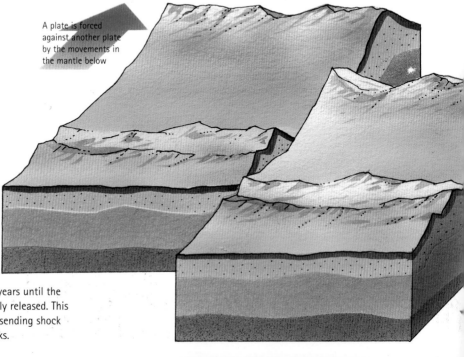

A plate is forced against another plate by the movements in the mantle below

How are earthquakes caused?

When Earth's plates push against each other, they place enormous stress on rocks near the top of the crust. Instead of rubbing smoothly past each other, they may lock together for years until the pent-up energy is finally released. This causes an earthquake, sending shock waves through the rocks.

What is a tsunami?

When an earthquake happens beneath the sea, it can create enormous tidal waves called tsunamis. Tsunamis can reach heights of 100 feet (30m) or more by the time they reach coastlines and can cause huge amounts of damage.

What should you do in an earthquake?

Probably the greatest danger in an earthquake is that a building will collapse on top of you. Standing in a doorway or taking shelter under a table could save your life. Architects and engineers try to construct buildings that resist collapse (left). These buildings have deep foundations in solid rock and are able to bend slightly.

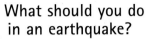

Trans-America Pyramid, San Francisco, CA

How are earthquakes measured?

Earthquakes are recorded by machines called seismographs (below) and are measured on two scales. The Mercalli Scale is based on the effects of earthquakes. The Richter Scale is based on the size of shock waves.

Mercalli Scale		Richter Scale
1	Very slight: detected by instruments	less than 3
2	Feeble: felt by people resting	3–3.4
3	Slight: like heavy trucks passing	3.5–4
4	Moderate: windows rattle	4.1–4.4
5	Rather strong: wakes sleeping people	4.5–4.8
6	Strong: trees sway, walls crack	4.9–5.4
7	Very strong: buildings crack	5.5–6
8	Destructive: buildings move	6.1–6.5
9	Ruinous: ground cracks	6.6–7
10	Disastrous: landslides	7.1–7.3
11	Very disastrous: railroad tracks break	7.4–8.1
12	Catastrophic: total devastation	8.1 and over

What damage can earthquakes cause?

Depending on the strength of the earthquake, areas can be completely devastated. The ground shakes and ripples, and huge cracks open up. Buildings collapse, and electricity lines, water mains, and gas pipes are destroyed. Fires often start, causing further chaos. Some earthquakes have caused the deaths of thousands of people. Approximately 30,000 people were killed by an earthquake in northern Turkey in August 1999.

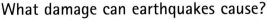

As the plates attempt to move past each other, tension builds up and will be released in the form of an earthquake

Quick-fire Quiz

1. Which fault line is on the western coast of North America?
   a) The San Andreas Fault
   b) The San Francisco Fault
   c) The Great American Fault

2. Where does most of an earthquake's damage usually occur?
   a) Under the ground
   b) In space
   c) At the epicenter

3. What is probably the greatest danger in an earthquake?
   a) Collapsing buildings
   b) Electric shocks
   c) Molten lava

4. Which type of damage would an earthquake measuring 7.1 on the Richter scale cause?
   a) Feeble
   b) Disastrous
   c) Catastrophic

Mountains

Formed over millions of years, mountains create some of the world's most dramatic landscapes. Most occur in ranges that stretch for hundreds of miles. Many of these ranges will continue to grow up before erosion eventually reduces them to the size of hills.

Alps
Atlas Mountains
Rocky Mountains
Himalayas
Andes
Great Dividing Range

Pressure applied by crust buckles rock

Fold mountains

How are mountains formed?

Volcanic mountains are formed when molten rock escapes through cracks in Earth's crust and builds up on the surface. Block mountains occur when a chunk of land is thrust above neighboring rock along fault lines in Earth's crust. The mountains in the great ranges are fold mountains. They are formed when two slabs of continental crust collide, buckling the rock and sediment between them (above). The Himalayas were formed in this way (right).

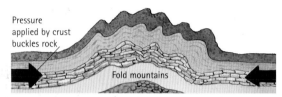

India hits Asia, crumpling both continental crusts and forming the Himalayan mountain range

Where are mountains found?

Mountains can be found all over the world (above). The greatest mountain ranges are the Rockies in North America, the Alps in Europe, the Andes in South America, and the highest of them all—the Himalayas in Asia.

How do mountains stay upright?

It is thought that Earth's crust "floats" on the mantle below. Mountains have "roots" that reach deep below ground level and support them.

What life can be found on mountains?

Animals and plants that live on mountains have to be able to survive extreme temperatures and high winds. Trees are unable to survive above a certain altitude known as the tree line. However, hardy alpine plants can grow higher up. Mountain animals such as llamas, yaks, goats, and hares have thick, woolly coats to keep out the cold.

Why are some mountains rugged and others smooth?

Young mountains, such as the Himalayas, have steep, rugged peaks and sides. Over time the peaks and sides will be eroded by water, rain, ice, and wind. This makes older mountains smoother and less high.

Edmund Hillary and Tenzing Norgay

Which is the highest mountain?

The world's highest peak is Mount Everest (below). It is part of the Himalayas in Asia and is 29,021 feet (8,848m) high. On May 29, 1953, New Zealand mountaineer Edmund Hillary and his Sherpa guide, Tenzing Norgay (right), made history by reaching the summit of Everest. Mauna Kea in Hawaii is 33,476 feet (10,203m) high. However, 19,680 feet (5,998m) of the mountain lies beneath the ocean.

Quick-fire Quiz

1. Which mountain range is found in South America?
a) The Alps
b) The Rockies
c) The Andes

2. Which type of mountains are in the great ranges?
a) Volcanic mountains
b) Fold mountains
c) Block mountains

3. What is the line above which trees are unable to grow called?
a) The tree line
b) The growth line
c) The altitude line

4. How high is Mauna Kea?
a) 3,476 feet
b) 23,476 feet
c) 33,476 feet

Volcanoes

An erupting volcano spewing hot, molten rock is one of the most dramatic sights on Earth. Volcanic eruptions are caused by disturbances in Earth's crust. There are about 500 active volcanoes in the world.

What are volcanoes?

Volcanoes are openings in Earth's crust from which hot, molten rock (magma), ash, and gas spurt. The magma, which is called lava after eruption, cools around the openings to form cone shapes. Volcanoes often occur in mountain ranges on land, but they can also form on ocean floors, rising above sea level (above).

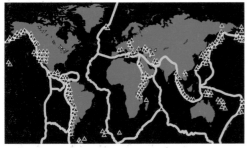

Pink triangles show active volcanoes. Plate boundaries are in yellow.

Where are volcanoes found?

Most of Earth's volcanoes are located along plate boundaries (above), where tectonic plates meet, because this is where crust is weakest. There are so many volcanoes surrounding the Pacific Ocean that it is known as the Ring of Fire. A few volcanoes occur away from plate edges, above "hot spots"—areas where Earth's crust is thin and magma can burn through. Some islands are the tops of volcanoes that have emerged from the ocean floor. The Hawaiian Islands are examples of this.

Magma chamber

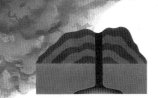
Cinder-cone volcano

Composite volcano

Shield volcano

Are there different types of volcanoes?

A volcano's shape depends on how thick the magma is and the force with which it was spewed out. A cinder cone is formed after a huge explosion, which occurs if there is a lot of gas in the magma. The cone of the volcano is made mostly of volcanic ash. A composite volcano erupts regularly and is usually very tall, made of alternating layers of lava and ash. The lava is thick and sticky and does not flow far before it solidifies. A shield volcano has several craters and is formed when magma is thin and runny. It spreads across a wide area to form a low dome shape.

What are geysers?

Geysers are found in volcanic areas where hot rocks lie near Earth's surface. Underground water is heated to boiling point by the rocks, then shoots into the air in a fountain. In New Zealand and Iceland the power from geysers and hot springs is used to make electricity. One of the world's most famous geysers is Old Faithful in Yellowstone National Park, which shoots up a jet of water and steam every 70 minutes.

Quick-fire Quiz

1. What is hot, molten rock called?
a) Volcanic ash
b) Red-hot rock
c) Lava or magma

2. Where is the Ring of Fire?
a) The Pacific Ocean
b) The Atlantic Ocean
c) North America

3. Which type of volcano is formed by runny lava?
a) A shield volcano
b) A cinder volcano
c) A composite volcano

4. How often does Old Faithful erupt?
a) Every 70 minutes
b) Every 70 hours
c) Every 70 days

What happens when a volcano erupts?

Deep beneath a volcano lies a magma chamber (left). Pressure builds up inside the chamber, and the magma escapes through a chimneylike vent. During an eruption rock and ash are spewed out with the magma.

What is a dormant volcano?

A dormant volcano is a volcano that has been quiet for hundreds of years. However, there is always a danger that a dormant volcano may suddenly erupt. A volcano that has permanently stopped erupting is said to be extinct.

Rocks, Fossils, and Minerals

Earth's many varied landscapes are all shaped out of rock. There are three main types of rock—igneous, metamorphic, and sedimentary—and they are all formed in different ways.

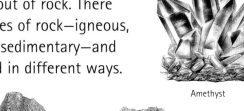

Amethyst

What are minerals?

All rocks are made up of building blocks called minerals. Minerals are natural chemical compounds, and nearly all consist of just eight chemical elements—oxygen, silicon, calcium, magnesium, potassium, aluminum, iron, and sodium. When minerals are cut and polished and are considered to be beautiful and durable enough to wear as jewelry, they are known as gemstones or gems (left). Gems are valued according to their hardness, density, color, and how they reflect light.

Opal

Diamond

Ruby

Emerald

What are "fiery" rocks?

After molten magma forces its way through cracks in Earth's crust, it gradually cools, forms crystals, and becomes a hard mass of igneous rock. The word "igneous" comes from the Latin word for fire. Granite (left) and basalt are examples of igneous rock.

Granite

What is metamorphic rock?

Metamorphic rock is igneous or sedimentary rock that has been changed by great heat or pressure. For example, magma under the ground can bake surrounding limestone and change it into marble. The forces that build new mountains also create metamorphic rock, changing soft mudstone into hard slate (left).

Slate

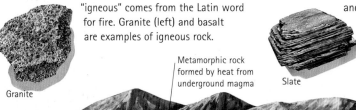

Metamorphic rock formed by heat from underground magma

Metamorphic rock formed by pressure from folding crust

Igneous rock

Slate

60

Magma chamber

Marble

How do fossils form?

Fossils are the remains of animals and plants that lived more than 10,000 years ago. Most fossils are formed in sedimentary rock.

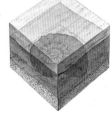

1 When a sea animal such as an ammonite dies, its body sinks to the seabed. The soft parts rot away, leaving the hard shell.

2 The shell is buried under more and more sediment. Over time this sediment hardens into rock.

3 Over millions of years the rock in which the fossil lies may shift, and the fossil could be thrust up to become part of a new mountain range.

4 Eventually the effects of weathering and erosion wear away the rock and expose the fossil.

How is limestone formed?

Limestone is a sedimentary rock. All sedimentary rock is made from sediments such as shells, sand, and mud that settle on the bottom of seas, lakes, and rivers. Sediments pile up in layers, and pressure from the higher layers squeezes water out from the lower layers. The squashed sediments cement together to form solid rock. Limestone is formed from the shells and skeletons of tiny sea creatures. Sandstone and chalk (right) are also sedimentary rocks.

Chalk

What use are rocks, fossils, and minerals?

Rocks are used as building materials, and some minerals are useful in industry—silicon is used to make glass, and diamonds make good cutting tools (some drills are tipped with diamonds). Coal, a fossil fuel, is mined from deep underground (below). It is the remains of prehistoric plants that built up in thick layers. The layers were flooded by the sea and covered with sand, which over millions of years compressed the layers into coal.

A seam of coal is mined deep beneath the ground

Quick-fire Quiz

1. Which type of rock is granite?
a) Igneous
b) Sedimentary
c) Metamorphic

2. Which of these is a sedimentary rock?
a) Chalk
b) Basalt
c) Marble

3. Which metamorphic rock can limestone be changed into?
a) Slate
b) Granite
c) Marble

4. In which type of rock are fossils usually found?
a) Igneous
b) Sedimentary
c) Metamorphic

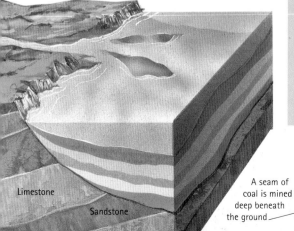

Limestone

Sandstone

Climate

Climate is the average weather conditions of a region, season by season. Many factors affect climate—global position, ocean currents, and the greenhouse effect. As these factors continue to change, so too will Earth's climate.

Why does Earth have seasons?

Earth has seasons because its axis tilts, so as it orbits the sun one hemisphere is always tipped closer to the sun than the other hemisphere is. When the Northern Hemisphere is closer to the sun—from March 21 to September 20—it will experience spring and summer, while the Southern Hemisphere will be in fall and winter. When the Southern Hemisphere is closer to the sun—from September 21 to March 20—it will have spring and summer, while the Northern Hemisphere will experience its fall and winter.

Spring in NH

Fall in SH

Summer in NH

Sun

Winter in NH

Winter in SH

Summer in SH

Fall in NH

Spring in SH

Key
NH Northern Hemisphere
SH Southern Hemisphere

Why are some places hotter than others?

Different parts of the world have different temperatures. Because Earth is round, the sun does not heat it evenly (below). Areas near the equator have a hot climate year-round because the sun is directly overhead. Farther away from the equator the sun's rays are spread over a much larger area, so it is not as hot. Although equatorial regions do not experience much change in temperature, they do have rainy and dry seasons.

Sun's rays spread over very large area—cold at North Pole

Sun's rays spread over large area—warm

Sun's rays directed at small area—hot at equator

Equator

Warm

Cold at South Pole

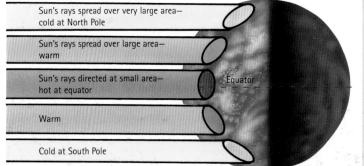

Pacific Ocean

South America

Australia   Warm water

Cold water

How do ocean currents affect climates?

Ocean currents bring warm or cold water to continental coasts. This water heats or cools air masses, and this affects the climate in the local area. Warm currents move west across the Pacific (above), providing southeastern Asia and northern Australia with a warm, humid climate.

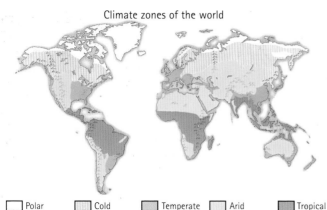

Climate zones of the world

Polar ■ Cold ■ Temperate ■ Arid ■ Tropical

How does global position affect climate?

Climate depends on many geographical factors—mountainous areas are cold, and places close to the ocean are wetter than inland regions. Global position also affects climate (left). Polar regions are snowy and icy, and even areas with simply "cold" climates may be frozen for months on end. Temperate climates have warm summers, cool winters, and rain. Arid desert areas are hot and dry, and tropical areas are hot and wet.

What is an ice age?

An ice age is a period when part of Earth is permanently covered by ice. Because the poles are frozen, we are in an ice age now. Some ice ages are more severe than others—millions of years ago ice sheets covered most of Earth during ice ages. The last severe ice age took place between about 20,000 and 80,000 years ago (right).

Average July temperatures

60°F
50°F
40°F
32°F

Severe ice age

200,000 160,000 140,000 80,000 40,000 20,000 present

Years before present

What is the greenhouse effect?

Some of the sun's heat is not absorbed by Earth and is reflected back into space. Gases in Earth's atmosphere, such as carbon dioxide, nitrogen oxide, and chlorofluorocarbons (CFCs), trap some of this heat and radiate it back to Earth. This is the greenhouse effect. Without the greenhouse effect, it would be too cold on Earth for life to exist. However, too many CFCs, which are released by industry, have entered the atmosphere, and this is causing too much heat to be trapped. This causes excessive global warming, which is harmful and alters Earth's climate over time.

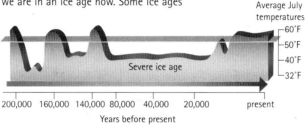

Sun's heat enters atmosphere

Some radiated heat escapes

Sun's heat reflected back into space

Radiated heat trapped in atmosphere causes global warming

Quick-fire Quiz

1. Why does Earth have seasons?
a) The sun's axis tilts
b) The equator tilts
c) Earth's axis tilts

2. When does the Southern Hemisphere have spring and summer?
a) March 21 to September 21
b) September 21 to March 21
c) January 21 to July 21

3. Which climate has warm summers and cool winters?
a) Cold
b) Temperate
c) Arid

4. What do places near oceans experience?
a) Cold weather
b) Dry weather
c) Wet weather

63

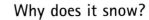

Weather

Weather is the day-to-day changes in atmospheric conditions— sunshine, rainfall, and wind speeds. Some areas have similar weather every day, while others have very changeable weather.

Why does it snow?

Tiny water droplets in clouds freeze to form ice crystals. These six-sided crystals can bind together and create beautiful snowflakes (left). The ice crystals are heavy, so they will fall from the clouds. If the temperature of the air below the clouds is less than 32°F (0°C), the ice crystals will remain frozen and fall as snow. If the air is above 32°F (0°C), the ice crystals will melt and fall as rain.

How are clouds made?

Water vapor in the air condenses into tiny droplets. The droplets are not heavy enough to fall as rain, and instead they group together to form clouds. Different conditions form clouds of different types and shapes (below). Cirrocumulus clouds look like ripples. Altocumulus clouds are white and puffy. Cumulus clouds are big, cauliflower-shaped clouds. Stratus clouds are flat and low-lying.

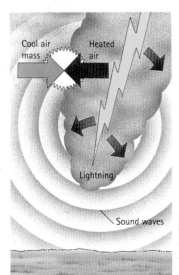

Cool air mass

Heated air

Lightning

Sound waves

What are thunder and lightning?

In a storm cloud air currents force water droplets to crash into each other until they become electrically charged. Lightning is the huge spark of electricity produced as the charge is released. Lightning heats the air around it so quickly that it produces a loud, booming noise—thunder (above). To work out how far away a storm is, count the seconds between the lightning and thunder—five seconds indicates one mile (1.6km).

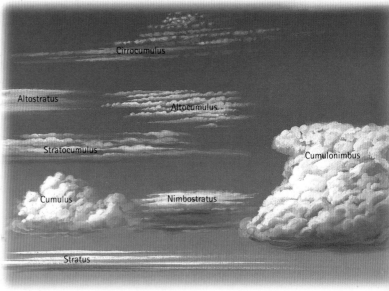

Cirrocumulus

Altostratus

Altocumulus

Stratocumulus

Cumulonimbus

Cumulus

Nimbostratus

Stratus

How are rainbows caused?

Rainbows, which appear in the sky after rain, are the reflection of sunlight in raindrops. The raindrops split the sunlight into a spectrum of colors— red, orange, yellow, green, blue, indigo, and violet (right). To see a rainbow, your back must be to the sun.

How is weather forecast?

The science of studying weather systems is called meteorology. Information on temperature, cloud type, wind speed, air pressure, rain, and snow is collected regularly from places all over the world. In addition to information from the ground, meteorologists can get an accurate picture of the weather from satellites in space (left). The information is sent to forecasting stations and plotted onto charts. Meteorologists can make fairly accurate forecasts up to a week ahead.

Weather satellite

What are tornadoes, hurricanes, typhoons, and cyclones?

A tornado is a twisting storm funnel about 330 feet (100m) wide. The winds inside the tornado can reach speeds of 220 miles per hour (355km/h). Tornadoes move in straight lines across land and are most common on the Great Plains (right). At the center, or eye, of a tornado is an area of pressure so low that it can cause buildings to explode. Hurricanes are much bigger storms that form over tropical waters in the Atlantic Ocean. They are so powerful that when they strike land, they can devastate crops, forests, and buildings. Storms that form over the Pacific Ocean are called typhoons, and ones that occur over the Indian Ocean are called cyclones.

Quick-fire Quiz

1. Which clouds are flat and low-lying?
a) Cirrus
b) Stratus
c) Cumulus

2. What are tropical storms that form over the Pacific Ocean called?
a) Hurricanes
b) Typhoons
c) Cyclones

3. What is the study of weather systems called?
a) Meteorology
b) Microbiology
c) Weatherology

4. What is lightning?
a) A spark of electricity
b) Crashing air currents
c) Loud, booming noises

Polar Regions

The North and South poles are at the north and south points of Earth's axis. The polar regions of the Arctic (north) and Antarctica (south) are the coldest areas on Earth (below). Ice and snow stretch as far as the eye can see.

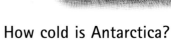

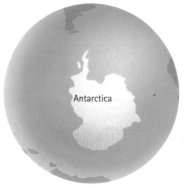

Arctic

Antarctica

Do any people live in Antarctica?

Only scientists live in Antarctica, and they normally stay only in the summer months. The land is not owned by any country, and the Antarctic Treaty, signed by 32 countries, ensures the land is used only for research. Tourism is increasing in the area, which makes waste disposal a problem—the freezing temperatures preserve waste, rather than rotting it away.

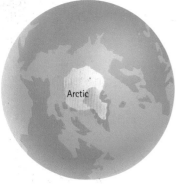

Is there any land in the Arctic Circle?

There is no land at the North Pole itself—just a mass of pack ice. However, most of Greenland and parts of Canada, Alaska, and Scandinavia lie within the Arctic Circle. Antarctica is a continental land mass covered by an ice sheet.

How cold is Antarctica?

The lowest temperature ever recorded on Earth was $-128.2°F$ ($-89.2°C$) at Vostok in Antarctica. Temperatures inland range from $-13°F$ ($-25°C$) to $-128°F$ ($-89°C$). Ice sheets are up to 9,840 feet (3km) thick, and the ice and snow reflect the sun's heat back into space. Icy winds can blow at speeds of up to 90 miles per hour (145km/h). It has not rained in Antarctica for two million years.

What are icebergs?

Icebergs are parts of the Arctic and Antarctic ice sheets that have broken off into the ocean. Icebergs vary in size and shape, and some can be the size of a small country. As much as 90 percent of an iceberg is underwater. This is why they are hazardous to ships, which are often unable to detect them.

What are glaciers?

A glacier is a large body of ice that moves slowly through mountain valleys and polar regions. Glaciers move less than seven feet (2m) a day, but they are so big that they can dramatically shape and carve the land they pass through. During the past ice ages, much of Europe, North America, South Africa, and Asia was covered by glaciers. When glaciers meet the ocean, chunks can break off into the sea and form icebergs (below).

Quick-fire Quiz

1. Where is the South Pole?
a) The Arctic
b) Antarctica
c) Greenland

2. Where are polar bears found?
a) The Arctic
b) Antarctica
c) Australia

3. How far do glaciers move each day?
a) Less than 7 feet
b) 7 to 15 feet
c) 15 to 27 feet

4. Which country lies within the Arctic Circle?
a) Ireland
b) Iceland
c) Greenland

What is tundra?

Tundra (above) is the land around the Arctic Circle between the northern conifer forests and the permanent ice sheets around the North Pole. The surface soil in the tundra thaws for only a few weeks in the summer, but below the surface the ground is permanently frozen. This means that vegetation cannot extend its roots very deep, and only small shrubs, mosses, and trees can grow there.

How do animals survive in polar climates?

Polar animals have thick coats or layers of fat (blubber) to keep warm. Polar mammals usually have small ears and snouts to avoid losing too much heat. Penguins, whales, seals, and seabirds fish in the icy seas, and musk oxen graze on plants in the tundra, where they live all year round. Polar bears live only in the Arctic, and penguins live only in Antarctica.

Arctic tern

Penguins   Seal   Musk ox   Polar bear

Deserts

Deserts are regions where the annual rainfall is less than 10 inches (25cm), but some deserts have no rain for several years. Deserts are the driest places on Earth and are often very windy. Few plants can survive in these conditions.

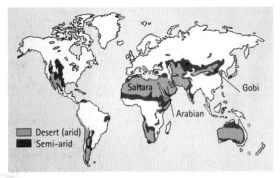

Desert (arid)
Semi-arid

Which are the largest deserts?

The three largest deserts in the world are the Sahara, the Arabian, and the Gobi (above). The Sahara covers about one third of Africa, measuring about 3,354,000 square miles (8,600,000km²). The Arabian Desert and the Gobi Desert in Asia measure 897,000 square miles (2,300,000km²) and 468,000 square miles (1,200,000km²), respectively. Australia has several deserts that cover a huge area of land.

Wind direction

Dunes "migrate" in direction of wind

How are dunes formed?

Many deserts have sandy mounds called dunes. Dunes are formed when the wind blows steadily from one direction. Sand grains lodge against stones or bushes, and over time the sand piles up, forming dunes. Whole dunes are moved along by the wind as sand on the gently inclined, wind-facing side of the dune is swept over the top of the dune (above). Dunes shaped like crescent moons are called barchan dunes.

Are deserts always hot?

Daytime temperatures can rise to a scorching 122°F (50°C) in some deserts. Once the sun sets, however, temperatures can drop dramatically, because there are few clouds over deserts to keep the day's heat in. Day and night temperatures in the western Sahara can differ by more than 113°F (45°C); the Gobi has a more temperate climate. Many people consider the polar regions to be cold deserts because they have no rain.

Are all deserts sandy?

Most deserts are rocky, not sandy. Only about 11 percent of the Sahara is sandy. Many deserts contain huge, strangely shaped rocks that have been formed by wind erosion.

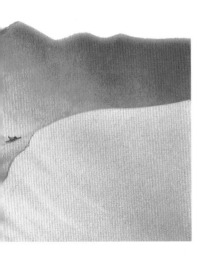

What is an oasis?

Deserts are very dry places. An oasis (above) is a small fertile area in a desert where water from under the ground reaches the surface. Many oases occur naturally, although they can be created artificially by digging wells in places where water lies close to the surface. Plants can grow near oases, but elsewhere some plants lie dormant and wait for rain.

Can people live in deserts?

Many people who live in deserts are nomads who wander from place to place in search of food and water. Permanent settlements are formed around oases, and because it is now possible to make artificial oases, more and more people are now living in desert lands.

What life is found in deserts?

Many desert animals, such as foxes, jackrabbits, and coyotes, are nocturnal, sleeping during the scorching hot day and coming out to find food at night, when it is cooler. Some desert animals are able to survive with little or no water—camels can go for many days without drinking. Desert plants store water in their fleshy stems and leaves. Cacti swell after rain and gradually get thinner as they use the water.

Quick-fire Quiz

1. Which is the largest desert?
a) The Arabian
b) The Gobi
c) The Sahara

2. What is a sandy mound in a desert called?
a) A castle
b) A dune
c) An oasis

3. Which people wander from place to place seeking food?
a) Nomads
b) Normans
c) Nocturnals

4. What are many desert animals?
a) Nocturnal
b) Amphibious
c) Heavy sleepers

Grasslands

Grasslands lie just beyond the edges of deserts and in the dry interiors of continents. In these regions rain falls during only one season of the year. The land is too dry to support many trees, but drought-resistant grasses flourish.

Why are grasslands good for grazing?

Large areas of the grasslands of North America, South America, Australia, and New Zealand are used to graze sheep or cattle (left). Because grass leaves grow from the base of the plant, they can survive and grow even if the tops of the plant are eaten. This makes grassland areas ideal for ranches, which rear livestock. Grasslands are also used to grow food crops like wheat and corn.

Where are grasslands found?

Grasslands are found all over the world, in the dry central areas of continents and on the edges of deserts (below). The grassland of Europe and Asia is called "steppe." In South America it is called "pampas," and in North America it is "prairie." The grasslands of Africa, India, and Australia are called "savanna." There are more than 8,000 different species of grasses around the world.

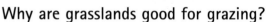

Prairie

Steppe

Savanna

Pampas

Savanna

Grasslands of the world

When were the prairies a "Dust Bowl"?

The grassland climate is very dry, and long droughts are common. In the 1930s a severe drought hit the prairies of the central United States. Overgrazing and poor farming reduced the ground to dust, and strong winds brought dust storms to the region. The area became known as the "Dust Bowl."

Which animals live in grasslands?

The animal species found in grasslands vary from continent to continent. The prairies of North America (left) were once home to buffalo, and they are still the habitat of falcons, coyotes, and prairie dogs. Kangaroos, koalas, emus, and kookaburras live in the Australian savanna. The savanna of Africa (below) shelters a rich variety of wildlife—from elephants and giraffes to lions and antelopes.

Quick-fire Quiz

1. What is Asia's grassland called?
   a) Steppe
   b) Pampas
   c) Savanna

2. How many species of grasses are there?
   a) More than 2,000
   b) More than 5,000
   c) More than 8,000

3. Where was the "Dust Bowl"?
   a) European steppe
   b) African savanna
   c) North American prairies

4. Where do kookaburras live?
   a) South American pampas
   b) African savanna
   c) Australian savanna

What is "slash-and-burn"?

Because grassland is useful for growing crops and grazing livestock, humans have looked for ways to extend it. Setting fire to vegetation during the dry season destroys woody plants and encourages new growth. The process is called "slash-and-burn."

Forests

Forests are huge areas of land covered with trees. There are many types of forests—coniferous, deciduous, and the spectacular tropical rain forests. A huge variety of wildlife and vegetation can be found deep within forests.

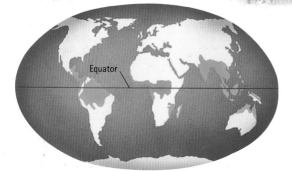

Equator

Rain forests of the world

How often does it rain in a rain forest?

Rain forests, or jungles, grow near the equator (above), where temperatures are high and the air is moist—it rains nearly every day. The conditions are ideal for wildlife. In fact, about half the world's plant and animal species are found in rain forests.

What is the rain forest's canopy?

There are several different levels in a rain forest. The forest floor is home to shrubs, climbing plants, moss, and fungi. It is very dark, and the floor is covered with decaying leaves and plants. The canopy (above) is the top of thousands of mature trees. It forms a kind of roof over the rain forest. Many forest animals, such as brightly colored birds and monkeys, live in it. Above the canopy a few taller trees break through, providing homes for big birds of prey.

How do rain forests help us breathe?

Rain forests play a vital role in Earth's oxygen cycle. The mass of vegetation in the vast rain forests takes in enormous amounts of carbon dioxide. The carbon dioxide is converted by the plants into oxygen, which is returned to Earth's atmosphere. This is one of the reasons why environmentalists are determined to halt the destruction of rain forests.

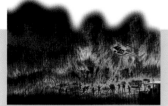

How do forest fires start?

Forest fires may be started by lightning, arson, or even the sun's rays magnified through an empty glass bottle. Fires often spread very quickly in forests—at speeds of up to 1.25 miles (2km) a minute. Firefighters battle against the huge fires, often helped by airplanes that dump huge loads of water onto the flames. Fires can rage for months, and the damage they cause is enormous—homes are destroyed, and air for thousands of miles around is polluted.

How do humans use forests?

Forests are rich resources for humans. They provide timber, food, and medicines. Timber, which can be burned for heating and cooking, is also used for building and for making products like paper. The sap from rubber trees can be made into rubber tires and gloves. Rain forests provide foods such as coffee, cocoa, nutmeg, and pepper. Many rain forest plants are used to develop medicines—quinine, used to treat malaria, comes from cinchona trees. The rain forests are now under threat of destruction as more and more trees are cut down.

What is the difference between a deciduous and a coniferous forest?

Deciduous trees, such as the oak (left), shed their leaves in winter. An oak tree can house more than 300 animal species. Coniferous trees, such as the fir tree (left), have hard, narrow leaves, or needles, that they keep all year round. For this reason conifers are known as evergreens. The biggest forest in the world is coniferous. It stretches across northern Asia and Europe. Coniferous forests thrive in cold areas with long winters, while deciduous forests grow in more temperate regions.

Fir tree (coniferous)   Oak tree (deciduous)

Quick-fire Quiz

1. What proportion of the world's plants and animals can be found in rain forests?
a) One fifth
b) One third
c) One half

2. Which type of forest grows in temperate regions?
a) Deciduous
b) Coniferous
c) Rain forest

3. Which tree does quinine come from?
a) Cinchona
b) Rubber
c) Palm

4. Which type of forest is the world's largest?
a) Deciduous
b) Coniferous
c) Rain forest

What do woodland animals eat?

Deciduous and coniferous forests are found in North America, Europe, and northern Asia. Most animals that live in these woodlands eat leaves and seeds, but some birds eat insects, and some animals eat meat—the wild boar eats mice as well as fungi and acorns. The gray squirrel leaps among the trees in search of fruit and birds' eggs, while deer nibble leaves from the lower branches of trees. Foxes emerge at night to hunt small mammals such as rabbits and mice.

Life on Earth

Simple organisms
3,000 million years ago
(m.y.a.)

Earth is the only planet in the universe that is known to support life. Millions of species of plants and animals currently live in the oceans and on the land, but 95 percent of all species that have ever existed are now extinct.

What is evolution?

Seed-eating

Berry-eating

Insect-eating

Cactus-eating

Evolution is the way in which the characteristics of living things change over time. According to Darwin's theory of natural selection, only "successful" animals will survive over time—animals with useless characteristics will either adapt or become extinct. Darwin noted that evolution had adapted the beaks of finches on the Galapagos Islands (left) to suit different foods.

Charles Darwin

When did life on Earth begin?

Life on Earth began about three billion years ago when chemicals dissolved in the oceans and simple bacteria grew. Then marine plants developed, producing oxygen that enabled marine animals to form. Over time life developed on land.

When did humans first appear?

Modern humans (*homo sapiens sapiens*) probably originated in Africa about 120,000 years ago. When European Neanderthals became extinct about 35,000 years ago, *homo sapiens sapiens* became dominant.

Modern mammals
10,000 years ago (y.a.)

Dinosaurs
220–75 m.y.a.

Homo sapiens sapiens
120,000 y.a.

Neanderthal
100,000–35,000 y.a.

Homo erectus
1.5–0.5 m.y.a.

Homo habilis
2–1.5 m.y.a.

Australopithecus
4–1 m.y.a.

Dryopithecus
15 m.y.a.

Early mammals
70 m.y.a.

How do plants differ from animals?

Plants, unlike animals, are able to produce their own food. They do this by photosynthesis—a process that enables them to convert water into energy with the aid of sunlight and natural solar cells, or chloroplasts (right).

Sunlight

Chloroplasts in leaf cells

74

Which is the most common type of animal?

Explorers and scientists have discovered more than one million animal species, and 97 percent of these are invertebrates. Invertebrates are animals without backbones, including insects, spiders, jellyfish, worms, and mollusks. Vertebrate species—animals with backbones—include reptiles, birds, fish, amphibians, and mammals.

Marine life
600–375 m.y.a.

Amphibians
375–275 m.y.a.

Reptiles
275 m.y.a.

Do animals always stay in the same habitat?

Many animals migrate to warmer climates to avoid the cold weather and food shortages of winter. The longest migration is that of the Arctic tern, which travels 24,800 miles (40,000km) from the Arctic to Antarctica each year (above). Some animals migrate to reproduce—loggerhead turtles swim up to 1,240 miles (2,000km) to their birthplace, where they lay eggs. Many animals do not migrate, and some are found naturally in only one particular part of the world—kangaroos are found only in Australia, ostriches live only in Africa, and giant anteaters are found only in South America.

Quick-fire Quiz

1. When did life on Earth begin?
   a) 300 million years ago
   b) 3 billion years ago
   c) 30 billion years ago

2. How many animal species have been found?
   a) 1 million
   b) 5 million
   c) 10 million

3. What percentage of animal species is invertebrate?
   a) 50 percent
   b) 79 percent
   c) 97 percent

4. Where do ostriches live?
   a) Africa
   b) Australia
   c) South America

2 Freshwater shrimp and snails eat the plants.

3 Trout feed on the shrimp and snails.

1 Water plants produce energy from sunlight, soil, and water.

What is a food chain?

Living things need energy. Plants, which convert light energy into food, are eaten by insects or other animals, which are then eaten by meat-eaters. When living things die, they rot and release nutrients into the ground. In this way energy is passed along a food chain. Animals and plants can belong to many different chains. The food web is the interconnection of different chains.

4 An otter preys on the trout.

6 Bacteria, flies, and maggots feed on the otter, which returns nutrients to the soil.

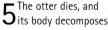

5 The otter dies, and its body decomposes.

Human Landscape

Humans have dramatically changed the face of Earth. Farming, industrialization, and the growth of towns and cities have all had a huge impact on the way we live and on the environment.

What is a city?

A city is a large, important town. It has a big population and is usually a center of commerce and industry. Most cities have grown over time from small towns or villages. Today nearly half of the world's population lives in cities, which are often overcrowded. To create more working and living space, many cities have tall buildings called skyscrapers (right).

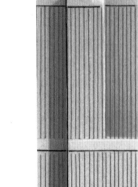

How many people are there in the world?

The world's population is over six billion. It has grown very quickly—in 1800 it was only about one billion. At the moment, around three people are born each second, but it is still difficult for experts to predict how much the population will grow in the future. Depending on future birth rates, the population in 2100 (right) could be 7.5 billion, 11 billion, or over 13 billion. Poorer countries often have higher birth rates than richer ones. This can cause long-term problems for the poorer countries because they have limited food supplies and resources.

The world's population is over six billion

13 billion
12 billion
11 billion
10 billion
9 billion
8 billion
7 billion
6 billion
5 billion
4 billion
3 billion
2 billion
1 billion

1600 1700 1800 1900 2000 2100

Which city has the largest population?

It is not easy to measure city populations. Statistics vary according to how and when populations are counted. Official population counts, or censuses, are carried out every few years and provide the most accurate estimates. Tokyo in Japan probably has the largest population (estimated at around 35 million), and Mexico City has the second largest (22 million). Bombay in India and São Paulo in Brazil follow with populations of around 20 million.

What is a developing country?

A developing country is a nation that has not experienced the development of new technologies and growth in wealth that many richer countries have. Most developing countries are located in the Southern Hemisphere, where extreme climates and lack of resources make progress difficult. Many developing countries have high levels of debt after borrowing money from developed countries and world banking organizations. A nation's wealth is judged by examining its gross national product (GNP)—income generated per year. Developed countries, like Japan, have higher GNPs than developing countries, like India (right).

India

How have changes in farming methods industrialized countries?

The increased use of machinery and improvements in farming methods have resulted in farming being less labor-intensive. This means that fewer farm workers are needed to work the land. In the past most people worked on farms, producing food for hundreds of people, but now many have left the countryside to take jobs in towns and cities. This enables countries to industrialize by developing their industries, factories, and economy. Many people in poorer countries still work in agriculture.

What is an aging population?

In a country with an aging population, the average age of the population is high. This is because the country has a low birth rate—fewer children are born—and because good medical care helps people live longer. Aging populations are usually found in developed countries. Developing countries, where people have more children and shorter life expectancies, have young populations. In Africa nearly 50 percent of the population is under the age of 15.

Quick-fire Quiz

1. What is today's estimated world population?
   a) 1.3 billion
   b) 3 billion
   c) 5.8 billion

2. How many people are born every second?
   a) One
   b) Three
   c) Ten

3. What does GNP stand for?
   a) General national population
   b) Great national possibilities
   c) Gross national product

4. Which countries usually have aging populations?
   a) Developed countries
   b) Developing countries
   c) African countries

Earth's Resources

Earth is rich in natural resources that we can use to make energy, goods, and materials. Many of these natural resources are extracted from deep within the ground or from under the ocean.

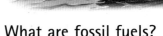

What is a renewable resource?

A renewable resource is a resource we can use without permanently reducing the amount available to us. Sunlight, wind, and water are all renewable resources, and there are many ways that we can produce energy from them (below). Coal, oil, gas, and wood are nonrenewable resources, and one day they will run out. Scientists believe that gas and oil supplies could run out in a few decades.

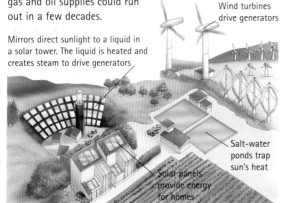

Wind turbines drive generators

Mirrors direct sunlight to a liquid in a solar tower. The liquid is heated and creates steam to drive generators

Salt-water ponds trap sun's heat

Solar panels provide energy for homes

What are fossil fuels?

Coal, oil, and natural gas are all fossil fuels. They are called this because they are made from the fossilized remains of plants and tiny animals. Oil is made from the remains of tiny sea creatures that lived millions of years ago. Oil rigs (above) are used to extract oil from deep beneath the sea bed. An oil rig is a platform with powerful drills that cut down into the rock. Once the oil has been reached, it is pumped up and sent down pipelines to land, where it is made into gasoline and other products.

How can we get energy from water?

Water is a very valuable source of energy. It can be used to produce electric and mechanical power. Hydroelectric plants use water from rivers, waterfalls, and dams to spin enormous wheels called turbines, which generate an electric current. Ocean waves are also a good source of power (right). Waves rock floats that absorb the energy and use it to drive pumps. The pumps force a liquid to spin the turbines and generate electricity.

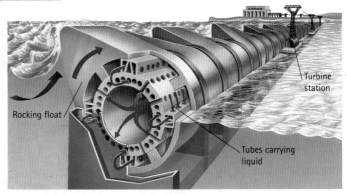

Turbine station

Rocking float

Tubes carrying liquid

What is nuclear energy?

Nuclear energy is created when tiny particles called neutrons are fired at uranium atoms, causing the atoms to split (below). This is called nuclear fission. It releases more neutrons and heat, which is used to generate an electric current. Fusion, which occurs on the sun's surface, also creates nuclear energy. This energy makes the sun shine.

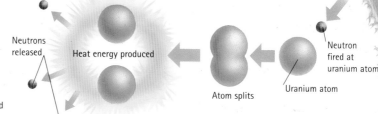

Sun's surface

Neutrons released

Heat energy produced

Neutron fired at uranium atom

Atom splits

Uranium atom

Quarry

Surface ores removed with power shovels

Shafts and tunnels access ores deep below surface

How are metals extracted from the ground?

Metal deposits near the ground's surface are the easiest to extract. Miners scoop them out, using explosives to break up any layers of rock in the way. If the metal ores are deep underground, miners have to tunnel through solid rock and cut them out. Stones used for building, such as marble and slate, are cut or blasted from the ground in a process called quarrying.

Is it possible to create new land?

Since medieval times land has been reclaimed from the sea. In the 1920s a large part of the Netherlands (right) was made usable, or reclaimed, by enclosing it with a massive dam. Today roughly one fourth of the land area of the Netherlands is reclaimed land. Italy, Japan, and England also have areas of reclaimed land.

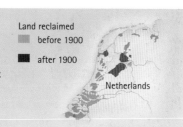

Land reclaimed

■ before 1900

■ after 1900

Netherlands

Do all countries have the resources they need?

Raw materials and energy sources are not evenly spread throughout the world. Russia, the United States, and Brazil are rich in minerals, but some countries must import raw materials. Heavy materials are transported by sea—oil is shipped in huge tankers (right).

Quick-fire Quiz

1. Which of these is a fossil fuel?
a) Coal
b) Wind
c) Sunlight

2. Which atoms are split to create nuclear energy?
a) Uranium
b) Cranium
c) Magnesium

3. Which of these is a renewable resource?
a) Coal
b) Wind
c) Oil

4. How much of the Netherlands is reclaimed land?
a) One eighth
b) One fourth
c) One half

Taking Care of Earth

Humans have done a great deal of damage to Earth. Forests have disappeared, natural vegetation has been cleared to make way for farmland and cities, and industrialization has polluted the oceans, rivers, and atmosphere. Governments and environmentalists have looked for ways to reduce the damage humans have caused.

What is recycling?

Many of Earth's natural raw materials have been used up by humans. Some materials, however, can be made into something new, or recycled. For example, old glass bottles and jars can be crushed and melted to make new glass objects. Aluminum cans, plastic bags and bottles, newspapers, cardboard boxes, and old clothes can also be recycled.

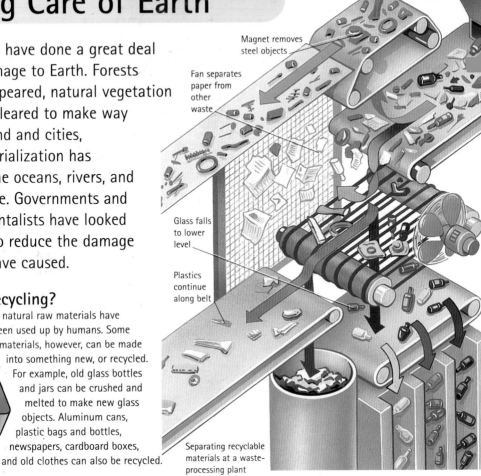

Mixed waste

Magnet removes steel objects

Fan separates paper from other waste

Glass falls to lower level

Plastics continue along belt

Separating recyclable materials at a waste-processing plant

Where is there a hole in the sky?

About 15 miles (25km) up in the atmosphere is a thin layer of ozone that protects Earth from the sun's ultraviolet rays. An excess of the chemical chlorofluorocarbon (CFC) has destroyed part of the layer, creating a hole over Antarctica. CFCs were once widely used in refrigerators, aerosol cans, and fast-food packaging, but they are now banned.

What are wildlife reserves?

Hunting and the destruction of natural environments have caused many animal species to become endangered or even extinct. Wildlife reserves provide a protected, natural wilderness where endangered species can live without risk from game hunters.

How is industrial land reclaimed?

1 Factories release smoke and chemicals into the atmosphere, polluting land and rivers. Garbage dumps and mines destroy natural vegetation.

2 Garbage dumps and old industrial areas can be cleared and covered with a thick layer of soil to be used as recreational land. Open-pit mines can be flooded to make new lakes.

Quick-fire Quiz

1. What is the term for making old materials into something new?
a) Rewinding
b) Rebuilding
c) Recycling

2. How high up is the ozone layer?
a) 1.5 miles
b) 15 miles
c) 25 miles

3. What produces acid rain?
a) Carbon dioxide and oxygen
b) Ozone and carbon monoxide
c) Sulfur dioxide and nitrogen dioxide

4. What does CFC stand for?
a) Cancer-forming chemical
b) Chlorofluorocarbon
c) Carbon fuel chemical

Acid rain

Waste gases produced by factories

What is acid rain?

Burning fossil fuels releases sulfur dioxide and nitrogen dioxide into the air, where they mix with water to form a weak acid. This eventually falls as acid rain (above). Acid rain can fall far away from the source of the pollution. It can kill many trees and acidify rivers and lakes, harming wildlife. Reducing our use of fossil fuels will help reduce the problem of acid rain.

How can we combat deforestation?

To prevent the destruction of rain forests, or deforestation, tropical timber is grown in plantations. Special fast-growing trees that can grow several yards each year are cultivated.

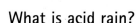

Web Addresses

www.enchantedlearning.com/subjects/rainforests
This is a magical site for both teachers and students, with information, games, and teaching materials on topics including rain forests, geography, oceans, and biomes.

www.funbrain.com/where/index.html
This is a great geography game, available at different levels and also as a two-player version, that will get you up to speed with world geography. Choose your map and pick your level, and then find out where things are in the world.

kids.earth.nasa.gov
This is NASA's planet Earth site for kids and is full of interesting information and activities.

www.kidsplanet.org
A fun, imaginative site for kids on all aspects of planet Earth, from the web of life explained by a garden spider to fact sheets, games, and ecological and environmental issues.

www.eduweb.com/amazon.html
www.eduweb.com/adventure.html
Explore the geography of the Ecuadorian Amazon through online games and activities. Understand how ecofriendly projects work by playing interactive games, such as Amazon Interactive, Tracking the Tiger Trade, Build-A-Prairie, and The Watershed Game.

www.nationalgeographic.com/kids
This site offers lots of information on planet Earth, zoology, and science, as well as games and activities.

mbgnet.mobot.org
Explore the different habitats of the world and learn about the people, animals, and plants that live in each area.

howstuffworks.com/rainforest.htm
An educational site offering useful and interesting articles about rain forests, the animals that live there, and what is happening to them in the world today. Includes links to other sites.

www.animalsoftherainforest.com
An educational rain forest site with large images covering a range of topics from wildlife to deforestation. Plus many links to other sites.

www.rainforestheroes.com/kidscorner/action
A site that offers practical solutions on how to protect rain forests. Includes activities to do at home that will help you understand all about rain forests.

www.thinkquest.org/library/index.html
The ThinkQuest Library is a collection of more than 5,500 educational web sites designed by participants in the ThinkQuest competitions. To see what they have created on planet Earth, enter subjects such as Earth, volcano, river, mountains, and ice age.

www.nwf.org/kids
This National Wildlife site offers games and ecotours led by "Ranger Rick," with lots of information and questions, backed up by a glossary. The site also features many cool things to do in order to better understand and help the planet.

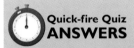
Quick-fire Quiz ANSWERS

Page 47 Earth's Formation
1. a   2. c   3. b   4. a

Page 49 Crust to Core
1. b   2. a   3. c   4. a

Page 51 Water
1. c   2. b   3. a   4. b

Page 53 Land
1. b   2. b   3. b   4. c

Page 55 Earthquakes
1. a   2. c   3. a   4. b

Page 57 Mountains
1. c   2. b   3. a   4. c

Page 59 Volcanoes
1. c   2. a   3. a   4. a

Page 61 Rocks, Fossils, and Minerals
1. a   2. a   3. c   4. b

Page 63 Climate
1. c   2. b   3. b   4. c

Page 65 Weather
1. b   2. b   3. a   4. a

Page 67 Polar Regions
1. b   2. a   3. a   4. c

Page 69 Deserts
1. c   2. b   3. a   4. a

Page 71 Grasslands
1. a   2. c   3. c   4. c

Page 73 Forests
1. c   2. a   3. a   4. b

Page 75 Life on Earth
1. b   2. a   3. c   4. a

Page 77 Human Landscape
1. c   2. b   3. c   4. a

Page 79 Earth's Resources
1. a   2. a   3. b   4. b

Page 81 Taking Care of Earth
1. c   2. a   3. c   4. b

1,000
QUESTIONS
& ANSWERS
FACTFILE

DINOSAURS

Contents

Digging up the Facts

Millions of years ago, dinosaurs ruled the earth, but they died out long before people existed. We only know about dinosaurs from their fossils—animal and plant remains that have been preserved in rocks, and which we can still see today.

How are fossils dug up?

When a dinosaur fossil is found, fossil experts called paleontologists carefully clear away the overlying rocks. They photograph, measure, and record the position of each bone. Then the bones are dug up, wrapped in layers of paper and plaster, and left to dry. This plaster "coat" protects the fossil on its journey to the museum, where the fossil is rebuilt. Sometimes a whole dinosaur skeleton is put together in this way.

How is a fossil formed?

When an animal or plant dies, it usually rots away. However, if it is buried quickly by mud or sand, parts of it may survive. Over millions of years it will turn into a fossil.

1 A dinosaur dies, and its flesh is eaten or rots away.

2 Its skeleton is covered by layers of mud or sand.

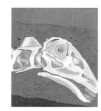

3 Slowly, mud turns to rock, and bones become fossils.

4 As the rock wears away, the fossil is revealed.

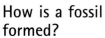

Bone

Skull

Footprints

Skin

Dung

Egg and baby

Insect in amber

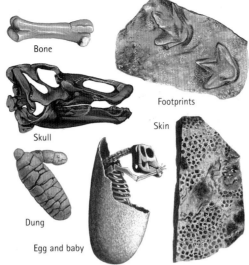

What kinds of fossils are there?

Fossilized bones and teeth are not the only dinosaur remains. Fossilized imprints of their scaly skin, footprints, and nests of eggs have all been found. Scientists can even tell what dinosaurs ate from their fossilized dung. Some fossils form in other ways. For example, an insect trapped in the sticky resin of a tree can be fossilized when the resin turns into hard amber.

Georges Cuvier

Mary Mantell

Gideon Mantell

Richard Owen

Edwin Cope

Othniel Marsh

William Buckland

Quick-fire Quiz

1. What are fossil experts called?
a) Fossiologists
b) Paleontologists
c) Rock collectors

2. Where are most fossils found?
a) Soil
b) Wood
c) Rock

3. Who invented the word "dinosaur"?
a) Mary Mantell
b) Edwin Cope
c) Richard Owen

4. What does *Megalosaurus* mean?
a) Fierce lizard
b) Big lizard
c) Toothed lizard

One name or two?

Dinosaur names are in Latin and have two parts—the genus name and the species name. They are written in italics, and the genus name has a capital letter, as in *Tyrannosaurus rex*. Similar species are grouped in the same genus, which is the name usually used.

Who found the first dinosaur bones?

Dinosaur bones were first found hundreds of years ago, but people thought they were from giants or dragons. In 1822, Georges Cuvier suggested that they belonged to giant reptiles. In 1824, William Buckland named the first dinosaur, *Megalosaurus* ("big lizard"). Fossil-hunters Mary and Gideon Mantell named a second dinosaur, *Iguanodon*, in 1825. Richard Owen first called them "dinosaurs" ("terrible lizards") in 1842. In America, over 130 kinds of dinosaurs were found by Edward Cope and Othniel Marsh.

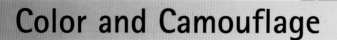

N o one knows for sure what color
dinosaurs were. A few pieces of
fossilized dinosaur skin have been found, but
the color faded millions of years ago. Perhaps
they had similar colors to reptiles today.

What use are colors?

Deinonychus

Skin color can help animals hide, attract a
mate, or send a warning to rivals. Like many
animals today, some dinosaurs may have
been camouflaged. This means their skin was
patterned to blend in with their surroundings. For
example, *Deinonychus* could have been sand-colored,
like a modern lion, to blend in with the sandy ground or dry, yellow
plants. Or perhaps it was striped, like a tiger, so that a pack could
hide among the vegetation until it was ready to attack.

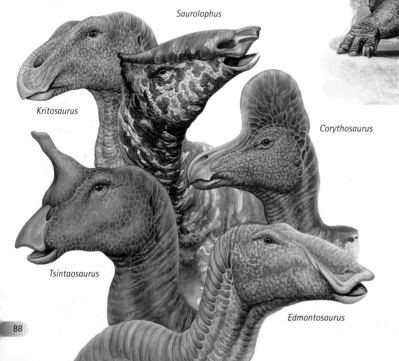

Saurolophus

Kritosaurus

Corythosaurus

Tsintaosaurus

Edmontosaurus

Could dinosaurs see in color?

No one knows for sure, but some
probably could. We do know that
some dinosaurs, called hadrosaurs,
had crests, frills, and inflatable air
sacs on their heads. The hadrosaurs'
heads and crests were probably
brightly colored so that they could
be seen easily. Perhaps the dinosaurs
also used their crests to send signals
to each other. Several modern-day
reptiles send signals in this way.

Were male and female dinosaurs different colors?

Mallard ducks

It is highly possible that they were. The male and female adults of many animals today, including some birds and lizards, are colored differently. The male may use his bright colors to attract a female or to warn other males to stay away. Females may have dull, drab colors so they are harder to spot when sitting on eggs or looking after babies. When artists first started drawing dinosaurs, they tended to make them all brown or green, but now dinosaurs are often shown with very colorful markings.

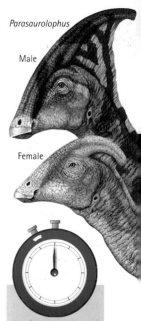

Parasaurolophus

Male

Female

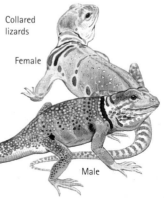

Collared lizards

Female

Male

Why would dinosaurs be striped?

A zebra's stripes break up its outline, making it hard for a predator to pick one animal out from the herd. Dinosaurs that lived in herds may have had stripes for the same reason.

Smooth or scaly?

Fossils and fossilized skin show that many dinosaurs were covered with lumps and bumps for protection. Several colorful reptiles today have similar skin, so some experts think dinosaurs were also brightly colored.

Quick-fire Quiz

1. Which of these had a large crest?
   a) Deinonychus
   b) Corythosaurus
   c) Kritosaurus

2. Why was dinosaur skin bumpy?
   a) For protection
   b) For warmth
   c) For camouflage

3. Why might dinosaurs have had stripes?
   a) To show off
   b) To confuse predators
   c) To attract mates

4. What is camouflage?
   a) Blending in with the surroundings
   b) Changing color
   c) Having bright warning colors

Dinosaur Giants

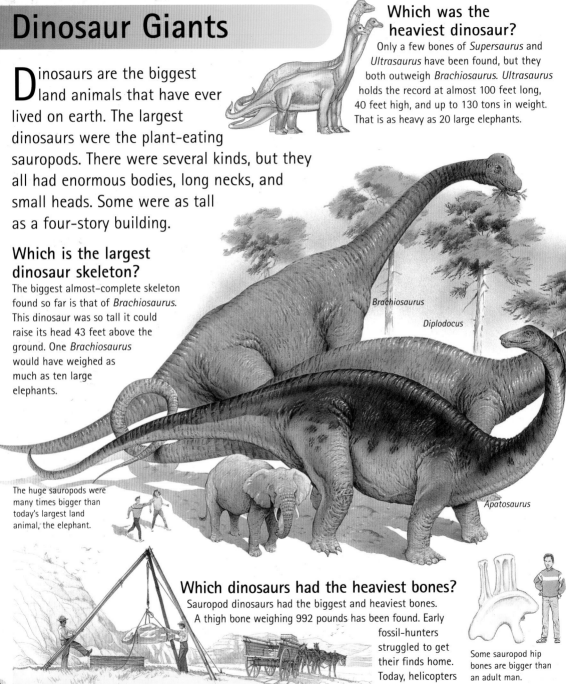

Dinosaurs are the biggest land animals that have ever lived on earth. The largest dinosaurs were the plant-eating sauropods. There were several kinds, but they all had enormous bodies, long necks, and small heads. Some were as tall as a four-story building.

Which is the largest dinosaur skeleton?

The biggest almost-complete skeleton found so far is that of *Brachiosaurus*. This dinosaur was so tall it could raise its head 43 feet above the ground. One *Brachiosaurus* would have weighed as much as ten large elephants.

Which was the heaviest dinosaur?

Only a few bones of *Supersaurus* and *Ultrasaurus* have been found, but they both outweigh *Brachiosaurus*. *Ultrasaurus* holds the record at almost 100 feet long, 40 feet high, and up to 130 tons in weight. That is as heavy as 20 large elephants.

Brachiosaurus

Diplodocus

Apatosaurus

The huge sauropods were many times bigger than today's largest land animal, the elephant.

Which dinosaurs had the heaviest bones?

Sauropod dinosaurs had the biggest and heaviest bones. A thigh bone weighing 992 pounds has been found. Early fossil-hunters struggled to get their finds home. Today, helicopters are often used.

Some sauropod hip bones are bigger than an adult man.

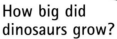

Were dinosaurs smart?

Dinosaurs may have been big, but they were not all very smart. Most of them, like this *Stegosaurus*, had a small brain. For its size, *Brachiosaurus* had the smallest brain of almost any known dinosaur. Its brain weighed only $1/100,000$ of its body weight. You are much brainier: a human brain weighs $1/40$ of an adult's body weight. But fossils show us that some dinosaurs had much bigger brains and were probably more intelligent.

How big did dinosaurs grow?

It is hard to figure out the size of the biggest dinosaurs because only a few bones have been found. Experts think that *Ultrasaurus* was the heaviest and that *Seismosaurus* was the longest (128–170 feet). That's longer than a blue whale—the biggest animal alive today.

Blue whale

Which was the biggest carnivore?

Tyrannosaurus rex was one of the biggest meat-eating dinosaurs. It grew up to 45 feet long and over 16 feet high. Its head alone was over 3 feet long. It could have opened its mouth wide enough to swallow you whole!

Which dinosaur had the biggest feet?

The front feet of sauropods such as *Brachiosaurus* were huge—up to 3 feet long. Some fossilized sauropod footprints are big enough to sit in. A sauropod's feet had to be big to support the dinosaur's great weight. Paleontologists can figure out an animal's size, weight, and speed from its footprints.

No dinosaur could ever really have lived like this.

Did dinosaurs live under water?

People once thought that *Brachiosaurus* was too big to live on land. They thought it supported its weight by living in water and breathing through the nostrils on the top of its head. We now know this is not true. The pressure of the water would have crushed its ribs and kept *Brachiosaurus* from breathing.

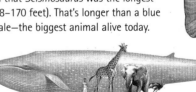

Quick-fire Quiz

1. How long was *Tyrannosaurus rex*'s head?
a) 3 feet
b) 13 feet
c) 30 feet

2. Which dinosaurs lived under water?
a) None of them
b) *Stegosaurus*
c) *Brachiosaurus*

3. Which is the most complete sauropod skeleton?
a) *Brachiosaurus*
b) *Tyrannosaurus*
c) *Ultrasaurus*

4. What is the biggest animal alive today?
a) Elephant
b) *Seismosaurus*
c) Blue whale

Small Dinosaurs

Not all dinosaurs were huge. Some were as small as modern-day lizards. Fewer fossils of small dinosaurs have been found because they were often eaten by other dinosaurs and their fragile bones were easily broken.

What did small dinosaurs eat?

1 Some small dinosaurs ate plants, while others fed on insects, worms, or small reptiles. Tiny *Lesothosaurus* lived in herds and fed on plants. It relied on speed to outrun predators.

What is the smallest dinosaur skeleton?

A *Mussaurus* ("mouse-lizard") skeleton found in Argentina in South America was tiny enough to fit into the palm of your hand. The skeleton was a baby dinosaur with a big head, eyes, and feet. Small eggs, about an inch long, were found nearby. An adult *Mussaurus* would have been about 10 feet long.

Which were the smallest dinosaurs?

One of the earliest and smallest meat-eating dinosaurs was *Saltopus*. At just 24 inches long, its body was the same size as that of a large chicken. *Saltopus* was a speedy hunter and could catch fast-moving lizards and flying insects. In 1984, a small plant-eating dinosaur, *Leaellynasaura*, was found in Australia. It was about the same size as *Saltopus*. However, some scientists think that the fossils were not fully grown and that adult *Leaellynasaura* may have been up to 7 feet long.

Leaellynasaura

Saltopus

2 *Compsognathus* was the size of a large pet cat. It moved quickly, using its speed to catch fast-moving prey like insects and lizards. One *Compsognathus* skeleton has been found with the remains of its last meal, a lizard, inside it.

3 *Hypsilophodon* was a speedy little dinosaur that grew to about 7 feet long. It lived in forests and used its horny beak to nip off juicy shoots from plants.

4 Wolf-sized *Oviraptor* may have darted along at up to 30 miles per hour. It hunted lizards and small mammals and raided other dinosaurs' nests to snatch the eggs.

How big were dinosaur babies?

Newly hatched dinosaur babies were very small. You could have held this baby *Protoceratops* in your hand. One baby *Troodon* fossil has been found that is only 3 inches long—the size of a large hen's egg.

Did small dinosaurs defend themselves?

Scutellosaurus was only the size of a cat, but this little plant-eater was no easy meal for big dinosaurs. It was protected by rows of small, bony knobs along its back and tail, and was the smallest armor-plated dinosaur.

Dinosaur Babies

For centuries, scientists puzzled over how dinosaur babies were born. Then, in 1923, an expedition to the Gobi Desert in Mongolia found a nest of fossilized dinosaur eggs, laid over 100 million years earlier. This proved that dinosaurs hatched from eggs.

Who found the first eggs?

Roy Chapman Andrews discovered the first dinosaur eggs in 1923 in the Gobi Desert. He worked for the American Museum of Natural History and led many exciting dinosaur-hunting expeditions. His team also discovered the remains of *Baluchitherium*, the largest land mammal that ever lived.

How big were dinosaur eggs?

Dinosaur eggs were laid in groups of ten to 40. The size of the egg varied according to the size of the adult, but they were small for such large animals. For example, a 100-foot-long female probably laid eggs about 25 inches long. A really huge egg would need such a thick shell that a baby could not break out of it.

Some dinosaur eggs had rough shells, and others were smooth.

Did dinosaurs build nests?

1 Some dinosaurs, such as the *Maiasaura* shown here, built nests. *Maiasaura* lived in herds. Every year the females gathered at the same nesting site. We know this because a huge nesting area has been found in Montana.

Did dinosaurs look after their babies?

Experts think that some kinds of baby dinosaurs, such as young *Maiasaura*, were not very well developed. The adults probably fed their newly hatched young on soft plant shoots until they were able to fend for themselves. The babies of other dinosaurs, such as *Orodromeus*, were well developed and could probably run soon after they hatched. So perhaps, like many reptiles today, these dinosaurs laid lots of eggs and left their hatchlings to look after themselves.

2 Female *Maiasaura* made low mounds of mud about 6 feet across. Each female dug out a nest and lined it with twigs and leaves.

Did dinosaurs sit on their eggs?

In 1993, an expedition in the Gobi Desert discovered the fossilized remains of an *Oviraptor* sitting on a nest of eggs. The find proved that some dinosaurs sat on their eggs to hatch them, in the same way that birds do today.

Quick-fire Quiz

1. Where were the first eggs found?
a) Sahara Desert
b) Gobi Desert
c) Kalahari Desert

2. Which dinosaur stole eggs?
a) *Troodon*
b) *Triceratops*
c) *Maiasaura*

3. Who found the first eggs?
a) Indiana Jones
b) Richard Owen
c) Roy Chapman Andrews

4. What were *Maiasaura* nests made of?
a) Stones
b) Mud
c) Paper

Did dinosaurs protect their young?

Armored dinosaurs like *Triceratops* may have defended their young by charging a would-be predator. Scientists think a herd of adult plant-eaters on the move defended their young by keeping them in the middle of the group.

3 Each female laid about 20 to 25 eggs in the nest. She covered them with plants to keep them warm.

4 The *Maiasaura* mother guarded her eggs carefully. Egg-thieves, such as *Troodon*, were always ready to snatch an easy meal.

5 The *Maiasaura* hatchlings broke out of their shells using a special, sharp tooth on their snouts.

Communication

Animals cannot talk to each other, so they communicate in other ways. They use sounds, smells, touch, and visual signals to tell each other what is going on. Dinosaurs may have used similar methods to "talk" to one another.

Why was making a noise useful?

Dinosaurs may have used sound to warn of danger or to keep in touch with other members of a large herd. *Parasaurolophus* may have hooted a warning if danger threatened. The duck-billed dinosaur *Edmontosaurus* may have blown up a bag of skin over its nose and bellowed loudly at rival males. Young dinosaurs may have squeaked to get an adult's attention.

What sounds did dinosaurs make?

Dinosaurs had complex ears and could probably hear well, so they may have used many different sounds to send signals to each other. Like reptiles today, most dinosaurs could probably hiss or grunt, and large ones may have roared. A few, like the hadrosaurs, probably made distinctive calls to each other through their horns, crests, and inflatable nose flaps. Scientists believe this is possible because when they blew through models of different hadrosaur skulls, they found that each skull made a different sound.

Tsintaosaurus

Edmontosaurus

Corythosaurus

Male peacock displaying

Lambeosaurus

Did dinosaurs display like birds?

Experts think that some male dinosaurs displayed to the females during the mating season. Just as peacocks display their colored feathers, male dinosaurs may have displayed bright head crests, spines, or neck ruffs to attract females and ward off rival males.

Did dinosaurs use their noses?

Fossils of dinosaurs' brains suggest that many dinosaurs had a good sense of smell and that most had well-developed nostrils. A strong sense of smell would have helped dinosaurs sniff out food. If, as some scientists think, dinosaurs gave off scent signals, they may also have used their sense of smell to find a mate. *Brachiosaurus* had huge nostrils on the top of its head. No one knows why, but perhaps they allowed the dinosaur to eat water plants and breathe at the same time.

Brachiosaurus

Parasaurolophus herd

Quick-fire Quiz

1. Which dinosaur group had head crests?
a) Hadrosaurs
b) Theropods
c) Lizards

2. Which dinosaur had an inflatable nose flap?
a) *Edmontosaurus*
b) *Brachiosaurus*
c) *Lambeosaurus*

3. Which dinosaur had a hollow crest?
a) *Tyrannosaurus*
b) *Brachiosaurus*
c) *Parasaurolophus*

4. Where were *Brachiosaurus's* nostrils?
a) On the end of its nose
b) On top of its head
c) It didn't have any

How did noisy noses work?

Hadrosaurs such as *Parasaurolophus* and *Lambeosaurus* had hollow crests. Air passages extended from the nose, through the crest, and down into the throat. The dinosaurs could hoot and honk as they breathed in and out. Different types of crests produced different notes.

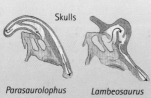

Skulls

Parasaurolophus   *Lambeosaurus*

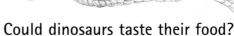

Could dinosaurs taste their food?

Many dinosaurs had tongues, and they could probably taste and smell their food, like most animals today. Reptiles such as snakes use their forked tongue to "taste" the air for traces of prey. But there is no evidence to suggest that any dinosaurs had tongues that could do this.

Plant-eaters

Most dinosaurs were herbivores. This means they ate only plants. Plant-eating dinosaurs came in all shapes and sizes, from small, two-legged dinosaurs to huge sauropods. Plants are hard to digest, so to get enough energy from their food, many spent most of the day eating.

Psittacosaurus

Lizard or bird hips?

Experts divide dinosaurs into two groups by the shape of their hips. Sauropod plant-eaters (1) had lizard hips. Their big stomachs unbalanced them, so they had to walk on four legs. Two-legged theropod meat-eaters (2) also had lizard hips. Plant-eating bird-hipped dinosaurs (3) evolved later. Many walked on two legs with their big stomach slung between their back legs. Armored bird-hipped plant-eaters were so heavy that they walked on four legs.

1

2

3

Did dinosaurs eat leaves?

Leaves were the main diet of many plant-eaters. *Psittacosaurus* probably snipped leaves off with its birdlike beak, then sliced them into smaller bits with its scissorlike teeth. Like the giraffe, *Brachiosaurus* used its long neck to graze on leafy treetops.

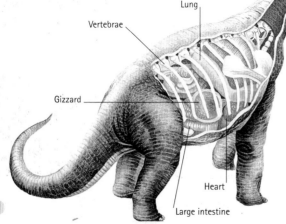

Lung

Vertebrae

Gizzard

Heart

Large intestine

Why were sauropods so big?

A sauropod's huge body was filled almost entirely with its organs. Sauropods, like *Brachiosaurus*, ate up to 450 pounds of plants a day, so they needed a big stomach and long intestines to digest this tough food. Experts once had to guess what a dinosaur's insides looked like, but in 1998, two dinosaurs from China were found with their organs intact. These should tell us more about what dinosaurs ate.

Lufengosaurus

1 2 3 4 5

Did plant–eaters have teeth?

Most plant-eating dinosaurs had teeth, and experts can tell what food a dinosaur ate by looking at them. *Lufengosaurus*, an early sauropod, had many small, peglike teeth with jagged edges. These were great for nipping off soft leaves, but no use for chewing, so *Lufengosaurus* swallowed its food whole.

Why were teeth different shapes?

The size and shape of a dinosaur's teeth depended on what it ate. The ornithopod *Heterodontosaurus* had sharp, narrow front teeth (1) for cutting and slicing. *Plateosaurus* (2) and sauropods like *Diplodocus* (3) and *Apatosaurus* (4) had peglike teeth to shred and crush food. *Stegosaurus* (5) had leaf-shaped teeth for slicing and munching soft plants.

Why did dinosaurs swallow stones?

Small stones have been found in the rib cages of many dinosaurs. Few dinosaurs could move their jaws from side to side, so they could not chew their food. They swallowed it whole and probably swallowed small stones, called gastroliths, to help them grind food as it churned in their stomachs. Chickens swallow grit to do the same thing.

Shunosaurus

Quick-fire Quiz

1. What are gastroliths?
a) Grinding teeth
b) Stomach stones
c) Plants

2. Which dinosaur had leaf-shaped teeth?
a) *Diplodocus*
b) *Apatosaurus*
c) *Stegosaurus*

3. Which dinosaur had a birdlike beak?
a) *Shunosaurus*
b) *Brachiosaurus*
c) *Psittacosaurus*

4. What did *Triceratops* eat?
a) Fruit and nuts
b) Ferns and horsetails
c) Grass

Did dinosaurs eat grass?

Grasses did not develop on earth until 25 million years after the dinosaurs died out. Instead, herbivorous dinosaurs ate other plants that were around at the time. Long-necked sauropods such as *Shunosaurus* used their simple, peglike teeth to munch on leaves, pine needles, and juicy shoots. A hadrosaur such as *Saurolophus* ate leaves from flowering plants and crunchy pinecones. It chopped off the leaves with its horny beak, then chewed them with its flat back teeth. Horned dinosaurs like *Triceratops* sliced up tough ferns and horsetails with their sharp beaks and teeth.

Leaves, pine needles, and shoots

Pinecones and shrub leaves

Ferns and horsetails

Saurolophus

Triceratops

99

Meat-eaters

All meat-eating, or carnivorous, dinosaurs were theropods. (Theropod means "beast foot.") They walked on two legs, and their three toes were armed with sharp claws. Some were fierce hunters, chasing and killing their prey. Others were scavengers, feeding on dead animals.

Did dinosaurs have sharp teeth?

The sharp, backward-pointing teeth of *Megalosaurus* are typical of many large meat-eating dinosaurs. They were good for gripping and ripping their prey. Other carnivorous dinosaurs had small, sharp teeth or crushing beaks.

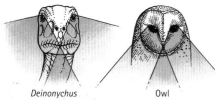

Deinonychus   *Owl*

Did meat-eaters have sharp eyesight?

Many hunters, such as *Deinonychus*, had good eyesight. It may have had forward-facing eyes and good binocular (overlapping) vision, like modern owls. This would have given it a single view of its prey and helped it judge distances.

Did all meat-eaters look alike?

Meat-eating dinosaurs came in all shapes and sizes. They ranged from chicken-sized *Saltopus* (24 inches) to huge *Tyrannosaurus* (40 feet long). Big theropods like *Tyrannosaurus*, *Allosaurus*, and *Dilophosaurus* hunted large plant-eaters, while speedy *Troodon* killed small reptiles and mammals. *Struthiomimus*, *Avimimus*, and *Oviraptor* used their strong beaks to catch and crush insects and eggs.

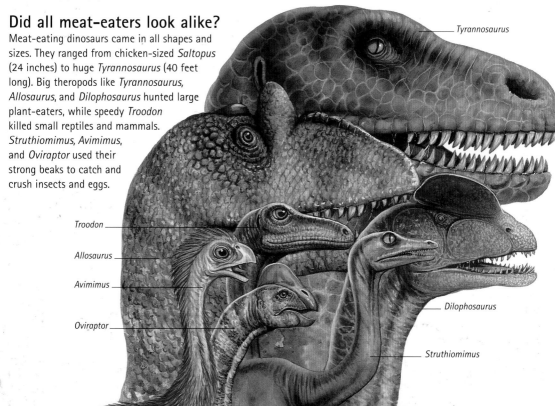

Tyrannosaurus

Troodon

Allosaurus

Avimimus

Oviraptor

Dilophosaurus

Struthiomimus

Did dinosaurs eat fish?

Experts believe that dinosaurs such as *Baryonyx* snapped up fish with their long, crocodile-like jaws. *Baryonyx* may also have speared fish with the huge, hooklike claws on its front feet, just as brown bears do today.

Which dinosaurs used claws to kill?

Deinonychus ("terrible claw") and its relatives specialized in using their claws to kill animals much larger than themselves. *Deinonychus* leapt at its victims, slashing them with the deadly, 5-inch claw on the second toe of its back foot.

Did dinosaurs hunt in packs?

Like today's wolves, some small meat-eating dinosaurs, such as *Deinonychus*, hunted in packs. This would have allowed them to hunt larger prey, such as a young *Diplodocus*, separating it from the rest of its herd.

Quick-fire Quiz

1. Which dinosaur was a cannibal?
a) *Diplodocus*
b) *Dilophosaurus*
c) *Coelophysis*

2. Which dinosaur ate fish?
a) *Oviraptor*
b) *Allosaurus*
c) *Baryonyx*

3. Which dinosaur name means "terrible claw"?
a) *Troodon*
b) *Deinonychus*
c) *Tyrannosaurus*

4. What did scavengers eat?
a) Dead animals
b) Bark
c) Leaves

Wolf pack

Were any dinosaurs cannibals?

Fossil remains of *Coelophysis* found in New Mexico had skeletons of young ones inside them. The bones were too big to belong to unborn *Coelophysis*. Experts believe that adult *Coelophysis* would eat their own young if food was short. Other dinosaurs may have been cannibals, too.

Did dinosaurs eat eggs?

Small, speedy meat-eaters such as *Troodon* snatched unguarded eggs from other dinosaurs' nests. Eggs were a good source of food—a complete meal in a shell! *Troodon* could sprint at about 30 miles per hour, so few lumbering plant-eaters could catch it.

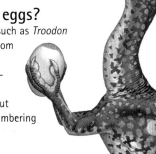

The Fiercest Dinosaur

Tyrannosaurus rex ("king tyrant lizard") lived about 70 million years ago. At over 40 feet long and three times as tall as a man, it was one of the largest and deadliest creatures that has ever lived on land.

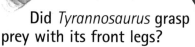

Did *Tyrannosaurus* grasp prey with its front legs?

Tyrannosaurus's arms and hands were too small to grasp its prey. They couldn't even reach its mouth. Its head and teeth were so strong and deadly that it did not need its arms to catch its prey.

Has a whole *Tyrannosaurus* skeleton ever been found?

Complete fossil skeletons are very rare, but in 1990, two almost complete *Tyrannosaurus* skeletons were found in the United States. Experts studying *Tyrannosaurus* skeletons believe that, unlike modern meat-eaters such as lions and tigers, the female *Tyrannosaurus* was probably bigger than the male.

Tyrannosaurus skeleton

Dilophosaurus

Allosaurus

Albertosaurus

How big were *T. rex* teeth?

Tyrannosaurus had teeth up to 7 inches long. These teeth had a razor-sharp point to stab prey, and rough, sawlike edges to rip through flesh. An adult had between 50 and 100 teeth. If one fell out, it simply grew another!

Were there other big meat-eaters?

The three meat-eaters above were related to *Tyrannosaurus*, but were not as big. Two huge, 8.5-foot-long fossil arms with clawed hands were found in Mongolia and named *Deinocheirus* ("terrible hand"). They may be from a species of *Deinonychus* that was even bigger than *Tyrannosaurus*.

Quick-fire Quiz

1. How long ago did *Tyrannosaurus* live?
a) 7 million years
b) 70 million years
c) 170 million years

2. How long were its teeth?
a) Up to 2 inches
b) Up to 5 inches
c) Up to 7 inches

3. Which dinosaur was related to *Tyrannosaurus*?
a) *Triceratops*
b) *Albertosaurus*
c) *Deinocheirus*

4. What does "*Tyrannosaurus rex*" mean?
a) Big, bad lizard
b) King tyrant lizard
c) Emperor reptile

Was *Tyrannosaurus* fast or slow?

Experts used to think that *Tyrannosaurus* stood upright and lumbered along, dragging its tail on the ground. By studying the more complete skeletons, they now think it leaned forward, with its tail sticking out as a balance, and that it could run fast. Judging from its skull and the size of its brain, experts think it also had good eyesight and hearing and an excellent sense of smell.

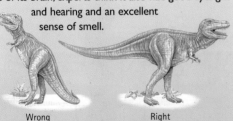

Wrong   Right

Was the fiercest dinosaur a scavenger?

Some experts think *Tyrannosaurus* was a scavenger that ate dead animals and stole prey from other predators. Others think it could run as fast as a racehorse (30 miles per hour) and was a fierce hunter. The latest finds show it probably did both.

Attack and Defense

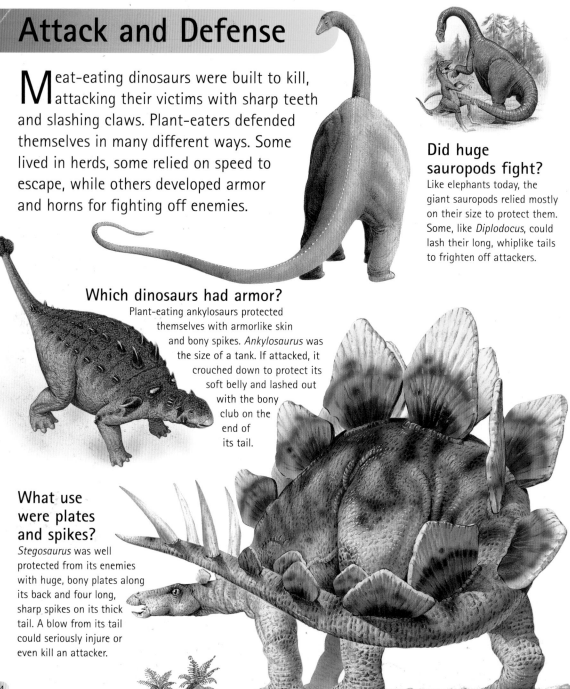

Meat-eating dinosaurs were built to kill, attacking their victims with sharp teeth and slashing claws. Plant-eaters defended themselves in many different ways. Some lived in herds, some relied on speed to escape, while others developed armor and horns for fighting off enemies.

Did huge sauropods fight?

Like elephants today, the giant sauropods relied mostly on their size to protect them. Some, like *Diplodocus*, could lash their long, whiplike tails to frighten off attackers.

Which dinosaurs had armor?

Plant-eating ankylosaurs protected themselves with armorlike skin and bony spikes. *Ankylosaurus* was the size of a tank. If attacked, it crouched down to protect its soft belly and lashed out with the bony club on the end of its tail.

What use were plates and spikes?

Stegosaurus was well protected from its enemies with huge, bony plates along its back and four long, sharp spikes on its thick tail. A blow from its tail could seriously injure or even kill an attacker.

Armor or radiators?

The plates along the back of *Stegosaurus* were covered with skin and had a lot of blood vessels in them. Some experts think they may have helped the dinosaur warm its body when it basked in the sun, and cool down by losing heat quickly in the shade. Other scientists think the plates were armor to protect it from carnosaurs (meat-eating dinosaurs) such as *Tyrannosaurus*.

Did plant-eaters have claws?

Most did not, but the plant-eating *Iguanodon* had two sharp thumb spikes. Perhaps it used them to stab attackers. Or maybe the males used them to fight each other.

Which dinosaurs had horns?

Plant-eating dinosaurs called ceratopsians developed horns and bony frills to protect themselves. They may have charged at enemies as a rhinoceros does, or maybe rival males fought by locking horns.

Quick-fire Quiz

1. Which dinosaur had plates and spikes?
a) *Stegosaurus*
b) *Diplodocus*
c) *Tyrannosaurus*

2. Which dinosaur had a tail club?
a) *Velociraptor*
b) *Ankylosaurus*
c) *Diplodocus*

3. How did *Iguanodon* protect itself?
a) With armor
b) With thumb spikes
c) With horns

4. Which dinosaurs had horns and bony frills ?
a) *Velociraptors*
b) Ceratopsians
c) Utopians

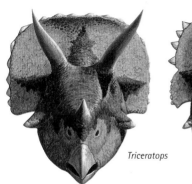

Triceratops

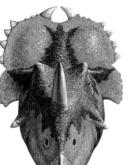

Centrosaurus

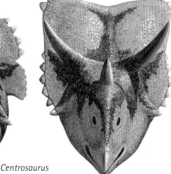

Chasmosaurus

What evidence is there?

A fossil found in Mongolia in 1971 showed a *Protoceratops* fighting like a rhinoceros, charging at a *Velociraptor* and smashing into it with its bony beak. The *Velociraptor*'s sharp claws had pierced the stomach and throat of the *Protoceratops*.

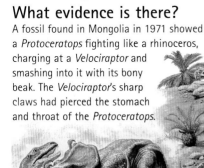

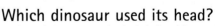

Which dinosaur used its head?

Pachycephalosaurus males had skulls with very thick tops. Rival males may have had head-butting contests to win a mate, like some wild sheep do today.

105

All Over the World

This map shows where dinosaur fossils have been found. Experts have divided the dinosaur age into three main parts: the Triassic, Jurassic, and Cretaceous Periods. Different dinosaurs lived in each period, so some fossils are older than others.

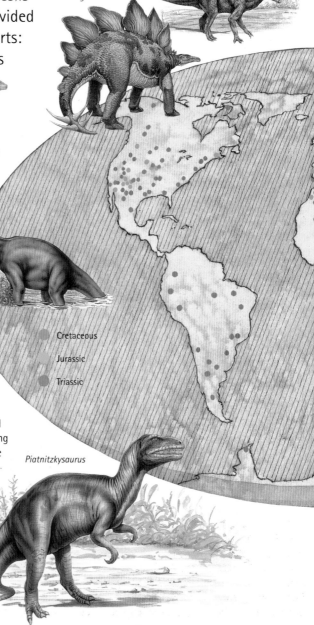

Stegosaurus

Maiasaura

Deinonychus

Diplodocus

Cretaceous

Jurassic

Triassic

Piatnitzkysaurus

Which dinosaurs have been found in North America?

Hundreds of dinosaur fossils, including *Diplodocus*, *Deinonychus*, and *Stegosaurus*, have been found in North America. The famous *Tyrannosaurus* and *Triceratops* have been found in North America, and nowhere else.

Which was the fiercest dinosaur in South America?

One of the biggest South American meat-eaters found so far is *Piatnitzkysaurus*, which was about 20 feet long and 10 feet high. It chased and killed prey in the same way as its larger North American relative, *Allosaurus*.

Did some dinosaurs live all over the world?

Some dinosaurs, such as *Brachiosaurus*, have been found in North America, Africa, and Europe. Some dinosaurs have only been found on one continent.

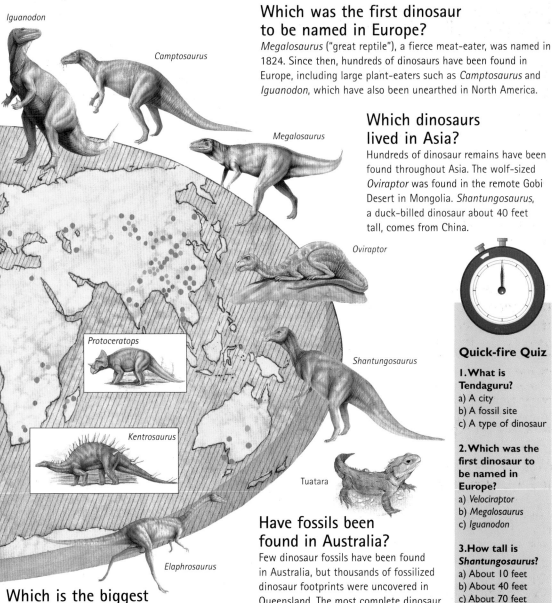

Iguanodon

Camptosaurus

Megalosaurus

Which was the first dinosaur to be named in Europe?

Megalosaurus ("great reptile"), a fierce meat-eater, was named in 1824. Since then, hundreds of dinosaurs have been found in Europe, including large plant-eaters such as *Camptosaurus* and *Iguanodon*, which have also been unearthed in North America.

Which dinosaurs lived in Asia?

Hundreds of dinosaur remains have been found throughout Asia. The wolf-sized *Oviraptor* was found in the remote Gobi Desert in Mongolia. *Shantungosaurus*, a duck-billed dinosaur about 40 feet tall, comes from China.

Oviraptor

Protoceratops

Shantungosaurus

Kentrosaurus

Tuatara

Elaphrosaurus

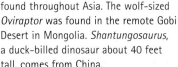

Quick-fire Quiz

1. What is **Tendaguru?**
a) A city
b) A fossil site
c) A type of dinosaur

2. Which was the first dinosaur to be named in **Europe?**
a) *Velociraptor*
b) *Megalosaurus*
c) *Iguanodon*

3. How tall is *Shantungosaurus?*
a) About 10 feet
b) About 40 feet
c) About 70 feet

4. Where does the tuatara live?
a) North America
b) Australia
c) New Zealand

Which is the biggest fossil site in Africa?

One of the biggest fossil sites in Africa is Tendaguru in Tanzania. Over 200 tons of dinosaur bones were found there between 1909 and 1912. Many kinds of dinosaurs were dug up, including the stegosaur *Kentrosaurus* and the small, bird-like *Elaphrosaurus*.

Have fossils been found in Australia?

Few dinosaur fossils have been found in Australia, but thousands of fossilized dinosaur footprints were uncovered in Queensland. The most complete dinosaur find is an iguanodon, *Muttaburrasaurus*. A few dinosaur fossils have also been found in New Zealand. The tuatara, a reptile that still lives there today, looks almost exactly the same as its ancestors that lived in the dinosaur age.

Living in Herds

Clues such as footprints and mass dinosaur graves show that some dinosaurs lived in groups. Plant-eating dinosaurs probably herded together for safety, as antelopes do today. Some meat-eaters may have hunted in packs.

Which dinosaurs probably lived alone?

Large meat-eating dinosaurs such as *Albertosaurus* were excellent hunters and had few enemies. They could have lived and hunted alone, just as tigers do today. However, the bones of 40 young and adult *Allosaurus* were discovered in a group in the United States, so perhaps they hunted in packs like lions.

Why did dinosaurs live together?

Many plant-eaters, like these *Edmontosaurus* hadrosaurs, lived in herds for protection. Many eyes keeping watch for a predator is better than one pair. It is also more difficult for a predator to attack a large, moving herd. These hadrosaurs probably hooted and honked to signal to each other if there was danger, such as a carnosaur, nearby.

Did herd members look after each other?

Fossilized footprints show that some dinosaur herds traveled with the young in the middle and the adults on the outside. If attacked, horned dinosaurs like *Triceratops* may have formed a circle around their young, with their horns pointing out toward the enemy, as musk oxen do today.

How do we know about dinosaur herds?

Vast tracks of fossilized dinosaur footprints all going the same way were discovered in North America. Experts believe they belonged to herds of dinosaurs. Huge numbers of dinosaurs have also been found buried together. One of these sites contained 10,000 duck-billed *Maiasaura*. This evidence shows that sauropods probably lived in groups.

Why did some herds die together?

In 1947, the fossilized remains of a large herd of *Coelophysis* were found at Ghost Ranch in New Mexico. The bones came from both young and old animals. Some experts think they probably all died together in a flash flood. Their bodies were carried along by the water and eventually dumped in a heap on a sandbank, where they fossilized.

Did dinosaurs travel far?

Some dinosaurs, like these iguanodons, probably traveled huge distances in search of food. Today, animals such as caribou and wildebeests do the same.

Did herds migrate?

Probably. Dinosaurs have been found in the Arctic and Antarctic, where there would have been plenty of food in the summer, but little in the winter. Experts think that dinosaur herds migrated away from the poles in the winter, as modern-day caribou do.

Did dinosaur herds have lookouts?

No one knows for sure, but in large herds of animals, some adults keep watch for predators. Dinosaurs probably did the same.

Which dinosaurs hunted in packs?

Carnivores like wolves and hyenas hunt in packs. Many small meat-eating dinosaurs, such as *Elaphrosaurus*, probably hunted in packs too. This would have allowed them to hunt and kill larger prey than if they hunted alone.

Fast and Slow

A dinosaur's shape, size, and speed were determined by how it lived. Hunters had to be fast to catch their prey. They ran on strong back legs, using their tails for balance. Huge plant-eaters could only move slowly. They did not need to chase food, and their huge size kept them safe.

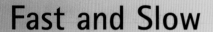

Iguanodon

Megalosaurus

How can we measure a dinosaur's speed?

Experts work out the speed at which a dinosaur moved from the space between its footprints and the length of its legs. The farther apart a dinosaur's tracks are, the faster it was moving. If the footprints are close together, it was probably walking slowly.

What can footprints tell us?

Fossilized footprints can show how dinosaurs moved. For example, *Iguanodon* walked on all fours, but could run on its back legs. The huge, three-toed prints of *Megalosaurus* show that it was a meat-eater and always moved on its back legs.

Which was the fastest dinosaur?

Ostrich-sized *Struthiomimus* was one of the fastest. It had no armor or horns to protect it and had to rely on speed to escape. It was as fast as a racehorse, reaching speeds of over 30 miles per hour.

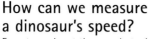

How fast did dinosaurs move?

1 Just like animals today, dinosaurs moved at different speeds at different times. *Tyrannosaurus* walked at 10 miles per hour, but ran much faster when attacking.

2 *Hypsilophodon* was one of the speediest dinosaurs. This plant-eater could race along at up to 30 miles per hour to escape from enemies.

3 *Apatosaurus* weighed 40 tons— as much as seven elephants. It walked at 6 to 10 miles per hour. If it had tried to run, the impact would have broken its legs.

4 *Triceratops* weighed as much as five rhinoceroses. It could also charge like a rhinoceros at speeds of over 15 miles per hour. Few predators would risk attacking it.

Which was the slowest dinosaur?

The huge sauropods, like *Brachiosaurus*, were the slowest-moving dinosaurs. At over 50 tons, they were too heavy to run, so they plodded along at about 6 miles per hour. Unlike smaller dinosaurs, these huge creatures were probably too big to have reared up on their hind legs.

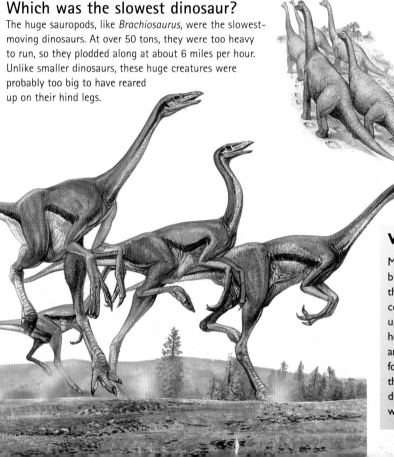

Quick-fire Quiz

1. How fast could *Triceratops* charge?
a) Over 15 mph
b) Over 25 mph
c) Over 55 mph

2. Which dinosaur could reach over 30 mph?
a) *Apatosaurus*
b) *Struthiomimus*
c) *Brachiosaurus*

3. Which of these shows how fast a dinosaur moved?
a) Its head
b) Its footprints
c) Its tail

4. Which legs did *Megalosaurus* use?
a) Its front legs
b) Its back legs
c) All four legs

Warm or cold blood?

Mammals and birds are warm-blooded, which means they make their own body heat. Reptiles are cold-blooded and have to warm up in the sun. To get the energy to heat their bodies, warm-blooded animals need about ten times more food than a cold-blooded animal of the same size. Studying how much dinosaurs ate may show if any were warm-blooded.

In the Sea

While dinosaurs ruled the land, other giant reptiles took over the seas. Mosasaurs, plesiosaurs, and pliosaurs were fierce predators, snapping up fish and other sea creatures. Giant turtles and crocodiles also hunted in prehistoric oceans.

Are all prehistoric sea reptiles extinct?

Most kinds of large sea reptiles died out with the dinosaurs, but turtles and crocodiles still exist. Prehistoric *Deinosuchus*, a 53-foot-long crocodile, however, was much bigger than any crocodile living today.

Deinosuchus

Kronosaurus

Mosasaurus

What did sea reptiles eat?

Sea reptiles ate fish, shellfish, and even each other! A *placodont* picked up shellfish with its long front teeth. It crushed them with its back teeth, spat out the shells, and swallowed the rest.

Teleosaurus

Ammonite (swimming shellfish)

Placodont

Who was Mary Anning?

Mary Anning was born in 1799 in Dorset, England. She grew up to be a great fossil-hunter and was so good that she earned her living by selling fossils. She found the first complete fossilized skeleton of a giant marine ichthyosaur when she was only 12 years old. Another of her amazing finds was the first complete skeleton of a plesiosaur.

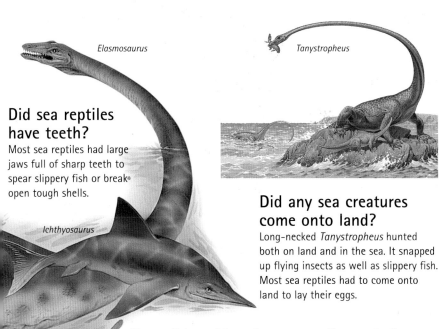
Elasmosaurus

Tanystropheus

Ichthyosaurus

Did sea reptiles have teeth?

Most sea reptiles had large jaws full of sharp teeth to spear slippery fish or break open tough shells.

Did any sea creatures come onto land?

Long-necked *Tanystropheus* hunted both on land and in the sea. It snapped up flying insects as well as slippery fish. Most sea reptiles had to come onto land to lay their eggs.

How did prehistoric sea reptiles swim?

Pliosaurs like *Kronosaurus* and plesiosaurs like *Elasmosaurus* had four strong paddles instead of feet. They moved them up and down to "fly" through the sea in the same way penguins do today. *Mosasaurus*, *Ichthyosaurus*, and crocodiles such as *Teleosaurus* swam by beating their tails from side to side. Sea reptiles could not breathe under water, so they swam to the surface to gulp in air.

Kronosaurus skeleton

How big were the sea reptiles?

One of the biggest sea reptiles was the pliosaur *Kronosaurus*. It was 55 feet long, with a huge head the size of a car. *Mosasaurus* was over 30 feet long, the largest lizard ever. Prehistoric turtles were also much bigger than their modern relatives. The largest, *Archelon*, was 13 feet long. Its huge front paddles powered it through the water at up to 10 miles per hour.

Archelon

Quick-fire Quiz

1. What was *Deinosuchus*?
   a) A fish
   b) A pliosaur
   c) A crocodile

2. How did sea reptiles breathe?
   a) At the surface
   b) Under water
   c) They didn't breathe air at all

3. Who found the first complete fossil ichthyosaur?
   a) Mary Mantell
   b) William Buckland
   c) Mary Anning

4. Which sea reptile gave birth to live young?
   a) *Elasmosaurus*
   b) *Ichthyosaurus*
   c) *Archelon*

Did sea reptiles lay eggs?

Most sea reptiles laid their eggs on land, like turtles today. But *Ichthyosaurus* gave birth to live young in the same way as sea mammals like this dolphin do today.

113

In the Air

When dinosaurs took over the land, other reptiles took to the air. The first reptiles to master flight were the pterosaurs. They ruled the skies for 166 million years, but died out at the end of the dinosaur age.

How big were pterosaurs?

Pterosaurs came in many sizes. *Quetzalcoatlus* was the largest. It had a human-sized body and a wingspan of over 40 feet—bigger than a hang glider! *Rhamphorhynchus* was the size of a crow, with a wingspan of 16 inches.

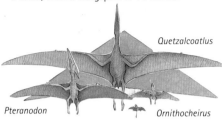

Quetzalcoatlus

Pteranodon

Ornithocheirus

Rhamphorhynchus

What did pterosaurs eat?

Pterosaurs' jaws and teeth help show what they ate. Most fed on fish, while some snapped up insects. *Pterodaustro* may have filtered tiny animals from the water with its sievelike bottom jaw. *Dzungaripterus's* pincerlike beak could prise shellfish from rocks. *Dimorphodon's* strong jaws were ideal for catching fish.

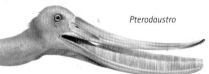

Pterodaustro

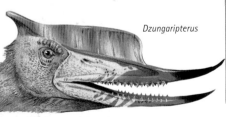

Dzungaripterus

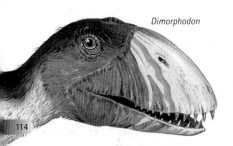

Dimorphodon

Pteranodon

Did pterosaurs build nests?

No one knows, but scientists think pterosaurs probably laid eggs. They may have laid them in nests and sat on them to keep them warm. Fossils show that baby pterosaurs were not well developed, so perhaps the adults fed them, as baby birds are fed today.

Furry and active?

Fossil evidence shows that some pterosaurs were covered with fur, which probably means they were warm-blooded, like birds. They also had big brains with large areas to control balance and sight.

When did reptiles first fly?

Reptiles first took to the air about 250 million years ago. Early flying reptiles, such as *Coelurosauravus*, were lizard-shaped with four legs. Their wings grew out from the sides of their bodies and were held rigid on long ribs. These reptiles used their wings to help them glide from tree to tree, but they could not flap them. One of the earliest gliding reptiles, *Longisquama*, had tall crests along its back. The crests may have opened out like wings to help it glide.

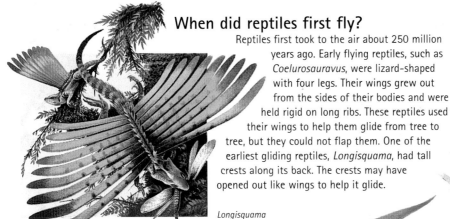

Longisquama

Coelurosauravus

Quetzalcoatlus

Bat

Did pterosaurs have tails?

All pterosaurs had tails. Early kinds, such as *Dimorphodon*, had long tails to increase lift and help them steer. Later types, such as *Pteranodon*, were called pterodactyls. They had much bigger wings and tiny tails.

Did pterosaurs have feathers?

Most pterosaurs were furry, not feathered, and their wings were made from sheets of leathery skin. In this way, they were more like bats than birds. The wings stretched from the pterosaur's body along its arm to the tips of its long fourth fingers. Their long wings were ideal for soaring on air currents.

Quick-fire Quiz

1. Which was the largest pterosaur?
a) *Pteranodon*
b) *Quetzalcoatlus*
c) *Pterodaustro*

2. What were pterosaurs' wings made of?
a) Feathers
b) Hair
c) Skin

3. What did most pterosaurs eat?
a) Fish
b) Dinosaurs
c) Insects

4. What were pterosaurs?
a) Dinosaurs
b) Reptiles
c) Birds

Death of the Dinosaurs

Dinosaurs died out about 65 million years ago. Studies show that they disappeared slowly in some places, but more suddenly in others. There are many theories to explain their extinction, but no one knows which is right.

Did a meteorite hit Earth?

One of the main theories is that a huge rock falling from outer space hit the earth. This meteorite threw up a cloud of dust, blocking out the sun's light and heat. The earth became much colder, and animals that could not cope with this died out. A huge crater that probably formed around this time has been found off the coast of Mexico. This evidence supports the idea that a meteorite caused the end of the dinosaurs.

Crater caused by a meteorite

United States

Gulf of Mexico

✳ Impact site

Did mammals eat dinosaur eggs?

One explanation for the death of the dinosaurs is that the number of small mammals increased. The mammals ate so many dinosaur eggs that few babies hatched. There are many strange theories, and this is one of the more unlikely ones.

Did plant life change?

The extinction of dinosaurs and other animals may have been gradual. Towards the end of the dinosaur age, the tropical climate in North America became cooler and more seasonal, and tropical plants were replaced by woodland plants. The dinosaurs seem to have migrated south, so perhaps they could not adapt to these changes in climate and plant life.

Did volcanoes make a difference?

Fossilized plant remains suggest that by 65 million years ago, the earth's climate had become cooler. Some scientists think this was caused by several huge volcanic eruptions that took place over a period of half a million years. Volcanoes send up gases and dust that can first heat the atmosphere, then cool it down, killing off life.

Were there other mass extinctions?

The end of the dinosaurs was not the first mass extinction. About 440 million years ago, almost half of the animal species died out, and another half died 370 million years ago. Over 95 percent of all living things died out about 345 million years ago, and 210 million years ago, at the end of the Permian Period, many land vertebrates died out. When these events happen, new species can take over the world.

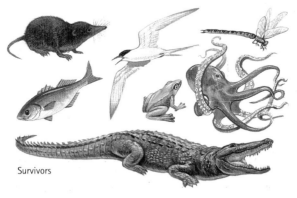

Survivors

Which animals died with the dinosaurs?

When the dinosaurs died out, so did many other reptiles, including mosasaurs, plesiosaurs, pliosaurs, and pterosaurs. Swimming shellfish like ammonites died too. Most other plants and animals, such as mammals, birds, frogs, fish, and other kinds of shellfish, survived. Not all reptiles died out either: turtles, crocodiles, snakes, and lizards still exist today.

Timescale

The earth formed about 4.6 billion years ago, and life developed about 1 billion years later. The oldest known fossils, which are of shellfish, are 600 million years old. Dinosaurs arrived 230 million years ago, and the first true humans about 2 million years ago.

First life: 3.5 billion years ago

When did dinosaurs live?

The dinosaur age, the Mesozoic Era, lasted from 250 to 65 million years ago. Scientists split this time into three main periods. Dinosaurs first appeared in the **Triassic Period**, 230 million years ago. The continents were a single land mass called Pangaea ("All-earth"), and dinosaurs could roam all over the world. During the **Jurassic Period**, 145 million years ago, Europe and Africa began to move away from the Americas. In the **Cretaceous Period**, the land masses separated, and different dinosaurs developed on the different continents.

Triassic

Early Jurassic

Early Cretaceous

When did animals move onto land?

Life began in the sea. Animals first moved onto land about 380 million years ago. Amphibians like *Eryops* could breathe air, but like frogs and toads today, they had to return to water to lay their eggs and to keep their skin moist. *Eryops* was the size of a pig. Its thick skin protected it and helped support its body weight on land.

DEVONIAN

CARBONIFEROUS

Eryops

Which animals first lived on land?

Although amphibians could live on land, they were not true land animals, as they had to return to the water to breed. The tiny tadpoles that hatched had to stay in the water until they developed into adults. Reptiles were the first vertebrates (animals with backbones) that could live completely on land. They laid their leathery eggs on land, and the baby developed inside the egg, feeding on the yolk. The newly hatched baby was fully formed and active.

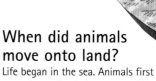

Tadpoles

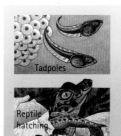

Reptile hatching

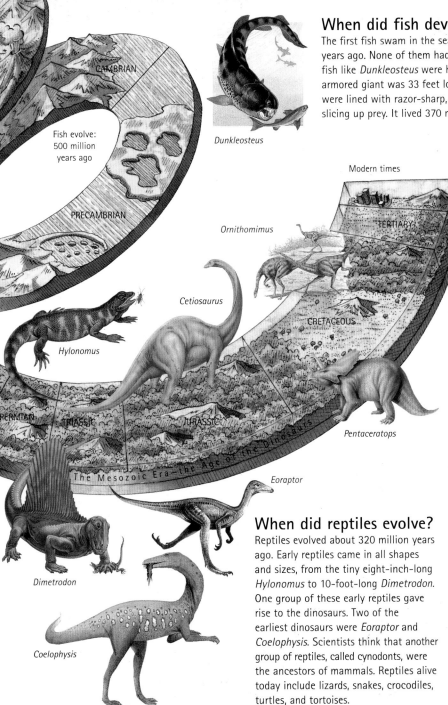

When did fish develop?

The first fish swam in the sea about 500 million years ago. None of them had jaws or fins. Later fish like *Dunkleosteus* were huge predators. This armored giant was 33 feet long, and its jaws were lined with razor-sharp, bony cutters for slicing up prey. It lived 370 million years ago.

Dunkleosteus

Fish evolve: 500 million years ago

CAMBRIAN

PRECAMBRIAN

Modern times

Ornithomimus

TERTIARY

Cetiosaurus

CRETACEOUS

Hylonomus

PERMIAN   TRIASSIC   JURASSIC

Pentaceratops

The Mesozoic Era—the Age of the Dinosaurs

Eoraptor

Dimetrodon

Coelophysis

When did reptiles evolve?

Reptiles evolved about 320 million years ago. Early reptiles came in all shapes and sizes, from the tiny eight-inch-long *Hylonomus* to 10-foot-long *Dimetrodon*. One group of these early reptiles gave rise to the dinosaurs. Two of the earliest dinosaurs were *Eoraptor* and *Coelophysis*. Scientists think that another group of reptiles, called cynodonts, were the ancestors of mammals. Reptiles alive today include lizards, snakes, crocodiles, turtles, and tortoises.

Quick-fire Quiz

1. What was the age of dinosaurs called?
a) Devonian
b) Mesozoic
c) Triassic

2. What was *Dunkleosteus*?
a) An amphibian
b) A reptile
c) A fish

3. What was the Triassic single land mass called?
a) Europe
b) Gondwana
c) Pangaea

4. What was *Dimetrodon*?
a) A reptile
b) A mammal
c) An amphibian

After the Dinosaurs

After the dinosaurs died out, other animals developed to take their place. Warm-blooded mammals took over as the ruling animals. They dominated the land and even took to the air. A few even went to live in the place where life first developed—the ocean.

What are the dinosaurs' nearest surviving relatives?

Many scientists now agree that birds are the closest living relatives of the dinosaurs. The first bird fossil to be found was *Archaeopteryx*. It had a reptilelike skeleton similar to that of *Deinonychus* and feathered wings like a bird. *Archaeopteryx* had a long, bony tail, three clawed fingers on each hand, and teeth. Modern birds have lost their teeth and their clawed wing fingers. Their small tail stumps hold their tail feathers.

Deinonychus

What were early birds like?

Very few fossils of early birds have been found. Several almost complete skeletons of *Hesperornis*, a diving bird that lived at the end of the dinosaur age, were found in the United States. *Hesperornis*'s wings were so small that it was almost certainly flightless, but its large feet may have been webbed to help it swim. It looked much more like today's birds than *Archaeopteryx* did, but it still had teeth in its beak and a fairly long, bony tail.

Why were mammals so successful?

There are several reasons. Early mammals had bigger brains and were more intelligent than reptiles. They were hairy and warm-blooded, so they could live in colder places. Most of them cared for their young for a long time, so perhaps more young survived. Also, different mammal groups had different kinds of teeth, so they could feed on a huge range of food without competing with each other.

What were the first mammals like?

The first mammals evolved about 215 million years ago. One of the earliest known mammals is *Morganucodon*. This mouse-sized hunter was warm-blooded but probably laid eggs like the Australian platypus. *Zalambdalestes* lived at the same time as the last of the dinosaurs, and gave birth to live young.

Zalambdalestes

Morganucodon

Smilodon

Archaeopteryx

Pigeon

When did mammoths die out?

Woolly mammoths died out about 10,000 years ago. The giant North American mammoth was over 14 feet tall. These huge beasts were preyed on by *Smilodon*, a saber-toothed cat with fangs as long as your hand (6 inches). When the mammoths died out, so did *Smilodon*.

Mammoths

Late arrivals?

The first humans evolved about two million years ago, but modern humans, or *Homo sapiens* ("wise person"), only arose about 100,000 years ago. In the Stone Age, 20,000 years ago, people lived in caves and hunted with stone tools.

Quick-fire Quiz

1. Which of these have no teeth?
   a) Modern birds
   b) *Archaeopteryx*
   c) *Hesperornis*

2. Which was the earliest known mammal?
   a) Mammoth
   b) *Smilodon*
   c) *Morganucodon*

3. How long ago did modern humans evolve?
   a) 20,000 years
   b) 100,000 years
   c) 5,000,000 years

4. Which animals dominated after the dinosaurs?
   a) Mammoths
   b) Amphibians
   c) Mammals

Web Addresses

www.enchantedlearning.com/subjects/dinosaur

Visit Zoom dinosaurs, designed for students of all ages and levels. This site offers information and activities, jokes, puzzles, and games. Take the opportunity to write your own story and view it online.

dsc.discovery.com/guides/dinosaur/dinosaur.html

Visit this lively, well-designed site where you can find out interesting facts about dinosaurs, prehistoric beasts, fossils, and human origins. Pick up lots of facts and check out the video gallery.

www.thinkquest.org/library/index.html

The ThinkQuest Library is a collection of more than 5,500 educational web sites designed by participants in the ThinkQuest competitions. To see what they have created on dinosaurs, enter subjects such as dinosaurs and fossils.

www.bbc.co.uk/dinosaurs

This is the British web site for the television program, *Walking with Dinosaurs*—the story of Big Al the Allosaurus. Visit this site to discover lots of dinosaur facts, games, and pictures.

www.abc.net.au/dinosaurs/default.htm

This is the U.S. site for the television program, *Walking with Dinosaurs*.

www.nmnh.si.edu/paleo/dino

Follow a virtual tour of the dinosaurs in the Smithsonian Museum of Natural History.

www.ology.amnh.org/paleontology/index.html

This is the kids' site from the American Museum of Natural

History. It offers a fascinating insight into dinosaurs and how we learn about them. Play games, collect "ology" cards, and find out about many fun things to do away from your computer.

www.nhm.ac.uk/science

This is the official web site for the British Natural History Museum in London, England—home to one of the best displays of dinosaur skeletons in the world.

www.nationalgeographic.com/dinoeggs

Join the online search for dinosaur eggs and watch them hatch.

www.kids.net.au/kidscategories/Kids_and_Teens/
School_Time/Science/The_Earth/Dinosaurs

Extensive information about dinosaurs. A search engine for children, educators, and teachers.

www.indyrad.iupui.edu/public/jrafert/dinoart.html

A site dedicated to dinosaur art and modeling. It features art from readers, galleries, books, and dinosaur kits.

www.dinofun.com

This is an interesting dinosaur site covering dinosaur facts and figures, as well as offering games, clip art, homework help, and useful resources for parents and teachers, including a list of museum exhibitions related to the subject.

www.acnatsci.org

This is the site for the Academy of Natural Sciences in Philadelphia. Visit their dinosaur exhibition and learn all about dinosaurs and the paleontologists that research them.

Quick-fire Quiz ANSWERS

Page 87 Digging up the Facts
1. b   2. c   3. c   4. b

Page 89 Color and Camouflage
1. b   2. a   3. b   4. a

Page 91 Dinosaur Giants
1. c   2. a   3. a   4. c

Page 93 Small Dinosaurs
1. c   2. c   3. a   4. b

Page 95 Dinosaur Babies
1. b   2. a   3. c   4. b

Page 97 Communication
1. a   2. a   3. c   4. c

Page 99 Plant-eaters
1. b   2. c   3. c   4. b

Page 101 Meat-eaters
1. c   2. c   3. b   4. a

Page 103 The Fiercest Dinosaur
1. b   2. c   3. b   4. b

Page 105 Attack and Defense
1. a   2. b   3. b   4. c

Page 107 All Over the World
1. b   2. b   3. b   4. c

Page 109 Living in Herds
1. a   2. b   3. b   4. c

Page 111 Fast and Slow
1. b   2. b   3. b   4. c

Page 113 In the Sea
1. c   2. a   3. c   4. b

Page 115 In the Air
1. b   2. c   3. a   4. b

Page 117 Death of the Dinosaurs
1. c   2. a   3. b   4. b

Page 119 Timescale
1. b   2. c   3. c   4. b

Page 121 After the Dinosaurs
1. a   2. c   3. b   4. c

1,000
QUESTIONS
& ANSWERS
FACTFILE
ANCIENT CIVILIZATIONS

Contents

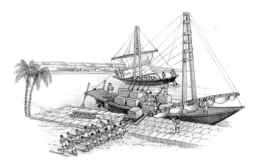

The First People

Early humans were nomads—
they lived in caves and tents,
moving from place to place in
search of food. Around 8000 B.C.,
people began to grow crops and
keep animals. These early farmers
settled in small villages, which later
grew larger and became cities.

Who painted caves?

Over 100 cave paintings have been discovered in
Europe, some dating back to about 25,000 B.C. Rock
paintings have been found in Africa and Australia. They
were painted by prehistoric people, who used natural
pigments to draw animals and hunting scenes.

Which was the largest ancient city?

The largest known ancient city is Çatal Hüyük in present-
day Turkey. By 6250 B.C., over 6,000 people lived there.
The mud-brick houses were one story high and had no
front doors. People entered by climbing a ladder and
crawling through a hole in the roof.

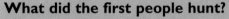

What did the first people hunt?

Stone Age people hunted wild animals for food.
One of the largest animals they
hunted was the
mammoth, a kind
of prehistoric
elephant.
No part
of a
mammoth
was wasted.
The flesh fed
a group of
prehistoric people
for weeks. Its furry
skin was used to make
clothes and tents. The
tusks and bones were used
to build huts and carved
to make jewelry.

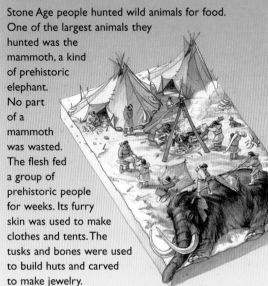

What gods did ancient people worship?

Early city-dwellers built religious
shrines, but little is known about
their gods. This clay figure, found at
a decorated shrine in Çatal Hüyük,
may have been a mother goddess.

Quick-fire Quiz

1. What was Çatal Hüyük?
a) A country
b) A kind of house
c) A city

2. What was a mammoth?
a) A prehistoric elephant
b) A prehistoric tiger
c) A prehistoric person

3. When were wolves tamed?
a) 2000 B.C.
b) 10,000 B.C.
c) 40,000 B.C.

4. What was made from palm leaves?
a) Rope
b) Paper
c) Bread

What did they eat?

People in Çatal Hüyük ate meat, nuts, vegetables, and fruits like apples and dates. The date palm tree had many other uses as well. The trunk provided timber, and the leaves were used to roof their houses or were woven into rope, mats, and sandals.

Did the first people keep animals?

People tamed wolves as long ago as 10,000 B.C. These were the first domesticated dogs and were used to herd other animals. In time, wild sheep, goats, cows, and pigs were kept as farm animals.

Early farm animals

What crops did they grow?

Early farmers sowed wild wheat and barley seeds. When wild wheat was cross-bred with a kind of grass, a new form of wheat with plumper seeds developed. The farmers ground these seeds between stones, mixed the flour with water, and made a new food—bread.

What were early villages like?

In Europe, the first villages were groups of houses in a fenced enclosure. The walls of the wooden houses were covered with mud, and the roofs were thatched with dry grass. Vegetables were grown in one part of the enclosure, and farm animals were kept in another.

River Valley Civilizations

The first great civilization, Sumer, developed in about 5000 B.C. between the Tigris and Euphrates rivers. The area was later called Mesopotamia (now Iraq). Sumer lasted 3,000 years. In that time, other civilizations grew along the Nile River in Egypt and the Indus River in Pakistan.

Did the Indus people build cities?

In the 1920s, two cities, Mohenjo-Daro and Harappa, were found in the Indus Valley. Dating from about 2000 B.C., they were built in a grid pattern, like modern American cities.

Who invented the wheel?

No one knows when the wheel was invented. The potter's wheel was used in Mesopotamia around 6,000 years ago. By about 3500 B.C., the Sumerians were using simple carts like this. Later they had wheeled war chariots, which were pulled by donkeys.

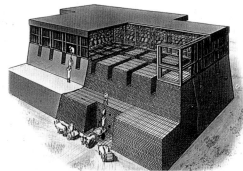

Granary in Mohenjo-Daro

Who invented writing?

Writing was probably invented by the Sumerians about 5,000 years ago. At first they drew pictures, but later these were turned into wedge-shaped symbols, which we now call cuneiform writing.

What crops did they grow?

Farmers in the Indus Valley grew many crops, including wheat, barley, melons, dates, and cotton. Each city had a huge, well-aired granary to store grain between harvests.

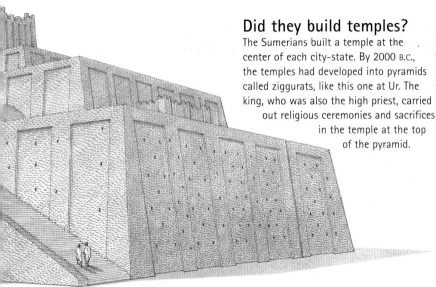

Did they build temples?

The Sumerians built a temple at the center of each city-state. By 2000 B.C., the temples had developed into pyramids called ziggurats, like this one at Ur. The king, who was also the high priest, carried out religious ceremonies and sacrifices in the temple at the top of the pyramid.

Quick-fire Quiz

1. What was a ziggurat?
a) A house
b) A pyramid
c) A palace

2. What kind of writing did the Sumerians use?
a) Cuneiform
b) Hieroglyphics
c) Letters

3. Where was Harappa?
a) Sumer
b) Egypt
c) Indus Valley

4. What did early Sumerians use to build their houses?
a) Wood
b) Stone
c) Reeds

What were river valley homes made from?

Most ancient peoples built homes from the materials around them. The Sumerians had no stones or trees, so they built houses from reeds and, later, sun-dried mud bricks. The Indus people lived in mud-brick houses built around courtyards. Each house had several rooms, a toilet, and a well. The Indus civilization lasted 800 years. It came to an end in about 1800 B.C.

Did they play games?

Rich Sumerians did not have to work all the time, so they relaxed by listening to music or playing games. This game board, found in a royal grave at Ur, dates from between 3000 and 2000 B.C. No one knows how it was played.

Did the Sumerians use money?

The Sumerians traded at huge markets. Each trader had his own seal for signing contracts. Sales were recorded on clay tablets. By about 3300 B.C., Sumerians were using clay tokens to buy goods. They may have had different tokens for different kinds of goods.

Who ruled Sumer?

Each Sumerian city-state had its own king. A king sometimes took over other cities, but none ever ruled all of Sumer. The royal families were very rich and wore fine clothes. A Sumerian princess wore a long dress with gold and silver jewelry.

Ancient Egypt

Over 5,000 years ago, two Egyptian kingdoms, Upper Egypt and Lower Egypt, grew up by the Nile River in North Africa. In 3100 B.C., King Menes united Egypt. It became a very powerful empire, which lasted until 30 B.C., when Egypt fell to the Romans.

How do we know about ancient Egypt?

The remains of tombs, written records, and wall paintings have helped build up a picture of ancient Egypt. Wall paintings show religious rituals, royal conquests, and scenes of everyday life.

Did Egyptians play games?

Like most ancient peoples, wealthy Egyptians spent their leisure time listening to music or playing board games. Their children played with toys such as balls, tops, dolls, and model animals.

Scribe

Who wrote letters?

Not all Egyptians could read and write. Men called scribes wrote letters for them. Scribes used hieroglyphics (picture writing) for royal and sacred writing, and simplified symbols for business letters. They used reed pens and a kind of paper called papyrus.

What did Egyptians eat?

Bread was the main food for most Egyptians. Wheat and barley were ground into flour. They mixed this with water to make dough, added flavorings such as garlic or honey, and baked it in clay pots.

Did they wear wigs?

Yes, the ancient Egyptians thought that hair was dirty, so they shaved their heads and wore elaborate wigs. They also wore makeup. They mixed powdered minerals, such as lead, copper, and iron oxide with water or oils to make bright lipstick, eye shadow, and blusher.

Were pharaohs rich?

Egyptian kings, called pharaohs, were worshiped and treated like gods. They owned the whole country—everybody and everything belonged to them, so they were very rich and powerful! The royal family lived in luxury, waited on by hundreds of servants.

Quick-fire Quiz

1. Who united Egypt?
a) King Nile
b) King Menes
c) King Egypt

2. When did Egypt fall to the Romans?
a) 300 B.C.
b) 30 B.C.
c) 3 B.C.

3. What did a scribe do?
a) Make wigs
b) Build tombs
c) Write letters

4. What crop was swapped for goods?
a) Dates
b) Grain
c) Garlic

Did Egyptians use money?

They did not use coins or paper money, but grain, an important crop, was used to pay taxes and exchanged for other items. For this reason, the Egyptians developed an accurate balance to weigh grain and other costly goods.

Why was the Nile River important?

The Egyptian Empire grew along the Nile River because it was good farming land. Hardly any rain fell in Egypt, but every July the Nile flooded, covering the surrounding soil with water and rich black mud. This mud was very fertile. The ancient Egyptians learned how to store enough of the flood water in canals to irrigate (water) the fields in the dry season. This meant they could produce enough crops to feed their own people and to sell some to other traders. Almost all of Egypt's wealth came from farming.

Priests and Mummies

The ancient Egyptians worshiped many gods and believed in life after death. To make sure their spirits could enjoy the afterlife, the Egyptians embalmed (preserved) the bodies of the dead. The priests were very powerful and helped people with sacred works.

Why were tombs robbed?

Robbers plundered tombs for the treasures they contained. Rich Egyptians were buried

with everything they would need in the afterlife—food, clothes, jewelry, and even models of servants. Lucky amulets like these were often placed among a mummy's bandages to ward off evil spirits.

Who was mummified?

Preserving a body was expensive. Only the royal family, top officials, and priests were mummified. The poor were buried in reed coffins or in holes in the sand. Some animals were mummified, including cats, dogs, baboons, and crocodiles, because they represented gods and goddesses. Cats, for example, represented the goddess Bastet.

What is a mummy?

A mummy is a body that has been preserved. The people who made mummies were called embalmers. After being dried out and rubbed with oils, the body was wrapped in bandages, which could be up to three miles long! A priest watched over the embalmers as they worked.

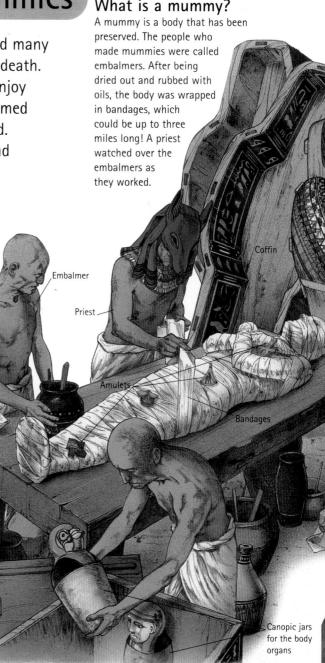

Coffin

Embalmer

Priest

Amulets

Bandages

Canopic jars for the body organs

Which pharaoh's tomb survived?

Most pharaohs' tombs were robbed. In 1922, however, archaeologists found the tomb of Tutankhamen, who was only 18 when he died. His tomb was still intact and full of priceless treasures, including his mummy and this ornate golden face mask.

Coffin-painter

What was painted on the coffin?

A body was placed in a nest of two or three coffins, each painted with hieroglyphics (word pictures), gods, pictures of the person's life, and spells to keep away evil spirits.

How was the brain removed?

An embalmer removed the brain by pulling it out through the nostrils with a bronze hook. They did not think the brain was important, so they threw it away!

How was a body preserved?

The soft body organs were removed, dried, and placed in vessels called canopic jars. The spaces were packed with rags or sawdust, and the body was stitched closed. It was then covered in a kind of salt called natron, which dried it out.

What was a death mask?

A death mask was a portrait of the dead person. It was put over the mummy's face so that the soul could recognize its body. Death masks were often made of painted wood, but most pharaohs had death masks of beaten gold.

Who wore a jackal's head?

When the priest said the final prayers over a body, he wore the mask of the jackal god, Anubis, god of the dead. At the tomb, the priest held the mummy during the "Opening of the Mouth" ceremony, to give the dead person the power to eat, move, and breathe.

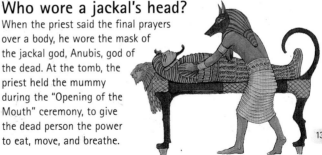

Pyramids and Tombs

Egyptian pharaohs of the Old and Middle Kingdoms (3,500 to 5,000 years ago) were buried inside pyramids. In the New Kingdom (3,000 to 3,500 years ago), pharaohs were buried in tombs in a valley on the west bank of the Nile at Thebes.

How was a pyramid built?

It took at least 4,000 craftsmen and thousands of laborers to build a pyramid. Most of the laborers were farmers who worked as builders to pay their taxes. They cleared the site, laid the foundations, and dragged the stones into place. Stonemasons used an assortment of tools to cut the hard blocks of limestone that covered the outside of the pyramids. They cut the stone into blocks that fit together perfectly.

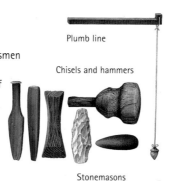

Plumb line

Chisels and hammers

Stonemasons

Which temple was moved?

In 1964, the temple at Abu Simbel was moved so that it would not be flooded when the Aswan Dam was built. The temple had been carved out of solid rock on the banks of the Nile River.

Why did Egyptians have funeral barges?

The mummified bodies of Egyptian pharaohs were placed on highly decorated boats so that they could travel to the next world. The boat was dragged to the tomb on a sled pulled by oxen.

Quick-fire Quiz

1. Where is the Great Pyramid?
a) Thebes
b) Giza
c) Abu Simbel

2. During which period were the pyramids built?
a) Old Kingdom
b) New Kingdom
c) Both Kingdoms

3. What was built on the west bank of the Nile?
a) Egyptian homes
b) Pharaohs' palaces
c) The pyramids

4. When was the last pyramid built?
a) About 2570 B.C.
b) About 1570 B.C.
c) About 570 B.C.

Where did the stones come from?

The inside of a pyramid was built from soft stone found locally. The outside was covered with smooth limestone from quarries up to 500 miles away. Huge blocks of stone, weighing up to 50 tons, were loaded onto barges in the flood season and shipped to the building site.

Where were the pyramids built?

All the pyramids were built on the west bank of the Nile. The Egyptians believed this was the land of the dead because it was where the sun set. They built their homes on the east bank, the land of the living, where the sun rose.

What is the Great Pyramid?

The Great Pyramid at Giza was built for King Khufu (c.2575 B.C.) from over two million stone blocks. The pharaoh was buried in a central chamber.

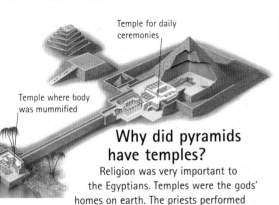

Temple for daily ceremonies

Temple where body was mummified

Why did pyramids have temples?

Religion was very important to the Egyptians. Temples were the gods' homes on earth. The priests performed special ceremonies before and after the pharaoh was put in the tomb, so temples were built in the pyramids.

Why did pyramid-building stop?

About 90 pyramids were built in total, the last one in 1570 B.C. But they were easy prey for robbers, so tombs for the pharaohs of the New Kingdom were carved from the cliffs in a hidden valley at Thebes instead. This is known as the Valley of the Kings. Although most of these tombs were also robbed, it was here that archaeologists Howard Carter and Lord Carnarvon found the untouched tomb of the boy king Tutankhamen.

Crete and Mycenae

The first European civilization began about 4,500 years ago, on the island of Crete. The Minoans, named after a famous king, Minos, were traders who ruled the Aegean Sea. In 1450 B.C., this civilization ended and the Mycenaeans, from mainland Greece, took over.

What was the minotaur?

The Minoans told how King Minos kept a minotaur, a monster that was half-man and half-bull, in a labyrinth (maze of tunnels) below his palace. Each year, he sacrificed 14 young Greeks to this terrible creature. The Greek hero Theseus was determined to kill the minotaur. With the help of King Minos's daughter, Ariadne, he found a way into the labyrinth, killed the monster, and escaped from the maze by following a thread he had unwound on his way through it.

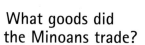

What goods did the Minoans trade?

Craftsmen made beautiful pottery and carved ornaments. Goldsmiths made fine jewelry, such as this bull's–head pendant. Minoan goods have been found in many neighboring countries, including Egypt.

Did Minoans build cities?

The Minoans built several cities, connected to each other by paved roads. Each had a fine palace. The grandest was at Knossos, in northern Crete. It had over 1,000 rooms, including luxurious apartments, workshops, and a school.

Minoan palace

Who went hunting?

The Mycenaeans loved to hunt wild animals, including lions, which roamed Greece until about 3,000 years ago. This fresco shows a boar hunt. Nobles hunted boar with spears and shields, and had dogs to help them. Hunters cut off the tusks from dead boars and used them to decorate their helmets.

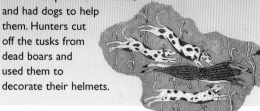

Did Minoans play sports?

Frescoes (wall paintings) show Minoans playing many sports. Boxing was popular, as was the dangerous sport of bull-leaping. One person held the bull's head, while the bull-leaper somersaulted between the bull's horns. A friend stood at the back to catch the bull-leaper.

What did Mycenaean palaces look like?

The Mycenaeans were the ruling Greeks from about 1450 B.C. to 1100 B.C. The remains of the palace of the Mycenaean king Nestor at Pylos, in southern Greece, show that it had richly decorated rooms built around a series of courtyards.

Mycenaean palace

Were the Mycenaeans warriors?

The Mycenaeans, unlike the Minoans, were warriors as well as traders and built fortified towns. The walls around the city of Mycenae were built from huge stone blocks. At the only entrance, the Lion Gate, a pair of stone lionesses stood guard. Warriors attacked their enemies from the top of the walls.

The Lion Gate

Quick-fire Quiz

1. Which of these civilizations began in Crete?
a) Egyptian
b) Mycenaean
c) Minoan

2. What was the minotaur?
a) Half-man, half-lion
b) Half-man, half-bull
c) Half-man, half-boar

3. Who killed the minotaur?
a) King Minos
b) King Nestor
c) Theseus

4. What was the main gate in Mycenae called?
a) The Lion Gate
b) The Bull Gate
c) The King Gate

Babylon

The Mesopotamian city-state of Babylon rose to prominence in 1900 B.C. Its power grew under Hammurabi the Great in the 1700s B.C. It collapsed in 1595 B.C., but rose again under Nebuchadnezzar, 1,000 years later. In 539 B.C., Babylon fell to the Persians.

Who made Babylon rich?

Nebuchadnezzar made Babylon one of the richest cities in the world. The main entrance, the Ishtar Gate, was decorated with glazed blue tiles. He brought plants and trees from Persia for the famous Hanging Gardens, which were one of the Seven Wonders of the Ancient World.

Did the Babylonians go to war?

The Babylonian army was well trained with good leaders. Both Hammurabi the Great and Nebuchadnezzar waged wars against surrounding lands. Skilled archers helped Nebuchadnezzar conquer lands, including Phoenicia, Syria, Judah, and Assyria.

What were their houses like?

About 4,000 years ago, most people in Babylon had simple homes. However, rich people built large, flat-roofed houses with wooden balconies around a central courtyard. They lived in great comfort, with many servants to cook and clean for them.

Whom did they worship?

The people of Babylon had many gods. Ishtar, the mother goddess, and Marduk, the dragon god, were the most powerful. One myth tells how Gilgamesh's pride angered the gods, who sent a Bull of Heaven to destroy him—but Gilgamesh survived.

Who lost the secret of eternal life?

Legend tells how Gilgamesh, a Babylonian hero and king, was given the secret of eternal life—a plant from under the sea. He found the plant, but he fell asleep on his way home with it. A snake gobbled up the plant, and Gilgamesh lost the chance to live forever.

Quick-fire Quiz

1. Who was the mother goddess?
a) Marduk
b) Ishtar
c) Gilgamesh

2. How many laws did Hammurabi make?
a) 282
b) 272
c) 262

3. What ate the secret of eternal life?
a) A snake
b) A bull
c) A genie

4. Who conquered Babylon in 539 B.C.?
a) The Greeks
b) The Egyptians
c) The Persians

What were genies?

The Babylonians believed that winged gods, or genies, protected royal palaces from demons and disease. This genie is holding a bucket and a pine cone, which were symbols of purification.

Who made good laws?

Hammurabi made 282 laws for his people to follow. Most were good laws, to protect the weak from the strong. They covered everything from fair rates of pay to rules for trading.

Did they have pets?

Some Babylonians probably had domesticated cats and dogs, but rich people kept more exotic pets. The first zoos were owned by wealthy princes, who gave each other presents of wild animals such as lions and leopards.

Did Babylonians do math?

Like earlier people in the region, the Babylonians used cuneiform writing, which can still be seen on clay tablets. Babylonian mathematicians figured out a system of counting based on the number 60. This was especially useful as 60 can be divided in many different ways. We still use this system today when we record the time (60 minutes in an hour, 60 seconds in a minute) and in measuring (there are 60 x 6 degrees in a circle). Babylonians recorded details of royal grants of land on boundary stones, which deterred land disputes between neighbors. The Babylonians were also great astronomers.

Assyrians and Hittites

The Hittites from Anatolia (now in Turkey) conquered most of Syria, Mesopotamia, and Babylon in the 1500s B.C. Their empire fell in 1200 B.C., and the Assyrians, from northern Mesopotamia, took over. In 609 B.C., the Assyrian Empire fell to the Babylonians.

What did they build?

The Assyrians built magnificent cities, temples, and palaces. The king often supervised the work from his chariot. Stones were brought from distant quarries, and oarsmen in skin boats towed them on rafts up the Tigris.

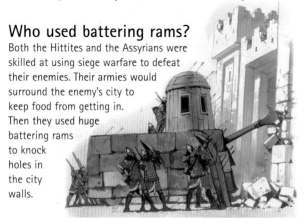

Who used battering rams?

Both the Hittites and the Assyrians were skilled at using siege warfare to defeat their enemies. Their armies would surround the enemy's city to keep food from getting in. Then they used huge battering rams to knock holes in the city walls.

Who was the last ruler of Assyria?

King Ashurbanipal was the last and greatest ruler of Assyria. He was a ruthless king, but he also built a great library where records and literature from Sumer and Babylon were stored on clay tablets. His palace at Nineveh had gardens stocked with plants from all over the world.

The Assyrian royal court

Who carved in stone?

The Hittites and Assyrians were great stonemasons. The Hittites carved huge pictures of their gods and goddesses into the rock face near their temples. The Assyrians left many finely carved stone sculptures, which tell us about their history and how they lived. Most of them show the kings and their conquests, but this one shows scenes of everyday life, such as people preparing and cooking food.

Carved stone being dragged to a new temple

Quick-fire Quiz

1. Who was Ashur?
a) A god
b) A king
c) A goddess

2. Where were the Hittites from?
a) Syria
b) Egypt
c) Anatolia

3. Where was Ashurbanipal's palace?
a) Babylon
b) Nineveh
c) Sumer

4. What animals pulled a war chariot?
a) Bulls
b) Lions
c) Horses

Winged lion

What gods did the Assyrians worship?

The Assyrians believed in many gods. Their chief god was Ashur, whose name was used for their capital city. Ishtar was the Assyrian goddess of war. The Babylonians also worshiped Ishtar, but believed that she was a mother goddess who helped protect their city. To ward off evil spirits, huge stone sculptures of winged lions with human heads were placed on each side of important doors and gateways.

Who drove war chariots?

Both the Hittites and the Assyrians used war chariots in battle. The two-wheeled chariots were drawn by horses, and skilled archers would shoot at the enemy as they raced along. The Assyrians were fierce warriors, fighting with swords, slingshots, and bows.

Assyrian war chariot

141

Ancient Sea Traders

The Phoenicians were the best sea traders of the ancient world. They lived in city-states on the coast of the Mediterranean Sea (now Lebanon) from about 1200 to 146 B.C. Their culture died out after the area was conquered by Alexander the Great.

Were the Phoenicians explorers?

The Phoenicians were skilled sailors and had fine ships. Around 600 B.C., the Egyptians paid the Phoenicians to explore West Africa. They also sailed to Britain, where they traded goods for tin and silver.

What goods did Phoenicians trade?

Phoenician craftsmen made fine cloth as well as pottery, ivory, and metal goods to sell. They also traded in the wood from cedar trees.

Letters from the Phoenician alphabet

𐤊 𐤀 𐤂 𐤃 𐤄 𐤉 𐤌 𐤅 𐤆

𐤆 𐤅 𐤋 𐤔 𐤎 𐤏 𐤐 𐤒 𐤑

𐤅 𐤕 𐤉 𐤉 𐤔 𐤉 𐤉

Who blew glass?

The Phoenicians were the first people to produce see-through glassware on a large scale. They also invented the process of glassblowing, which allowed them to make fine glassware like this.

Could Phoenicians read and write?

The Phoenicians must have been able to read and write, because they were among the first people to use an alphabet for writing words, instead of using pictograms. Their alphabet had 30 consonants, and there were no vowels. These letters became the basis for all modern alphabets.

How did the Phoenicians get their name?

The name came from the Greek word "phoinos," meaning "red." They were called this because they made a rich, red-purple dye from a sea snail called a murex. Cloth dyed with this was expensive. In Roman times, only emperors were allowed to wear murex-dyed robes.

Murex

Who founded the city of Carthage?

Carthage was the largest Phoenician city. According to legend, the founder of Carthage was the Phoenician princess Dido. After landing on the coast of North Africa, Dido asked the local ruler for land to build a city. He said she could take an area of land that could be enclosed by an ox-hide. Clever Dido had the hide cut into thin strips so that she could mark out a large plot of land. Carthage became one of the most important trading cities in the area.

Did they build temples?

The Phoenicians built many temples and shrines to their gods. Their main god was the warrior god, Baal. Occasionally, in times of trouble, the priests and priestesses sacrificed children to the gods.

Phoenician priestess

Where were Phoenician colonies?

The Phoenicians spread throughout the Mediterranean, setting up colonies in many foreign lands, including Marseilles (France), Cadiz (Spain), Malta, Sicily, Cyprus, and Carthage (now Tunisia) in North Africa. From Carthage they traded with local Africans, buying precious ivory, animal skins, and wood.

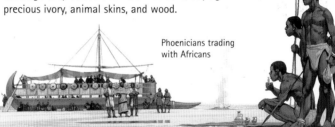

Phoenicians trading with Africans

143

Ancient Greece

By 500 B.C., Greece had grown to include many small, independent city-states around the Mediterranean. Each city-state had its own government and laws. The most important city-states were Athens and Sparta.

Who were the Spartans?

Sparta, a city-state in southern Greece, was a mighty military power. All Spartan men were in the army, and boys left home at seven to start training as soldiers. Women did not fight, but had to be physically fit so their babies would be healthy and strong.

What was an acropolis?

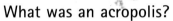

Each Greek city-state had a walled city with an acropolis (a fort) and an agora (a large, open space used for meetings and markets). In time, the acropolis became a religious center.

Who left Athens?

Criminals or unpopular politicians could be ostracized, or banished. Each year, Athenians wrote the name of a person they wanted banished on pieces of pottery called "ostraka." Anyone with more than 6,000 votes had to leave for 10 years!

Did Greeks play sports?

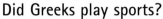

The ancient Greeks enjoyed competitive games. The most famous, the Olympics, were first held in 776 B.C. and took place every four years. At first, there was just one race. By 500 B.C., the Games lasted five days.

Who won an olive wreath?

On the final day of the Olympic Games, the winners received their prizes—crowns of olive leaves cut from a special grove near the temple of Zeus. Afterward they were guests of honor at a victory feast.

Who played outdoors?

Greek plays were performed in large, open-air theaters. The semicircular theater in Athens held over 10,000 people. All the actors were male, and they wore brightly painted masks to show which characters they were playing.

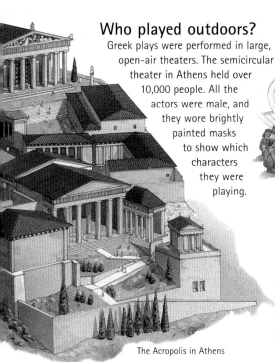

The Acropolis in Athens

Who read the future?

The Greeks had many gods and goddesses. The chief god was Zeus, who lived with other important gods on Mount Olympus, the highest mountain in Greece. If the Greeks wanted to know about the future, they visited shrines called oracles. Priests and priestesses at an oracle spoke on behalf of the gods. The most famous oracle was at the temple of Apollo, the sun god, at Delphi.

Did they enjoy music?

The Greeks liked singing and dancing, and music was played at most social occasions. Poetry was sung or chanted, accompanied by music. The main stringed instrument was the lyre, which was sometimes made from a tortoise shell.

Whose speeches were timed?

In Athens, all men who were not slaves were citizens and could speak at the Assembly. At this meeting they could give their opinions on political matters. Each speaker was timed with a water clock, so he could not talk for too long!

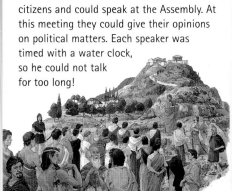

Quick-fire Quiz

1. Where was the future told?
a) An Assembly
b) An acropolis
c) An oracle

2. What was the lyre?
a) A bird
b) A musical instrument
c) An Olympic sport

3. How often were the Olympic Games held?
a) Every year
b) Every four years
c) Every ten years

4. Who could speak at the Assembly?
a) Citizens
b) Slaves
c) Everyone

Greek Life

Greek architecture, the arts, sports, and science flourished during the Golden Age (600 to 300 B.C.). Athens became the center of Greek culture. In 338 B.C., King Philip of Macedonia conquered Greece. His son, Alexander the Great, spread Greek learning to North Africa and the Middle East.

Where did people shop?

In the agora, or marketplace, you could buy everything from food to fabrics, silverware to slaves. Fast-food sellers supplied tasty snacks, and you could even visit a doctor.

What were Greek houses like?

Greek houses were made of sun-dried mud bricks built around a central courtyard. Most houses had one story, but some wealthier homes had bedrooms on a second floor. Greek men, women, and slaves all lived in separate quarters.

How do we know about ancient Greek life?

Archaeologists have found marble and bronze statues and pottery bowls, vases, and cups decorated with scenes from Greek life. These tell us what the Greeks wore and how they lived.

What did ancient Greeks eat?

Basic foods were bread, olives, figs, and goat's milk cheese. Meat was expensive, but fish was cheap along the coast. Women prepared the food, and everyone ate in the courtyard.

What did the Greeks wear?

Everyone wore a chiton, a large cloth rectangle fastened at the shoulders. Saffron yellow was a favorite color, but purple, red, and violet were also fashionable. Wealthy women piled their hair into elaborate styles and wore makeup, earrings, necklaces, bracelets, and rings.

Did Greeks take baths?

Few homes had bathtubs, but the gymnasium, a public sports ground in Athens, had plunge pools and steam baths. Women and children washed using bronze basins, and some homes had terra-cotta hip baths. Slaves helped their masters wash.

Where did people relax?

The agora was a place to relax and meet friends. Men met there to listen to storytellers recounting tales or to hear philosophers such as Socrates discuss politics.

Quick-fire Quiz

1. What was an agora?
a) A school
b) A marketplace
c) A temple

2. Who went to school?
a) Boys
b) Girls
c) No one

3. What was a chiton?
a) A stool
b) A book
c) A robe

4. Who conquered Greece in 338 B.C.?
a) King Philip
b) Alexander
c) Socrates

Did they have furniture?

Wealthy Athenians lived in heated homes with fine furniture. They lounged on padded couches and ate from small tables inlaid with ivory. Their wooden beds had leather thongs to support a mattress and lots of cushions.

Did Greek children go to school?

Rich Athenian boys went to school between the ages of seven and 18. They studied math, reading, writing, music, and poetry in the morning and did athletics and dancing in the afternoon. The girls stayed at home, learning to spin, weave, and run a household.

The Persians

About 3,000 years ago, Persia (now Iran) was ruled by two powers, the Medes and the Persians. In 550 B.C., the Persian king, Cyrus the Great, seized power. He made Persia the center of a huge empire, which lasted until 330 B.C., when Alexander the Great took control.

Who was Alexander the Great?

Alexander the Great became king of Greece in 336 B.C. and set out to conquer the Persians. He was a great soldier and a clever leader. Within 12 years he had taken over Persia and built an empire stretching from Egypt to India.

Who made Persia great?

King Darius I ruled Persia from 521 to 486 B.C. His powerful empire included Egypt and the Indus Valley. He taxed all the people he conquered, and the tributes they brought him included food, animals, fine cloth, gold, and jewels. He built roads to link the empire and introduced a standard currency to increase trade.

Who were the Parthians?

The Parthians moved into Persia in about 1000 B.C. and lived under Persian rule. After the death of Alexander the Great, the Parthians took over the area. They were fierce warriors. A favorite trick was to pretend to retreat, then turn in their saddles to fire back at the surprised enemy.

What religion did the Persians follow?

Many Persians worshiped Mithras, the god of light, truth, and justice. Persian legend says that he killed a magic bull and that every animal and plant sprang from its blood. Later, Mithras was popular with Roman soldiers, who built temples to him. Around 600 B.C., a Persian prophet called Zoroaster founded a new religion, Zoroastrianism, which is still followed today in parts of Iran and India.

Quick-fire Quiz

1. Who founded the Persian Empire?
a) King Cyrus
b) King Darius
c) King Philip

2. When was the Battle of Salamis?
a) 380 B.C.
b) 480 B.C.
c) 580 B.C.

3. Who was Zoroaster?
a) A god
b) A soldier
c) A prophet

4. What was a trireme?
a) A palace
b) A sword
c) A ship

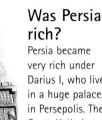

Did Persia have an army?

The Persians had a large, well-trained army. The soldiers were armed with spears, daggers, and bows and arrows. They wore leather tunics strengthened with scales to protect them in battle.

Did the Persians and Greeks fight?

The Greeks and Persians were at war for many years. At the Battle of Salamis in 480 B.C., the Persian fleet was forced to retreat by the might of the Greek triremes. A trireme was a swift ship powered by over 150 oarsmen grouped in three banks on either side of the ship.

Was Persia rich?

Persia became very rich under Darius I, who lived in a huge palace in Persepolis. The Great Hall alone held 10,000 people. When Alexander the Great invaded, he is said to have taken 4,500 tons of gold from the Persian cities of Persepolis and Susa.

149

Ancient China

The first emperor of a united China was King Zheng of Qin. In 221 B.C., he defeated the rulers of all the kingdoms that made up China and founded the Qin dynasty, from which China got its name.

What is a dynasty?
Each kingdom in ancient China was governed by a series of ruling families, called dynasties. Many of these dynasties lasted for hundreds of years. The longest reigning dynasty, the Zhou dynasty, ruled for over 800 years, from 1122 B.C. to 256 B.C.

What was the terra-cotta army?
When King Zheng became emperor, he changed his name to Shi Huangdi ("First Emperor") and ordered that a splendid tomb be built. It was guarded by a terra-cotta army—7,000 life-size clay soldiers. The soldiers had real crossbows and spears, with life-size clay horses and chariots.

Who was Confucius?
Confucius, or K'ung Fu-tzu, was born in China in 551 B.C. He was a great thinker who believed that the emperor should care for his people like a father, and that the people should love and obey him. For over 2,000 years his teachings influenced the way China was ruled.

Who invented paper?
The Chinese invented many useful things. Around A.D. 100, a man named Tsai Lung rolled a paste of hemp and wood into a sheet, which he stretched and dried. He had invented paper. About 800 years later, the Chinese printed the first paper money.

What are yin and yang?
The Chinese believe everything in nature is in harmony. Confucius depicted this by the yin and yang symbol. The dark yin interlocks with the light yang, and each one contains a tiny bit of the other.

Who invented the compass?

The ancient Chinese were great scientists and inventors. During the Han dynasty, scientists invented the first magnetic compass with a dial and a needle. At first, they did not use it for navigation, as we do now, but to make sure that their temples faced the right way. The Chinese were very skilled sailors. Hundreds of years before the Europeans, the Chinese built sea-going ships that had many sails and were steered by rudders. Chinese sailors traveled as far as Africa to trade. They were also skilled mathematicians and astronomers. The Chinese were the first to make maps using a grid system and to figure out that a year has 365.25 days.

Who built the Great Wall?

The Great Wall of China was built for Shi Huangdi between 214 and 204 B.C. by thousands of poor farmers. Short bits of wall were joined up to make the longest wall in the world, stretching over 1,400 miles. The wall is up to 50 feet high and is wide enough for a bus to drive along the top.

Who defeated an emperor?

Life was hard for most peasants during the Qin dynasty. They had to pay taxes and work for Shi Huangdi. After his death, the peasants rebelled against the new emperor, his son. They raised a large army, and in 209 B.C., the emperor was defeated.

Peasants during the Qin Dynasty

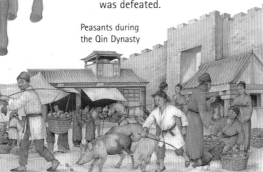

Quick-fire Quiz

1. What did the terra-cotta army guard?
   a) A palace
   b) A tomb
   c) A city

2. Who invented paper?
   a) K'ung Fu-tzu
   b) Shi Huangdi
   c) Tsai Lung

3. How high is the Great Wall?
   a) 5 feet
   b) 50 feet
   c) 100 feet

4. When was Confucius born?
   a) 551 B.C.
   b) 151 B.C.
   c) 51 B.C.

The Celts

Between 750 and 50 B.C., the Celts were the most important peoples in Europe. There were many different Celtic tribes, but they all spoke the same kind of language and had similar lifestyles. Eventually, the Romans conquered most of their lands.

What were Celtic homes like?
A Celtic house often had walls made of branches covered with clay, and a thatched roof of straw or reeds. Most homes had one large room, where the family cooked, ate, and slept. There were no windows. A central fire provided heat and light.

Were the Celts warriors?
Celtic men and women were renowned fighters, and battles between tribes were common. Many warriors painted their faces and bodies blue to look as fierce as possible. Some went into battle naked, but others wore tartan tops, capes, and pants and carried fine bronze shields.

Were the Celts interested in arts and crafts?
The Celts were great poets and musicians and made beautifully decorated metalwork. Wealthy warriors carried fine shields. They often wore an armband made from gold and a delicately carved neck ring, called a torque. Celtic jewelry and weapons were decorated with abstract or geometric designs.

Shield

Armband

Why were cattle important?

The Celts were farmers. They depended on meat to get them through the winter, so cattle were very important. On the feast of Beltane on May 1, which marked the start of summer, Druids (priests) chased cattle through bonfires to expel evil spirits and disease.

A bull's-head decoration from a cauldron found in Denmark

Quick-fire Quiz

1. What was a torque?
a) An earring
b) A neck ring
c) A belt

2. When was Beltane celebrated?
a) November
b) February
c) May

3. What was a Druid?
a) A priest
b) A warrior
c) A king

4. What is Stonehenge?
a) A feast
b) A city
c) A monument

What are Celtic myths about?

Few Celtic myths have survived. The best known come from Ireland and Wales. A collection of Welsh tales called *The Mabinogion* tells the mythical history of early Britain. In the Irish myth shown here, a giant brings a king a magic cauldron, which represents plenty, fertility, and rebirth.

Who built Stonehenge?

Stonehenge, in England, was built by Stone Age people around 2750 B.C., long before the Celts. The arrangement of the huge circle of standing stones marked the midsummer sunrise and the midwinter moonrise. Historians think this monument was used as a place of worship and to study the stars. Later, Celts may have used it as a meeting place for worship and to make sacrifices to their gods.

Could Celts read and write?

Celts did not read or write. Their myths, laws, and religion were passed down by word of mouth. Druids taught poetry, history, and the law. At feasts, musicians and storytellers called bards told tales of brave heroes.

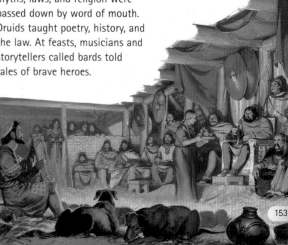

153

Life in Ancient Rome

At first, ancient Rome was ruled by kings, but in 509 B.C., the Romans set up a republic with elected leaders. Rome gradually took over other lands, and by A.D. 150 the empire stretched across Europe into Africa.

Who were looked after by wolves?

According to Roman legend, King Numitor was deposed, and later, his baby grandsons, Romulus and Remus, were thrown into the Tiber River. They were rescued and raised by a wolf. When they grew up, the brothers built Rome.

Where did rich Romans live?

Many rich Romans had a country home (a villa) and a town house (a domus). Houses were built around a courtyard and had lots of rooms, running water, a kitchen, heating, and sometimes even a bathroom.

Did Romans wear makeup?

A rich Roman woman powdered her face with chalk or white lead and painted her lips with red ocher. She took a long time to get ready for the day, even though slave girls helped her dress and style her hair.

Who ruled Rome?

The Roman republic was ruled by the Senate, a group of elder citizens. Each year, the Senate elected two consuls to lead Rome. The Senate met to decide how Rome was to be run and to advise the consuls, who were the most powerful people in Rome.

Where did the poor live?

Poor Romans lived in tiny apartments in high-rise buildings. Many buildings were not very stable, and they sometimes fell down with people still inside. They did not have kitchens, so people had to buy hot food from vendors. Their laundry was strung between buildings because they had no yards. They threw their trash into the streets, making the city dirty and smelly. Water had to be collected from a public water trough. Only rich people had water piped into their homes.

Did rich Romans have feasts?

Rich Romans enjoyed having friends over for a feast. They served dozens of tasty dishes such as oysters, stuffed dormice, roast peacock, and boiled ostrich. The Romans did not sit on chairs to eat—instead they lounged on couches. They ate with their fingers or with a spoon. Some rich Romans were so greedy they tried every dish and then, in order to make room for more, made themselves throw up. They even had a special room for this, called the vomitorium.

Quick-fire Quiz

1. When did Rome become a republic?
a) 509 B.C.
b) 409 B.C.
c) 309 B.C.

2. Who ruled the republic?
a) The emperor
b) The Senate
c) The king

3. What was a gladiator?
a) A public bath
b) A country house
c) A fighter

4. Who brought up Romulus and Remus?
a) Rich women
b) A wolf
c) The consuls

Who fought for sport?

The Romans loved to go to the amphitheater to watch violent shows, which they called games. At the amphitheater, gladiators fought each other, often to the death. Some gladiators had to fight wild animals like lions with spears, flaming torches, or even their bare hands.

Gladiator

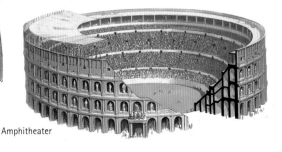

Amphitheater

Where did Romans relax?

Most Romans went to the public baths to relax. These were more like recreation centers than places to wash. You could play games, read, chat to friends, work out in the gym, or take a stroll in the gardens. You could even get your hair cut or have a massage.

155

The Roman Empire

The Roman republic ended in 27 B.C., when Emperor Augustus set up the Roman Empire. In A.D. 395, the empire split into two. The western part, based in Rome, fell to tribes the Romans called "barbarians" in A.D. 476. The eastern part, ruled from Constantinople (now Istanbul), lasted until A.D. 1453.

Did the Romans build bridges?

The Romans were very clever builders and engineers. They built huge stone bridges called viaducts to carry roads, and stone channels called aqueducts to carry water across valleys. They also built many fine cities, linking them with long, straight roads.

Which Roman leader was murdered?

Julius Caesar was a great general who made himself dictator (sole ruler) for life. Although he brought peace and passed good laws, the Senate thought he was too powerful. On March 15, 44 B.C., a group of senators stabbed him to death.

Julius Caesar

What did the Romans trade?

Roman trade routes spread throughout Europe and into China and India. Their ships took many goods such as wine, olive oil, and farm products, as well as works of art, to distant ports. They brought back exotic goods like wild animals, ivory, and silk.

Roman ship

Where did Roman soldiers live?

Soldiers on the move lived in leather tents. At other times, they lived in large forts with workshops, stables, and hospitals. The men shared simple rooms, but the officers had houses.

How did Romans protect their cities?

In later times, the Romans needed to protect their cities from attack by the barbarian tribes that swept across Europe. They built thick walls around their towns and forts, which were then more easily defended by soldiers.

What did Roman soldiers wear?

Roman soldiers wore armor of metal strips joined together with straps, over a woolen tunic. They carried a shield to protect the lower body. When on the move, they carried everything on their backs—weapons, tools, and a kit bag.

Why was Rome so successful?

A well-organized, full-time army was the key to Rome's success. Highly trained soldiers were split into legions of 6,000 men made up of ten cohorts, and then into centuries of 100 men, which were commanded by centurions (officers). Few foreign fortresses could stand against the might of a Roman attack.

Who met in the catacombs?

Early Christians were persecuted by the Romans, who thought they were plotting against the emperor. The Christians met secretly in the catacombs (underground burial chambers) beneath Rome. Many Christians were put to death in the arena to entertain the crowds. Some were made to fight unarmed against gladiators or lions. Emperor Constantine was converted to Christianity in A.D. 313, and about 60 years later it became the empire's official religion.

How were soldiers like a tortoise?

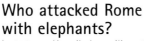

When they attacked an enemy fort, Roman soldiers held their shields over their heads so that they overlapped. They called this formation a "testudo" (tortoise).

Who attacked Rome with elephants?

In 218 B.C., Hannibal, a military leader from Carthage in North Africa, led 10,000 soldiers and 38 elephants through Spain and across the Alps to attack Rome. Hannibal won three important victories, but only 12 elephants survived.

Quick-fire Quiz

1. Who attacked Rome with elephants?
a) Augustus
b) Hannibal
c) Caesar

2. What was a centurion?
a) An army officer
b) A fortress
c) A senator

3. What does an aqueduct carry?
a) Oil
b) Wine
c) Water

4. What are catacombs?
a) Stone bridges
b) Public baths
c) Burial chambers

The Mayan Empire

The Maya Indians built a vast empire that covered parts of Mexico, Guatemala, and Honduras in the jungles of Central America. It reached its peak from A.D. 300–800, but over the next 200 years, it collapsed and was taken over by the Toltecs.

What clothes did the Maya wear?

Mayan men wore simple loincloths. If it was cold, they also wore a cloak called a manta. Men dressed up in elaborate headdresses decorated with quetzal or macaw feathers. The more important the person, the bigger his hat! Women wore simple smock dresses.

What were Mayan cities like?

The Maya were the first people in America to build big cities. These cities, which lay deep in the jungle, were full of grand pyramids, temples, and palaces built of local limestone. The walls were covered with plaster and were sometimes painted red. This color was important in the Mayan religion. Walls were sometimes decorated with paintings of gods and hieroglyphics.

God-king   Noble   Warrior   Priest

Who ruled the Maya?

Every Mayan city-state had its own royal family. They were ruled by a warrior god-king who led his people into battle. Next in importance were nobles, warriors, and priests. Then came craftsmen and merchants, and last were peasants and laborers. The Maya worshiped the jaguar, and noble Mayan warriors wore jaguar skins and headdresses. They thought that this would help make them as fierce and brave as a jaguar in battle.

Did the Maya build pyramids?

The Maya built huge, stone-stepped pyramids with temples and an observatory at the top. The Castillo, the main pyramid in the Mayan city of Chichén Itzá, has four stairways, each with 91 steps. These, together with the step at the temple entrance, add up to 365—the number of days in a year.

Did they study the stars?

The Maya were expert astronomers who studied the moon, stars, and planets. They were also skilled mathematicians and had a complicated calendar for counting the days and years. They used their knowledge to predict special events such as an eclipse.

Could the Maya read and write?

The Maya wrote in hieroglyphics (picture writing). They carved important inscriptions on huge stone monuments called stelae. They also wrote detailed accounts of important events on animal skins or in books made of bark. When the Spanish conquered the area in the early 1500s, they burned most of these books.

Did the Maya play games?

The Maya played a sacred ball game called Pok-a-tok. The players, who were bandaged to prevent injury, bounced a solid rubber ball to each other using their elbows, hips, and thighs. The game was won by the first team to hit the ball through a stone ring mounted on a wall.

What gods did they worship?

The Maya had over 150 gods. The most important was the sun god, who went into the underworld at sunset and became the jaguar god. The Maya sometimes sacrificed captured enemies to their gods.

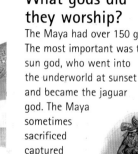

Quick-fire Quiz

1. What is the Castillo?
a) A city
b) A pyramid
c) A book

2. What was a manta?
a) A hat
b) A dress
c) A cloak

3. What were Mayan cities built from?
a) Limestone
b) Mud
c) Wood

4. What were stelae?
a) Monuments
b) Temples
c) Priests

Timeline

 ey dates in the development of ancient civilizations are recorded here—from the first cave paintings, through the establishment of great empires, to the empires' eventual collapse.

25,000 B.C. to 2000 B.C.

c.25,000 B.C. Stone Age people painted cave walls
c.10,000–9000 B.C. Start of agriculture in Near East
8000–7000 B.C. First permanent houses built; walled cities developed in Near East and Turkey
5000 B.C. People began farming in Nile Valley in Egypt
4000–3000 B.C. Sumerian civilization in Mesopotamia invented cuneiform writing and used the plow and the wheel
3372 B.C. First date in Mayan calendar
3000 B.C. Lower and Upper Egypt united under a single pharaoh
3000 B.C. Troy flourished as a city-state in Anatolia
c.2800 B.C. Stonehenge built in England
2800–2400 B.C. City-states of Sumer at their most powerful
2500 B.C. Rise of Indus Valley people
2700-2200 B.C. Old Kingdom in Egypt; first step pyramids built
2690 B.C. Huang Ti ("Yellow Emperor") ruled in China; according to legend, silk was discovered by his wife, Hsi-Ling Shi
2600 B.C. Sphinx and Great Pyramids built in Egypt
2500 B.C. First European civilization, the Minoans, developed on Greek island of Crete
2360 B.C. Arabians migrated to Mesopotamia and set up Babylonian and Assyrian kingdoms

2250 B.C. Hsai dynasty in power in China
2050 B.C. Start of Middle Kingdom of Egypt
2000 B.C. Hittites arrived in Anatolia (now Turkey)
2000 B.C. Mycenaeans invaded Greece

1999 B.C. to 1000 B.C.

1925 B.C. Hittites conquered Babylon
1830 B.C. King Sumu-abum established first Babylonian dynasty
1814–1782 B.C. Assyria extended empire
1792–1750 B.C. Hammurabi the Great ruled Babylon; empire declined after his death
1760 B.C. Shang dynasty founded in China

1750–1500 B.C. Hittites spread throughout area and invaded Syria
1650–1450 B.C. Mycenaean power centered on Mycenae and Pylos
1550–1050 B.C. New Kingdom in Egypt; Valley of Kings used for pharaohs' tombs
1500–1166 B.C. Egypt at peak of power
1500 B.C. Aryans invaded Indus Valley
c.1500 B.C. Maya farm land in Central America; developed a calendar and writing
1450 B.C. Minoan civilization collapsed and Mycenaeans took over
1350–1250 B.C. Assyrian Empire expands
1200 B.C. Trojan Wars: Mycenaeans invaded and destroyed Troy in Anatolia
1200 B.C. Hittites' empire collapsed after invasion of Phoenicians; Phoenicians became the world's most powerful sea traders
1150 B.C. Israelites arrived in Canaan
1100 B.C. Mycenaean civilization collapsed
c.1122 B.C. Zhou dynasty came to power in China after defeating armies of Shang dynasty
1050 B.C. Phoenicians developed alphabet, which formed the basis for all modern alphabets
c.1000 B.C. Dorians invaded Greece; start of Dark Ages
c.1000 B.C. Kingdom of Kush established in Africa
1000 B.C. Israel ruled by King David

999 B.C. to 500 B.C.

900–625 B.C. Assyria and Babylon at war
c.814 B.C. Carthage founded
800 B.C. Greek poet Homer wrote about Trojan Wars and Greek legends
800 B.C. Olmecs in Mexico built temples
753 B.C. Traditional date for founding of Rome
750–600 B.C. Celts appeared in Central Europe and spread throughout western Europe
c.750–682 B.C. Kingdom of Kush defeated Egypt; Nubians rule over Egypt
729 B.C. Assyrians ruled Babylon
700 B.C. Assyrians took over Phoenicia and Israel
700–500 B.C. Rise of Athens and other Greek city-states
689 B.C. Assyrians destroyed Babylon
671–664 B.C. Assyrians ruled Egypt
668–627 B.C. Ashurbanipal increased power of Assyria
609 B.C. Assyrian Empire ended
605–562 B.C. Nebuchadnezzar rebuilt Babylon
c.600 B.C. Zoroaster reforms the ancient Persian religion
c.600 B.C. Earliest Mayan pyramids built
590 B.C. Babylonians took over Jerusalem
551 B.C. Confucius was born in China
c.550 B.C. Persian Empire became powerful
539 B.C. Persians took over Babylon and Phoenicia
525–404 B.C. Persians ruled Egypt
509 B.C. Roman republic founded
508 B.C. Athens became a democracy
500 B.C. Italian Etruscan Empire very powerful

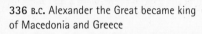

499 B.C. to A.D. 1

490–479 B.C. Persian Wars between Greeks and Persians; Greeks defeated Persians in 479 B.C.
c.477–405 B.C. Golden Age of Athens
463–221 B.C. Time of warring states in China
450–400 B.C. Etruscan Empire declined
431–404 B.C. Peloponnesian Wars between Athens and Sparta; Sparta won in 404 B.C.
390 B.C. Celts attacked Rome
338 B.C. Philip of Macedonia conquered Greece

336 B.C. Alexander the Great became king of Macedonia and Greece
333–323 B.C. Alexander the Great conquered Phoenicia, Egypt, Persia, and parts of India
321–184 B.C. Mauryan Empire founded in India
300 B.C. Maya started to build stone cities
275 B.C. Romans took over all of Italy
265 B.C. Romans began to conquer Europe
264–146 B.C. Carthage at war with Rome (Punic Wars)
250 B.C. Celtic tribes at peak of power
221 B.C. Emperor Qin united China in first dynasty
206 B.C.–A.D. 220 Han dynasty in China
218 B.C. Hannibal invaded Rome on elephants
202 B.C. Hannibal defeated by Romans
146 B.C. Carthage defeated; North Africa became part of Roman Empire
55 B.C. Julius Caesar invaded Britain but had to retreat
52 B.C. Caesar conquered Celtic Gaul (France)
45 B.C. Caesar became dictator of Rome
44 B.C. Caesar assassinated
30 B.C. Egypt taken over by the Romans
27 B.C. Octavian becomes first Roman emperor, Augustus

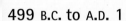

A.D. 1 to A.D. 800

A.D. 43 Romans conquered Britain
A.D. 61 Celtic Queen Boudicca led revolt against Romans in Britain
A.D. 64 Rome destroyed by fire
A.D. 79 Mount Vesuvius erupted, covering Pompeii (Roman city) in ash
c.A.D. 150 Roman Empire most powerful
A.D. 250 European barbarian tribes attacked Rome
A.D. 284 Roman Empire split into east and west
A.D. 268 Goths sacked Athens and Sparta
A.D. 330 Constantinople (now Istanbul) became capital of eastern Roman Empire
A.D. 300–700 Mayan civilization at height
A.D. 406 Vandal tribe overran Gaul
A.D. 410 Rome sacked by Visigoths; Romans left Britain
A.D. 455 Rome sacked by Vandals
A.D. 476 Last western Roman emperor deposed; eastern empire continued until A.D. 1453 as Byzantine Empire
A.D. 800 Mayan cities abandoned; civilization collapsed; Toltecs took over

Web Addresses

www.bbc.co.uk/history/forkids

This history web site, for children between the ages of seven and nine, offers many games, videos, animations, and activities. It covers various topics, including the Romans, the ancient Greeks, and the Vikings.

www.cultures.com

Devoted to present-day and ancient cultures, this site also features the *Illustrated Encyclopedia of Greek Mythology* and the *Illustrated Encyclopedia of MesoAmerican Cultures.*

www.pbs.org/nova/pyramid/explore

This section of the PBS web site offers information on the Vikings, the Roman Empire, and the ancient Greeks.

www.bbc.co.uk/history/topics

This site covers a multitude of topics, including the Egyptians, the Romans, and the ancient Greeks.

www.historychannel.com

This site offers a variety of topics relating to ancient civilizations.

www.thebritishmuseum.ac.uk

Explore the museum's collection of artifacts belonging to other cultures, both ancient and modern, in Africa, the Americas, Asia, Britain, Europe, Greece, Japan, the Middle East, the Pacific Rim, and ancient Rome.

www.louvre.fr/louvre.htm

Investigate the Louvre Museum in Paris, France, for a fine collection of artifacts from Egypt, Greece, and Rome.

www.eduweb.com

Participate in fun, educational web adventures on this site.

www.thinkquest.org/library/index.html

This library of more than 5,500 entries has been created by teachers and students worldwide. For information on ancient civilizations check out Rome, Egypt, Greece, Incas, and Mayans.

www.civilization.ca/civil/egypt/egypte.html

This is a clearly written, informative site on Egyptian civilization— with links to many relevant topics such as religion, archaeology, and architecture.

touregypt.net/kids

This is a kids' site featuring Egyptian history, an ABC of Egypt, an Egyptian coloring book, and galleries of childrens' Egypt-inspired drawings and paintings.

www.historyforkids.org

This site covers many eras of history. You can either search the site or click on an icon for information on an ancient civilization.

members.aol.com/donnclass/Chinalife.html

A fun site about daily life in ancient China, which includes a "cheat sheet" summary of 11,000 years of Chinese history.

www.andes.org

A cultural site featuring songs, dances, jokes, and pictures of the Andean people living in the Cusco region of Peru.

www.ancientsites.com

A site for all history lovers. Most of it is free, although it also includes extended features that are available on subscription.

www.civilization.ca/civil/maya/mminteng.html

Lots of historical and social information about Mayan culture.

Quick-fire Quiz
ANSWERS

1. b   2. b   3. c   4. b

Page 133 Priests and Mummies
1. b   2. a   3. b   4. c

Page 127 The First People
1. c   2. a   3. b   4. a

Page 135 Pyramids and Tombs
1. b   2. a   3. c   4. b

Page 129 River Valley Civilizations
1. b   2. a   3. c   4. c

Page 137 Crete and Mycenae
1. c   2. b   3. c   4. a

Page 131 Ancient Egypt

Page 139 Babylon
1. b   2. a   3. a   4. c

Page 141 Assyrians and Hittites
1. a   2. c   3. b   4. c

Page 143 Ancient Sea Traders
1. a   2. b   3. b   4. c

Page 145 Ancient Greece
1. c   2. b   3. b   4. a

Page 147 Greek Life
1. b   2. a   3. c   4. a

Page 149 The Persians
1. a   2. b   3. c   4. c

Page 151 Ancient China
1. b   2. c   3. b   4. a

Page 153 The Celts
1. b   2. c   3. a   4. c

Page 155 Life in Ancient Rome
1. a   2. b   3. c   4. b

Page 157 The Roman Empire
1. b   2. a   3. c   4. c

Page 159 The Mayan Empire
1. b   2. c   3. a   4. a

1,000
QUESTIONS
& ANSWERS
FACTFILE

KNIGHTS
AND CASTLES

Contents

First Knights

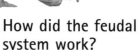

The king

Knights were noblemen who fought on horseback and often lived in castles. This lifestyle began in the early Middle Ages in France and spread across Europe. Knights were successful because they were part of a system that helped kings win wars and govern their kingdoms. It was known as the feudal system.

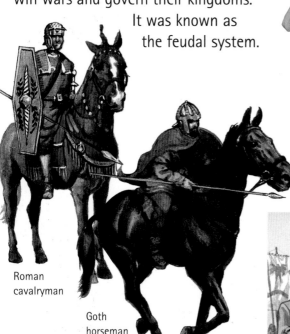

Roman cavalryman

Goth horseman

How did the feudal system work?

In a country with the feudal system, the king owned all the land, but he distributed some of the land to his lords, who were knights. This gift provided a knight with an income, but in return he had to fight for the king and help run the kingdom. In turn, the knight allowed peasants to make a living from his land, as long as they also worked for him.

Who were the first knights?

Knights and feudalism arrived when Charlemagne (right) created his empire in the 800s. Earlier the Romans had used mounted soldiers, but their role in battle was limited. Some of the European peoples ruled by the Romans, such as the Celts and Goths, were good horsemen and fought on horseback. But they had no feudal system and so were not true knights.

Who was Charlemagne?

Charlemagne was the king of the Franks, a people who occupied France and western Germany. From his base at Aachen, he built up a huge empire. He set up local lords as governors of each area, giving them land in return for service—creating an early feudal system. In the year 800 he was given the title of Roman Emperor, although the true Roman Empire had fallen 300 years earlier.

Why were the Normans so powerful?

The Normans (left) were a people who originally came from Scandinavia and settled in northwestern France. They were good builders who erected many strong castles. Like their Viking ancestors, they were skilled soldiers, sailors, and boat builders. Unlike the Vikings, they also had a feudal system. All these factors helped them create a kingdom in France and England and rule it effectively. The Normans also carved out dominions in southern Italy and the Middle East.

What were mottes and baileys?

Mottes and baileys were the first true castles. When the Normans conquered England, they needed castles quickly as bases for their lords. They made a soil mound, called a motte, and built a wooden tower on top as a stronghold. Next to this they fenced off a yard, called a bailey, where they built a hall, stables, a chapel, and other buildings. A ditch or moat surrounded the castle.

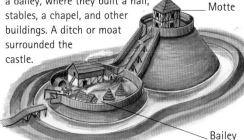

Motte

Bailey

How could you tell a high-ranking Norman?

A high-ranking Norman (above) rode a horse, carried a kite-shaped shield, and wore mail armor. He wielded a sword and a lance, and on his lance he tied a small flag, called a pennon, which showed he was a noble.

Were wooden castles weak?

Wooden castles were well protected by their mottes and moats, but they were easy to knock down or to attack with fire. Most of them were eventually replaced by stronger stone buildings.

Quick-fire Quiz

1. What title was Charlemagne given in 800?
a) Lord of the Franks
b) King of France
c) Roman Emperor

2. Who were the Normans' ancestors?
a) Vikings
b) Franks
c) Britons

3. What did a Norman noble tie on his lance?
a) A helmet
b) A handkerchief
c) A pennon

4. What was a castle courtyard called?
a) The motte
b) The bailey
c) The stronghold

Building a Castle

Many skilled craftsmen were needed to build a castle—masons cut and built with stone, carpenters made floors and roofs, and metalworkers shaped bars and fastenings for doors. The master mason, who designed the castle, supervised all these activities and made sure the building was extremely strong.

How long did it take to build a castle?

The Normans could finish a wooden castle in a few days, but a big stone castle (right) could take years to construct. Castle builders had no modern tools. They had to rely on simple aids like pulleys for lifting heavy loads, and they climbed up wooden scaffolding and ladders to reach the tops of high walls.

How did stonemasons cut large blocks of stone?

Stonemasons (above) used large, two-man saws to cut stone roughly. They then measured the stone with compasses and miter squares before shaping it more precisely with chisels. They did as much work as they could at the quarry in order to save time and energy. By removing all the unwanted stone, the masons did not have to cart too much extra weight to the construction site.

Why do the stairs spiral up to the right?

Coming down stairs going this way, a right-handed defender could easily use his weapon. An attacker coming up the stairs had less room to swing his sword.

How did they build the walls?

Castle builders liked to use neat, rectangular stone blocks shaped with a mallet and chisel for the walls—if they could get them. These would be bonded together tightly with cement (right) so that an attacker would find it difficult to break them down. Laid carefully, these blocks could even be used for the curves needed for round castle towers. For extra strength, rubble and cement were packed into the main walls (see page 171).

How did workers lift large stones?

Carrying heavy lumps of stone up to the castle battlements was hard work. Masons used a rope and pulley, linked to a simple wooden crank (left), to haul the stone into place. At the end of the rope they could attach a basket to carry small stones, or a pair of metal pincers to grip a larger block.

Why did they "turn" timber?

Carpenters used a tool called a lathe to make rounded items, like posts. Powered by a long, springy pole (right), the lathe could spin a piece of wood quickly. The carpenter held his chisel on the wood, removing the corners and giving it a round shape. This process is called turning.

How were planks cut from enormous tree trunks?

Medieval carpenters used a pit and a long, two-handled saw (above) to cut along the length of a tree trunk. One man stood inside the pit, pulling the saw down, while the other held the top end of the saw, guiding it carefully along. As they sawed, the workers drove wooden wedges into the gap to keep the cut open. One large trunk could make several planks.

Quick-fire Quiz

1. What gave the lathe its power?
a) A springy pole
b) A waterwheel
c) A motor

2. What was scaffolding made from?
a) Stone
b) Metal poles
c) Wooden poles

3. What did masons use to grip large stone blocks?
a) Hands
b) Metal pincers
c) Baskets

4. How many men usually worked at a saw pit?
a) One
b) Two
c) Three

Castle Designs

Castle builders tried all kinds of different designs to make their buildings stronger. One of the simplest was the square stone tower, or keep. But a keep was not enough on its own and was usually surrounded by extra walls. Later, builders added towers, gatehouses, and more walls.

Why were some towers round?

Round towers were stronger than square towers, because they did not have weak corners. In addition, defenders could fire arrows in many different directions from a round tower, giving them more chance of hitting their enemies. Not all towers were round, but their importance for defense made them increasingly popular.

What was a shell keep?

A shell keep was a circular stone wall on top of a soil mound. Many of these were built on the sites of old motte and bailey castles. Around the inside of a shell keep was a wall walk, where archers could stand to shoot through the battlements. Below this were structures, such as the hall, built against the outer wall.

Why have extra sets of walls?

Early castles had just one set of walls. This made it fairly easy for an attacker to break inside, so builders began adding extra sets of walls (right). This slowed attackers down. It also meant that defenders could trap their enemies between two walls, making them sitting targets for defending archers.

Outer bailey

Ditch

Wooden hoardings

Where was the castle strongest?

In early castles the stronghold was usually the keep. But when keeps went out of fashion, the gatehouse (above) became the strongest part. Gatehouses had thick walls, twin towers, and one or more strong gates, called portcullises (see page 189). Outside the main walls lords sometimes built a barbican, a strong outer courtyard that an enemy would have to take before attacking the main castle.

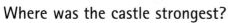

How thick were the walls?

Stone castle walls could be several yards thick. The thicker they were, the harder they were for attackers to knock down. If they were really thick, enemies might not even try to attack them. Castle walls were actually two parallel walls with a gap between them. The gap could be filled with rubble to make them even stronger.

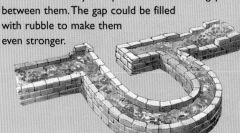

What was a concentric castle?

A concentric castle was a castle with two parallel sets of walls, one inside the other. As well as giving an enemy two barriers to get through, these twin walls provided defenders with two firing platforms. The outer wall was often lower than the one on the inside so that one group of defending archers could fire safely over the heads of the others.

Battlements

Chateau Gaillard (begun 1196)

Keep

Inner wall

Inner bailey

Round tower

Outer wall

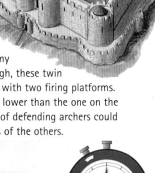

Quick-fire Quiz

1. Where did archers stand in a shell keep?
a) In the courtyard
b) On the wall walk
c) On the catwalk

2. Why did archers like round towers?
a) They gave more lines of fire
b) They were warm
c) They were spacious

3. What was a portcullis?
a) A type of tower
b) A strong gate
c) A thick wall

4. What were extra walls for?
a) To accommodate more soldiers
b) To prevent mining
c) For defense

171

Parts of the Castle

A castle had one or more courtyards, with main rooms in buildings along the insides of the courtyard walls. Near the great hall, where everyone ate, were the pantry and the kitchen. Stables, workshops, and extra living rooms were located in wall towers or in buildings separate from the great hall.

Where were the stables?

Stables were usually built in one of the castle courtyards. Like many buildings inside the walls, they could be large, but were often built of timber. Near the stables was a workshop for the farrier, the craftsman who made and fitted horseshoes.

What was in a keep?

Because the keep was one of the strongest parts of the castle, everything of value was kept in its basement. The lord's hall was above this. Further floors were used by members of the lord's household.

Were dungeons really prisons?

The basement rooms in castle towers, now called dungeons, were storage rooms, not prisons. Weapons, equipment, and food would be kept there. Prisons were rare in the Middle Ages, and the only people held prisoner for long periods were nobles captured in battle. The nobles could then be set free in return for ransom—money (right) from their families.

Where was the bathroom?

Castles did not have bathrooms like those in modern houses. When people washed, they used a bowl of water. For toilets there were garderobes. A garderobe consisted of a wooden seat above a stone drain, which emptied through the castle wall directly into the moat. Garderobes smelled bad and must have been cold, because the drain usually led straight out into the open air.

How was the food cooked?

Castles had no modern kitchen appliances, so most food was cooked over the fire (left). The cook roasted meat on a spit, which could be turned with a handle so the food was cooked on all sides. Other foods were boiled in a large iron pot over the flames. Castle kitchens also had ovens for baking the bread that everyone ate with their meals.

Quick-fire Quiz

1. What was in the keep basement?
   a) The hall
   b) The storage room
   c) The kitchen

2. What did a farrier make?
   a) Castles
   b) Horseshoes
   c) Bread

3. Why might you be imprisoned?
   a) For a minor crime
   b) For a serious crime
   c) For ransom

4. Why were garderobes cold?
   a) They were used only in winter
   b) They drained into the open air
   c) They had large windows

How were wall towers used?

Wall towers (left) were used in all kinds of ways. Guards could get the best view of the surrounding country from the top of the stair turret and could fire at an enemy from the battlements around the roof. In the rooms below, there were more windows to shoot from. In peacetime these rooms, which often had fireplaces, provided accommodation for the soldiers or members of the lord's family.

Did castles have gardens?

Many castles had gardens where vegetables and herbs were grown for cooking. In the later Middle Ages, when castles became more luxurious, some even had ornamental gardens. There the flowers, herbs, shrubs, and trees were arranged in neat patterns.

Castle Life

What kind of music entertained the guests?

Minstrels (right) played instruments and sang songs. The fiddle was popular, but after the Crusades many minstrels took up an Arab instrument, the lute. In Wales musicians played the harp, while the harplike psaltery was played all over Europe.

During peacetime the lord and his followers collected rent from tenants and made sure the castle was in good repair. Knights went hunting to bring extra food for the table. Women and girls spun wool, cooked, and mended clothes. In the evening everyone came together for a meal in the great hall.

Where did everyone sleep?

Medieval castles had no bedrooms. The lord and his family usually slept in the solar (right), a private room next to the hall. Most of the rest of the household slept in the hall itself. After the evening meal they took down the tables and leaned them against the wall, then put straw-filled mattresses on the floor. Others slept where they worked. Cooks, for example, slept in the kitchen.

What was on the menu?

People ate whatever farmers could provide, plus what could be hunted. If food was plentiful, the diet included meat such as venison and boar together with beef, pork, and mutton from the farm. Bread and vegetables were served with the meat, often on a trencher—a dinner plate of firm bread. This was washed down with ale or wine (right). In lean times people ate meat preserved with salt and flavored with herbs to hide the salty taste.

Trencher

Did women have rights?
Medieval women had few rights. Few were educated, and most had to endure a life of household chores. If a woman had property, it passed to her husband when she died. For the lady of the manor, things could be different. She helped run the manor if her husband was away and might even have to defend the castle.

Who was the boss?
The lord was the boss, and everyone had to obey him. His power covered almost every aspect of life, from how his land should be farmed to who rode into battle with him. The only area that the lord did not control was religion—his power was second to that of the local bishop and clergy.

Who helped the lord?
A number of servants, from the steward to the reeve, helped run the lord's manor (see pages 192-193). Others did menial duties in the castle (above). Pages served at the lord's table, while grooms looked after his horses. He might have a clerk—who could also be the chaplain—to keep records and write letters. But the lord's constant companion and most important personal servant was his squire (see pages 176-177).

(see pages 192-193) ... (see pages 176-177)

How did people keep warm?
Compared with houses today, castles and manor houses were cold and drafty, even when heated with blazing log fires. To keep down the drafts, the lords lined their walls with tapestries. People wore several layers of thick, wool clothing in the winter, and the rich added garments trimmed with fur (right) when the weather was really cold.

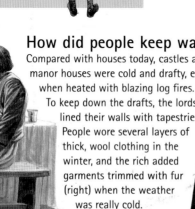

175

Becoming a Knight

To become a knight, a young man had to belong to a noble family. As a boy he began his training as a page and learned how to behave in a noble household. As a teenager he became a squire, learning knightly conduct and how to handle weapons and horses. Finally, in a ceremony known as dubbing, he became a knight.

Serving at table

Practicing with a lance

How did a boy become a page?

If a boy was the son of a noble family, he did not go to school. Instead, when he was about seven years old, he was sent away to be a page in the household of another lord. Here he learned good manners and skills such as carrying food to the table (right) and serving his lord and lady.

What did a squire do?

A squire was a knight's personal servant and helper. His duties included looking after all the weapons and tending the horses. Before a battle the squire helped his master put on armor. He may even have had to fight beside his lord, providing aid if the knight was wounded. By doing all these things, a squire learned how to behave as a knight.

Did knights pray?

In the Middle Ages religion played a big part in most people's lives. When a squire was to be made a knight, he often spent the whole night before the dubbing ceremony in prayer in the castle chapel (left). This vigil was a sign that he would take his vows seriously to serve his king faithfully for the rest of his life.

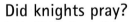

How did squires practice sword play?

For practice, knights and squires often used a sword and a small, round shield called a buckler. To build up strength, squires were sometimes given swords that were heavier than those actually used in battle. Pages or young squires might be given wooden swords to practice with.

Exercising

Helping the knight

Practicing swordplay

Dubbing

How did squires exercise?

Squires kept in shape by practicing swordplay, wrestling, throwing the javelin, and all kinds of other sporting activities. They made sure that they were strong in case they had to go into battle.

Quick-fire Quiz

1. At what age did a boy become a page?
a) About four
b) About seven
c) About seventeen

2. Why could being a squire be dangerous?
a) Lords were cruel
b) You may have had to fight in battle
c) You had no shield

3. What was a small, round shield called?
a) A buckler
b) A helm
c) A hand shield

4. What was used to dub a knight?
a) A shield
b) A lance
c) A sword

Were knights and squires well-mannered?

Knights and squires were supposed to behave with good manners. They were meant to be considerate to women and courteous to all. But they did not always live up to this ideal. Sometimes squires got together in rowdy gangs and went around causing mischief. On one occasion they even burned down part of a town.

What was dubbing?

Dubbing was the ceremony at which a squire was made into a knight. The squire kneeled in front of his lord or the king, who tapped him on the shoulder with his sword. The new knight was then presented with a sword and spurs. There was often a celebration afterward.

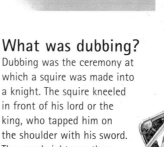

Heraldry

In the Middle Ages every noble family had a coat of arms that acted as its badge. A knight wore his coat of arms into battle and when competing in a tournament so that he could be recognized easily. Coats of arms were always designed in a similar way, using the same range of colors and basic patterns.

Groom's arms

Bride's arms

Combined coat of arms

How was a coat of arms designed?

The herald chose the colors, shapes, and other designs that were suitable for the family who were to bear the arms. He made sure that the design was different from all others—every coat of arms had to be unique. When two noble families were united by marriage, the couple could have their two coats of arms combined (above), with the bride's and groom's arms on opposite sides of the shield.

What did heraldic symbols mean?

Many of the symbols used in heraldry have special meanings. Designs such as the diagonal bar (left) showed that the bearer's parents were not married. This was important in the Middle Ages, because an illegitimate son would not be able to inherit his father's title or lands.

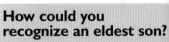

What were a herald's duties?

A herald was an officer in the household of the king or great lord. As well as designing coats of arms (above), it was his job to organize ceremonies and tournaments. In war the herald carried messages between opposing armies (left). Therefore, it was essential that he could recognize every coat of arms, to deliver the message to the right person.

How could you recognize an eldest son?

An eldest son used his father's coat of arms, but with an added element. While the father was alive, the son's coat of arms was marked with a symbol called a label. The label ran across the shoulders and looked like a horizontal line with three thicker, downward-pointing lines joined to it. When the father died, the eldest son removed the label.

How were knights identified on the battlefield?

A knight's shield and his surcoat—a loose robe worn over the armor—were decorated with his coat of arms. This made it easy to see who was who in the confusion of battle. Heralds also used coats of arms to identify casualties after the battle (below).

Quick-fire Quiz

1. Which of these was a herald's job?
a) Carrying messages
b) Fighting
c) Looking after the horses

2. Where were the supporters placed?
a) Above the shield
b) Below the shield
c) On either side of the shield

3. What was red called in heraldry?
a) Sable
b) Scarlet
c) Gules

4. What mark denoted an eldest son?
a) Bar
b) Label
c) Chevron

What was the language of heraldry?

Coats of arms were described in a special language based on Old French. Each of the colors had its own name in this language—for example, red was called "gules," and black was referred to as "sable." Experts on heraldry still use this language to describe coats of arms today.

What were supporters?

The supporters were a pair of figures that stood on either side of the shield in a coat of arms, as if they were holding it up. These figures were often animals and could be real beasts, such as lions or antelope, or mythical ones, such as unicorns or griffons. Supporters were not normally shown on a knight's surcoat, but were included in the full coat of arms.

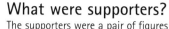

Horsemanship

Whether fighting, hunting, or traveling, a knight spent much of his time on horseback. A horse was the knight's most valued possession. As a page or squire he was shown how to ride and how to care for his mount. As he got older he learned how to fight on horseback using a sword and a lance so that he could fight for his king and take part in tournaments.

How many horses did a knight own?

Most knights had several horses, which were used for different tasks. A knight would have one or two warhorses (destriers), a powerful horse for hunting (a courser), and perhaps another one for traveling. Knights also kept packhorses in their stables. These were used to carry luggage when the knight and his household were traveling or when items had to be sent across the country.

What was a destrier?

A destrier was a warhorse. Destriers were large, powerful stallions that could carry their owners swiftly into battle. The best and costliest destriers were said to come from southern Europe, especially from Italy and Spain. The name "destrier" comes from the Latin word for "right," perhaps because the horse led with its right leg, swerving away from an opponent in battle.

How could you stop a horse in its tracks?

If footsoldiers were going into battle against mounted knights, they might scatter fearsome-looking, spiked objects called caltrops on the ground. A caltrop had four metal spikes, arranged so that whichever way the caltrop landed, one spike pointed up. A caltrop could injure a horse that stepped on it.

Caltrop

How did a knight control his horse?

A knight controlled his horse with both his feet and his hands. He placed his feet in a pair of stirrups and used them to grip his mount. This meant that the knight's hands were free to hold the reins or to wield a sword or a lance. The leather reins were connected to a bit that was placed in the horse's mouth. By changing the tension of the reins, the knight could make his horse speed up, slow down, or turn a corner.

Stirrup

Were spurs cruel?

A good rider would use his spurs only sparingly—for example, when urging his horse to give an extra burst of speed. Even so, a jab from the single, long, metal spike of a prick spur must have hurt; rowel spurs, with their rings of shorter spikes, did less damage.

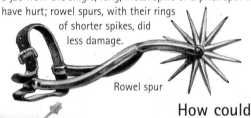

Rowel spur

Armored horse

How could a knight protect his horse?

Some knights had armor made for their warhorses, because it was just as dangerous for a horse in battle as it was for the animal's rider. Horse armor was usually made up of a shaffron, or headpiece, and a crinet, a series of metal plates that covered the neck. Because plate armor was expensive, the rest of the horse sometimes went unprotected into battle.

Quick-fire Quiz

1. How many spikes did a prick spur have?
a) One
b Two
c) Three

2. What was a caltrop used for?
a) Killing soldiers
b) Controlling horses
c) Injuring horses

3. Where were the best warhorses bred?
a) Holland and Germany
b) Spain and Italy
c) Britain and Ireland

4. What was a knight's most valued possession?
a) His sword
b) His horse
c) His armor

Weapons and Fighting

The most feared sight on a medieval battlefield was a line of enemy knights charging directly at you. Well armored, mounted on warhorses, and wielding weapons that they had spent years training to use, knights were fast, powerful, and difficult to stop. A knight's favorite weapon was the sword, which could be used either on foot or from a horse, but he was adept with other weapons.

What was a double-edged sword used for?

A two-edged sword was used for cutting and slashing blows. This type of weapon was very effective against an enemy who was not wearing armor, especially if it was a "great sword" with a large grip that the knight could hold in both hands. He could then use all his strength to deliver powerful, cutting blows.

Mace

Shield

Sword

Dagger

Crossbow

Battle-ax

Arrows

Longbow

Did knights use only swords and daggers?

In addition to the sword, the knight used several other hand weapons (above and right), including the battle-ax and the mace. The mace was especially fearsome because its raised metal ridges or spikes concentrated the power of the blow, knocking the enemy sideways.

How did the Normans use their shields?

Norman soldiers held their large, kite-shaped shields in front of them to give plenty of protection. If a group of men was fighting in a row, they moved their shields together (below) to form a wall that archers or even mounted warriors found difficult to break through.

How did you use a flail?

A flail consisted of a wooden handle linked by a chain to a spiked metal ball. A knight normally used the flail when fighting on foot. He aimed to strike at an enemy's head, knocking him out or piercing his armor.

How could you injure someone who was wearing mail?

To do serious injury to an opponent in mail (see page 184), a knight needed a sword or dagger with a narrow, sharp point, to get through one of the gaps between the metal rings. Archers (right) also found that they could pierce mail by using narrow metal heads on their arrows.

When was a lance used?

A lance was a long, heavy, polelike weapon, which was most effective at the start of a battle. Wielded by mounted knights charging swiftly, it could kill a man with a single thrust. After the charge the knight discarded the lance and drew his sword—a better weapon for one-on-one fighting.

How were swords made stronger?

Armorers gave blades extra strength by altering their shape. A blade with a cross section like an elongated diamond was the strongest. Both cutting and stabbing swords (below) were made with blades in this shape.

Quick-fire Quiz

1. How did you hold a "great sword"?
a) Close to the chest
b) With one hand
c) With two hands

2. Which blade shape gave greatest strength?
a) Diamond
b) Rounded
c) Hollow

3. What did a weapon need to pierce mail?
a) A narrow point
b) Extra power
c) Plenty of weight

4. Where was a knight most likely to use a flail?
a) On horseback
b) On foot
c) In a boat

Armor

Every knight wanted to go into battle well protected. In the early Middle Ages knights wore mail, but armor made up of metal plates became more popular. Knights liked plate armor because it protected them well from arrows and sword blows, while allowing them to move with great freedom. But only a rich man could afford a full suit of plate armor.

What did the armorer do?

Armorers (below) were skilled craftsmen who made both armor and weapons and could beat pieces of metal into sturdy breastplates or helmets. They did this by hammering a sheet of metal on an anvil or on a rounded object called a former. This gave the piece the right curve. Suits of armor often came back damaged from battle, so armorers also spent a lot of time on repairs.

How could you "knit" with metal?

By making mail. Mail, or chain mail as it is sometimes called, was a form of armor made up of thousands of tiny, linked metal rings. By varying the number of rings in a row, the armorer could shape mail into garments such as shirts, head coverings, leg guards, and even mittens. Mail was popular until plate armor became fashionable in the late 1200s.

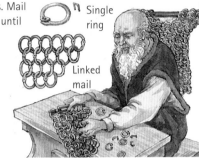

Single ring

Linked mail

Conical helmet   Basinet   Great helm (jousting)   Frog-mouthed (jousting)   Barbute

Why were there so many types of helmets?

Fashions in helmets changed just like fashions in clothes. In the late 1300s knights often wore the basinet, a helmet with a pointed visor and a collar of mail, which offered excellent protection. By the mid-1400s they were wearing lighter helmets, called barbutes. For jousts and tournaments a rich knight might wear a highly decorated great helm.

What did a knight wear under his armor?

Under his armor a knight wore a padded jacket called an arming doublet. The doublet had sections of mail sewn under the arms and in other places to protect areas where there were gaps between the plates.

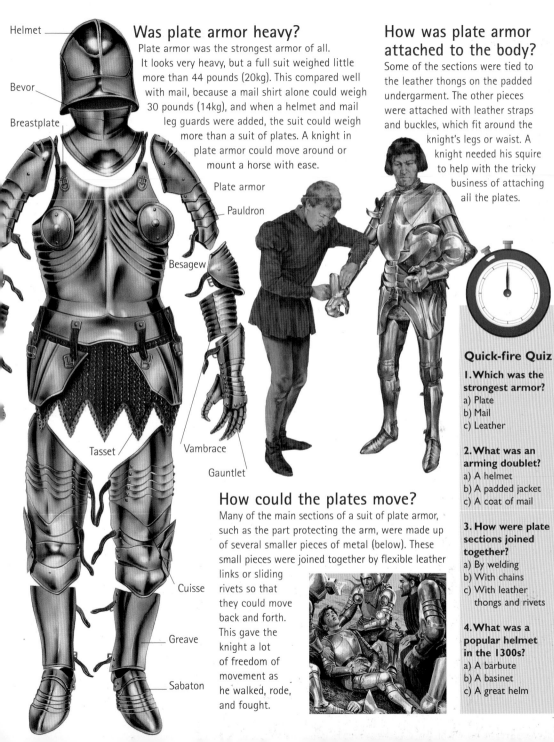

Helmet

Bevor

Breastplate

Was plate armor heavy?

Plate armor was the strongest armor of all. It looks very heavy, but a full suit weighed little more than 44 pounds (20kg). This compared well with mail, because a mail shirt alone could weigh 30 pounds (14kg), and when a helmet and mail leg guards were added, the suit could weigh more than a suit of plates. A knight in plate armor could move around or mount a horse with ease.

Plate armor

Pauldron

Besagew

Tasset

Vambrace

Gauntlet

How was plate armor attached to the body?

Some of the sections were tied to the leather thongs on the padded undergarment. The other pieces were attached with leather straps and buckles, which fit around the knight's legs or waist. A knight needed his squire to help with the tricky business of attaching all the plates.

Quick-fire Quiz

1. Which was the strongest armor?
a) Plate
b) Mail
c) Leather

2. What was an arming doublet?
a) A helmet
b) A padded jacket
c) A coat of mail

3. How were plate sections joined together?
a) By welding
b) With chains
c) With leather thongs and rivets

4. What was a popular helmet in the 1300s?
a) A barbute
b) A basinet
c) A great helm

How could the plates move?

Many of the main sections of a suit of plate armor, such as the part protecting the arm, were made up of several smaller pieces of metal (below). These small pieces were joined together by flexible leather links or sliding rivets so that they could move back and forth. This gave the knight a lot of freedom of movement as he walked, rode, and fought.

Cuisse

Greave

Sabaton

Siege

When enemy forces arrived to attack a castle, the castle's owner and his men pulled up the drawbridge and got ready for a siege. The siege could end peacefully, especially if the defenders ran out of food and were forced to surrender. But if there was a fight, the attackers could use all kinds of powerful weapons to force their way in.

How effective were archers?

The longbow was one of the medieval soldier's most awesome weapons. Its deadly arrows could fly almost 1,000 feet (300m), and a skilled archer could fire up to 12 arrows a minute. Castle defenders had to hide behind the battlements to avoid the arrows' sharp metal points.

What were siege engines?

The devices used by medieval armies to attack castles were known as siege engines. They were fearsome weapons that hurled missiles at the enemy or knocked down walls. The trebuchet and the mangonel were catapults powerful enough to fling heavy rocks. The ballista, a giant crossbow, shot bolts that were often tipped with blazing rags. Weapons on wheeled platforms could be moved into position to find their target. Reloading very large devices was slow work, but their devastating power struck fear into the enemy.

Mangonel

How could an attacker get through walls?

One way was to batter down the walls using a ram, a huge tree trunk mounted on wheels. A group of men, protected by the ram's roof, struck the walls repeatedly with the ram until they toppled. Alternatively, attackers could try wheeling a wooden siege tower up to the walls and climbing over. Both the ram and the tower were covered with animal skins to protect their wooden structures from flaming arrows.

Siege tower

Ram

What was mining?

Mining was another way of bringing down castle walls. The miners dug a tunnel under the walls, using wooden props to keep the tunnel from collapsing. Once they finished digging, they lit a fire in the tunnel. This set the props alight, so that the walls above no longer had anything to support them. If all went according to plan, a section of the castle walls collapsed, and the attackers swarmed into the castle. If the defenders saw a mine being dug, however, they could retaliate by digging their own tunnel into the mine and fighting off the attackers.

Tunnel entrance, far away from the walls

Miners set fire to wooden props

Workers bring wood for the fire

Soldiers remove vital foundation rocks

Trebuchet

How did a catapult work?

Catapults worked like giant slings to launch missiles at or over walls. Trebuchets used counterweights; the mangonel's sling was held by ropes, which were then released. It took many men to reload the largest catapults.

Defense

Everything about a castle was designed to make it easy to defend. The walls were thick to withstand attacks from siege engines, while windows were small to keep out arrows. Battlements, towers, and hoardings all gave good lines of fire.

What was a moat?

A moat was a barrier between the castle and its attackers. Many castles were surrounded by dry ditches, but a water-filled moat gave more protection. An attacker could walk across a dry ditch and start mining—digging holes under the walls to make them fall down. With a moat it was virtually impossible for the enemy to undermine the castle walls.

What were murder holes?

Murder holes were small openings in the ceiling, usually within a castle gatehouse. They enabled defenders to look down at anyone passing through the gate below. If the person below was an enemy, the defender could shoot arrows or pour boiling liquid through one of the holes.

How was an embrasure used?

An embrasure was a hole in the wall where an archer could stand. The hole was splayed on the inside so that the archer could stand to one side of the opening, out of reach of enemy fire. When the archer was ready to shoot, he moved quickly to the opening, fired his arrow, and then ducked back out of range.

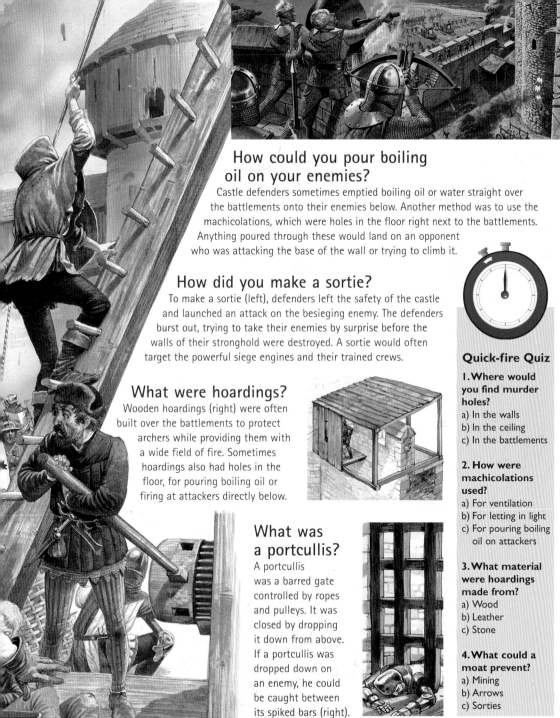

How could you pour boiling oil on your enemies?

Castle defenders sometimes emptied boiling oil or water straight over the battlements onto their enemies below. Another method was to use the machicolations, which were holes in the floor right next to the battlements. Anything poured through these would land on an opponent who was attacking the base of the wall or trying to climb it.

How did you make a sortie?

To make a sortie (left), defenders left the safety of the castle and launched an attack on the besieging enemy. The defenders burst out, trying to take their enemies by surprise before the walls of their stronghold were destroyed. A sortie would often target the powerful siege engines and their trained crews.

What were hoardings?

Wooden hoardings (right) were often built over the battlements to protect archers while providing them with a wide field of fire. Sometimes hoardings also had holes in the floor, for pouring boiling oil or firing at attackers directly below.

What was a portcullis?

A portcullis was a barred gate controlled by ropes and pulleys. It was closed by dropping it down from above. If a portcullis was dropped down on an enemy, he could be caught between its spiked bars (right).

Quick-fire Quiz

1. Where would you find murder holes?
a) In the walls
b) In the ceiling
c) In the battlements

2. How were machicolations used?
a) For ventilation
b) For letting in light
c) For pouring boiling oil on attackers

3. What material were hoardings made from?
a) Wood
b) Leather
c) Stone

4. What could a moat prevent?
a) Mining
b) Arrows
c) Sorties

The Crusades

In the late 1000s Christian rulers tried to take control of the Holy Land—the part of the Middle East where Jesus had lived. At that time the Holy Land was ruled by the Muslims—followers of Islam—to whom the area was also sacred. It was the start of a bitter conflict—the Crusades.

Who went on the Crusades?

All kinds of people went on the Crusades. Some were kings, such as Richard I of England and Philip II of France. Others were nobles, and many were men-at-arms who went with their lords to the east. A large number of poor peasants also went on crusade, inspired by leaders such as the French monk Peter the Hermit.

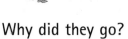

Why did they go?

Many crusaders were men who genuinely believed that it was right to fight for control of the Christian sites in the Holy Land. But others went just for the adventure or because they thought that they could benefit, either by looting after battles or by setting themselves up as lords in the east. Many of the latter were the younger sons of nobles, who would not inherit any of their parents' wealth back home.

What was the Children's Crusade?

In 1212 Nicholas, a 12-year-old boy from Cologne, Germany, led thousands of children across the Alps and into Italy on their way to the Holy Land. Another boy, Stephen, from France, led another group of children. Both groups failed. Stephen and his followers were captured and sold as slaves; the followers of Nicholas died in Italy.

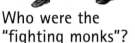

Who were the "fighting monks"?

The fighting monks were groups of men who took religious vows but were still allowed to fight the Muslims. There were several groups, or orders, of fighting monks—the Knights Templar (named after their headquarters near the Temple in Jerusalem), the Knights of St. John (famous for their work healing the sick), and the Teutonic Knights (who originally came from Germany).

What did the Crusades achieve?

Although the crusaders set up states in the Middle East, these were soon reconquered. Only the ruins of their great castles, such as Krak des Chevaliers (below), survive. But they brought useful knowledge back to Europe, as well as new medicines and eastern inventions such as the windmill.

Who was Saladin?

Saladin was a Muslim leader in the 1100s who ruled Egypt and part of Syria. He defended his lands from crusaders and defeated the Second Crusade. When the Third Crusade began, Saladin fought Richard I of England. Again Saladin was victorious and greatly reduced the crusaders' power.

Saladin

How many crusades were there?

There were eight separate crusades from Europe to the Holy Land between the 1000s and the 1200s. The most successful was the first (1096–99), which was led by a group of French and Norman barons. It ended with the capture of Jerusalem. In 1271 the last crusader territory in the Holy Land was lost to the Muslims.

Quick-fire Quiz

1. Which French king led a crusade?
a) Philip I
b) Philip II
c) Richard I

2. Who led the First Crusade?
a) French and Norman barons
b) Richard I
c) German lords

3. Which was the most successful crusade?
a) The fourth
b) The second
c) The first

4. What were the Knights of St. John known for?
a) Healing the sick
b) Helping the poor
c) Fighting for St. John

The Lord's Manor

A manor consisted of a lord's castle, church, houses for the peasants, and farmland. The lord was the most important person. He was the landlord, boss, and judge, and the peasants had to do what he told them. These peasants were known as serfs or villeins; they had no freedom.

Who looked after the money?

The person who kept the accounts on the manor was the steward (left). He had to be educated, although most accounting systems were primitive. Later a group of merchants in Italy invented the system of double-entry bookkeeping, which is still used by accountants today. As well as looking after the money, the steward managed the lord's farm and also acted as judge in the manorial court if the lord was away.

What did the bailiff do?

The bailiff was a peasant farmer who had his own land. As well as his own fields, he looked after the day-to-day running of the lord's personal land, making sure that all the jobs were done correctly and at the right time. In addition, the bailiff was responsible for repairs and building work on the manor, bringing in any workers, such as stonemasons or carpenters, to get these jobs done. He was second in importance to the steward.

What was life like for the workers?

Life was hard for peasants. Men spent nearly all their time working in the fields. Women had to cook, look after the house, and make the family's clothes. For children there was no school. Boys helped in the fields while girls learned how to spin, sew, and cook. Sunday and religious holidays were the only days off. For some, local markets (below) offered a welcome break from the hardships of daily life.

Who kept watch on the peasants?

The reeve (right) was the person who kept an eye on the peasants. He was a peasant himself, chosen by his peers, and he worked closely with the bailiff. He was most often seen out in the fields, making sure that everyone was working hard. But if any of the workers had a problem, the reeve could tell the bailiff, who would then decide what to do or whether to report the matter to the lord.

Reeve

Who worked the lord's land?

The lord's land was divided into two sections. Most was allotted to the peasants, who were allowed to work the land in return for services to the lord and a share of the produce. The rest of the lord's land was called the demesne. This was farmed by the lord with help from the peasants, who owed him some of their labor each week.

Who dealt with criminals?

The lord held his own court in his hall for minor crimes. Punishments included whipping, beating, fines, or being locked in the stocks. Serious offenses were judged by the county sheriff and could be punished by death by hanging. The church had its own laws and courts (above) for dealing with lawbreakers among the clergy.

Quick-fire Quiz

1. Who was judge in the court when the lord was away?
a) The bailiff
b) The reeve
c) The steward

2. Who farmed the demesne?
a) The lord
b) The sheriff
c) The reeve

3. How many years did a peasant spend at school?
a) Ten
b) Six
c) None

4. What caused so many women to die young?
a) Overwork
b) Black Death
c) Childbirth

What happened when people were sick?

Medieval medicine was basic. Some herbal medicines worked well, but other remedies, such as bloodletting, did no good. As a result, many people died of minor illnesses, and few lived beyond the age of 40. Life was especially hard for women, many of whom died in childbirth. The most feared illness was the bubonic plague, or the Black Death (right). It killed a third of the population of Europe in the 1300s.

Peacetime Pursuits

In the Middle Ages people had to create their own entertainment. Poor families filled their limited spare time with simple games and storytelling. For noble families life was easier, but even knights had to mix some of their pleasure with work. Many liked to hunt, but the main reason for hunting was to provide food.

What was chivalry?

Chivalry was a code of conduct that all knights were supposed to follow. A knight was expected to be considerate, especially toward women, and to treat enemies with respect. Many did not live up to this, but the Middle Ages are often known as the "Age of Chivalry."

What were the favorite games?

Peasant children usually played games, such as leapfrog and tag, that did not need any equipment, since ordinary families could not afford toys. Noble families had more money, and a knight's children were sometimes given toys, such as wooden swords and shields or miniature models of men-at-arms.

What were pastimes for adults?

Some people liked to play board games, such as chess (above), which appealed to noblemen because it is like a battle. Otherwise, knights and their ladies looked forward to visits from musicians and actors who arrived from time to time and performed in return for board and lodging.

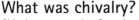

How did a falconer exercise his birds?

Falconers trained their birds to hunt and bring back prey. One way to exercise a falcon was to let it hunt for animals as it would in the wild. An alternative was to use a lure—a fake bird on the end of a long string. The falconer twirled the lure around in the air, encouraging the bird to pounce on it.

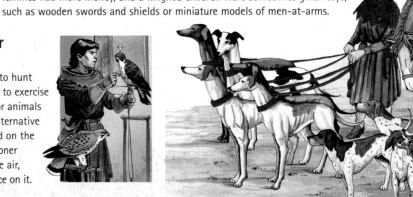

Why did girls learn to spin?

In the Middle Ages most manors kept sheep for meat and for wool. It was the job of the women and girls to spin the wool into yarn, which was then woven into cloth. A simple spindle or wooden spinning wheel was all that was needed, so almost every medieval girl learned to spin to produce yarn.

How did people like to be entertained?

One of the favorite pastimes was telling stories. Few people could read, but popular tales were handed down from one generation to the next by word of mouth. People liked to listen to stories about the exploits and loves of knights in times gone by. Some of the favorites were about the adventures of the mythical English king Arthur (right) and his Knights of the Round Table.

Which creatures did knights most enjoy hunting?

Knights hunted animals that they could eat. They liked to chase large creatures that provided plenty of meat—and offered a challenge to the hunter. Deer and wild boar were favorites. When these animals were scarce, smaller creatures like hares were hunted. Poorer people might have hunted birds or rabbits. In the Middle Ages there were few imported foods, and everyone had to eat what could be grown on the local land. Hunting made the diet more varied. Hunting also offered knights useful riding practice for war.

Quick-fire Quiz

1. What animals did knights hunt?
a) Falcons
b) Dogs
c) Deer

2. Which king was a favorite of storytellers?
a) King Alfred
b) King Arthur
c) King Albert

3. What are the Middle Ages sometimes called?
a) Age of Innocence
b) Age of Chivalry
c) Bronze Age

4. Which board game was popular with noblemen?
a) Chess
b) Checkers
c) Solitaire

Tournaments

Knights needed to practice fighting, so they often engaged in mock combat as a rehearsal for war. Many people liked to watch the knights fight, so tournaments soon became great festivals to which spectators came from far and wide. As well as mock battles, knights also fought one-to-one on horseback in the joust and with swords in foot combat.

What happened in a joust?

In a joust (right) two mounted knights hurtled toward each other and tried to knock each other off their horses as they passed. The weapon they used was the lance—either a pointed lance for the "joust of war," or a safer, blunt lance for the "joust of peace." Both types of jousts were stunning spectacles. Knights wore special armor for the joust. Their breastplates had metal rests for their lances, and they wore helmets that covered the entire head. Only a narrow slit was left in the helmet to allow the knight to see his target.

How did squires practice for the joust?

Jousting was dangerous, so knights invented a safer way to practice. Squires rode toward a quintain, a device with two moving arms attached to a wooden post. One arm held a shield, the other a heavy weight. The squire had to hit the shield with his lance, then ride past swiftly to avoid being hit by the swinging weight, which quickly spun around at him.

What if you weren't a knight?

Men who were not knights could train for war by practicing archery. Archers organized competitions, with everyone trying to hit the gold circle in the center of the target. To protect spectators, there was a barrier or a mound of soil, called the butts, behind the targets.

What drew spectators to the tournament?

Many people liked the pageantry seen at the tournament. This included the knights' shields decorated with their coats of arms, the banners, and the brightly patterned cloths—called caparisons—on the horses. As the knights rode through the streets to the tournament, onlookers could easily recognize those they supported from all the badges and heraldry.

Who took part in tournaments?

It was mostly knights who took part, and they were usually members of the country's powerful families. Large-scale mock battles, called melees (right), involved many knights, and sometimes foot soldiers too. Tournaments were hosted by the king or one of his highest-ranking lords. As well as giving battle practice, tournaments showed people how strong the king was and how many knightly followers he had.

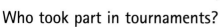

197

The Last Castles

After the 1400s nobles stopped building castles as secure strongholds. Instead they built elegant houses in which to enjoy a life of comfort. This came about because of changes in the way nobles lived and how battles were fought. Some families still lived in buildings that looked like castles from the outside, but would have been of little use in war.

Were cannons effective against castles?

The first cannons (above), used from the 1300s onward, did not always work very well. They made a lot of noise, but damaged few castles. But as time went on, cannons became larger and more reliable and could blow huge holes in castle walls. This meant that, by the 1500s, castles were no longer as secure from attack as they had been.

Was armor bullet-proof?

Yes. Armorers normally tried to make their plates thick enough to stop a bullet. As firearms became more common from the 1400s, people were anxious to be protected by their armor. Armorers often fired bullets at their breastplates before the armor left the workshop. The mark left by the bullet reassured the wearer that he would be safe.

How did leather replace armor?

By the 1600s light cavalry soldiers (left) were doing the jobs of knights on the battlefield. Many of these horsemen found that a jacket of pale leather—called a buff coat—gave them enough protection from sword cuts. Buff coats were worn with a metal breastplate and helmet, to shield the most vulnerable parts of the body.

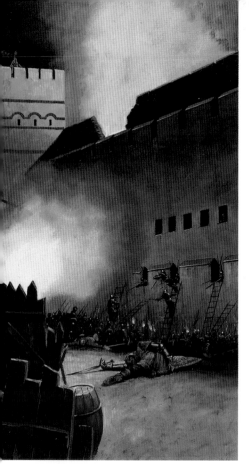

Why did knights stop building castles?

In 1453 the Ottoman Turks laid siege to Constantinople (modern Istanbul), the capital of the Byzantine Empire (left). When their firearms battered down the walls and the Turks swarmed into the great city, it seemed to be the end of an era. Lords realized that there was little point in building stone castles for defense. At the same time the feudal system was breaking down. Knights were no longer powerful, and other people—especially merchants—were getting richer. The age of castles was at an end.

Are there new castles?

Many nobles in the late 1700s and 1800s wanted to revive the Age of Chivalry. They designed their homes in the style of castles by adding towers, gatehouses, thick walls, and pointed windows, to create buildings like Schloss Neuschwanstein in Germany (above).

Why are so many castles ruined?

A castle could be damaged in a siege or "slighted" by an enemy to make it unusable. Some lords abandoned their castles because they wanted a more comfortable home. Local people would use much of the stone to build new houses.

Quick-fire Quiz

1. Who might wear a buff coat?
a) The lady of the manor
b) A squire
c) A cavalry soldier

2. How did armorers test plate armor?
a) By firing bullets at it
b) By hammering it
c) By heating it

3. How did castle windows change over the centuries?
a) They got smaller
b) They got bigger
c) They were filled in

4. Which weapon was the greatest threat to castles?
a) Siege tower
b) Cannon
c) Catapult

How did castles change?

Lords still lived in castles after the 1400s, but these castles were no longer built to withstand a siege. Nobles added features that gave them more comfort, such as luxurious bedrooms. Inside walls were lined with wooden paneling, and decorated plasterwork adorned the ceilings. Castle owners also put in bigger windows, so the rooms were much more light and airy than in medieval castles.

Timeline

This timeline records the key dates in the history of castles and knights. Most of the story takes place in a period known as the Middle Ages, or the medieval era. This period is called the "Middle" Ages because it is midway between the end of the Roman Empire (in the 400s) and the Renaissance (in the 1400s). The period does not have precise dates, but many historians say that the Middle Ages lasted from 500 to 1500.

A.D. 1 to 800

1–500 Romans use light cavalry troops to support footsoldiers. They build forts throughout Europe to defend their empire.

350–550 Western Roman Empire disintegrates.

410 Goths sack Rome.

622 The Islamic religion is established.

634 Omar I, caliph of the Arab Muslims, conquers Holy Land from Byzantines.

771 Charlemagne becomes king of the Franks. He uses mounted warriors to defend his lands.

790s Vikings begin raids on Britain and mainland Europe.

800 to 1000

800 Charlemagne is crowned Holy Roman Emperor by Pope Leo III.

800-1000 Rulers in western Europe begin to grant land to their nobles in return for services—the feudal system is established.

800-1150 The current style of architecture is the Romanesque, featuring rounded arches, thick walls, and tunnellike barrel vaults.

911 The Viking leader Rollo settles with his followers in northwestern France. They become known as the Normans, and their territory Normandy.

950 The stone keep at Doué-la-Fontaine, France, is built. This is now the oldest stone keep to survive.

987-1040 Foulques Nerra of Anjou builds 27 castles as part of his war with the Count of Blois.

1000 to 1100

1000 The Normans spread the fashion for castle-building around many areas of Europe. They begin by building wooden motte-and-bailey castles, but later construct castles using stone.

1000-1200 Many Italian towns become independent states, each defended by its own stone walls and castle. Italian lords each build their own stone tower, and some cities have many towers, with lords competing to build the tallest.

1066 William of Normandy invades England and defeats King Harold II at the Battle of Hastings. As his nobles take over they build castles all over the country to increase their power.

1071 William of Poitiers, said to be the first troubadour (medieval poet and singer), is born.

1090 Christian writers lay down rules of conduct for knights. The rules become the code of chivalry.

1095 Pope Urban II preaches the First Crusade.

1096-99 The First Crusade. Jerusalem is captured from the Muslims.

1100 Tower keeps become popular in many areas. In England and France stocky, square towers are common; German knights prefer more slender towers surrounded by strong curtain walls.

1100 to 1200

1100–1200 Many crusader castles are built.

1113 The Knights of St. John are founded in Jerusalem.

1118 The Knights Templar build their first headquarters near the Temple in Jerusalem.

1142 Crusaders take and rebuild Syria's greatest castle, the Krak des Chevaliers.

1147–49 The Second Crusade.

1150 The Gothic style replaces the Romaneqsue as the favored building style.

1160 Castle builders experiment with differently shaped keeps. Round keeps and many-sided designs are tried.

1170 Many Norman mottes with wooden towers are converted into stone shell keeps.

1180 Philip Augustus, one of the greatest French kings, comes to the throne; he will build many castles in his kingdom.

1188–92 The Third Crusade.

1190 The Teutonic Knights are founded. They build many castles in Europe.

1190 The keep goes out of fashion. Builders concentrate on courtyard castles with strong gatehouses.

1196 Richard I begins work on Château Gaillard, France. One of the strongest castles, it will withstand a siege for over a year.

1200 to 1300

1200 Rounded wall towers become popular.

1202–04 The Fourth Crusade.

1212 The Children's Crusade.

1217–22 The Fifth Crusade.

1228–29 The Sixth Crusade.

1220 Frederick II, one of the greatest castle builders, becomes Holy Roman Emperor.

1248–54 The Seventh Crusade.

1270 Rise of the concentric castle.

1270 The Eighth Crusade.

1272 Edward I comes to the throne of England. He launches military campaigns against the Scots and Welsh and builds many castles to control the population.

1291 Sultan Baybars storms the Christian city of Acre, and the crusading movement comes to an end.

1300 to 1400

1302 Battle of Courtrai. Flemish peasants armed with pikes defeat mounted French knights, proving that knights are not invincible in battle.

1312 The Knights Templar are dissolved.

1320s Cannons are first used in Europe.

1330 Plate armor becomes more fashionable.

1337–1453 The Hundred Years' War between England and France.

1347–51 The Black Death kills around one third of the population of Europe.

1380 Castle builders start to use gun loops so that defenders can fire out safely.

1400 to 1600

1400 Decline of castles begins.

1415 Battle of Agincourt. Henry V of England defeats army of French knights.

1450 Thicker walls are built to protect castles from pounding by cannon.

1453 The city of Constantinople, capital of the Byzantine Empire, falls to the Ottoman Turks, ending the Byzantine Empire.

1476–77 France fights wars with the Duchy of Burgundy; the widespread use of pikes and handguns shows that the age of the knight is coming to an end.

1500s Lords convert their castles into more comfortable residences or build palaces.

1509 Henry VIII builds forts (strongholds designed for guns where no one lives permanently) rather than true castles.

1600 to 2000

1650 Star-shaped forts used to defend many towns in France.

1800 People begin to be interested in castles as symbols of the Age of Chivalry.

1854 French architect Eugène-Emmanuel Viollet-le-Duc begins to publish books about medieval building, renewing interest in castles and showing how they were built.

1869 Work is started on Neuschwanstein, the fairy-tale castle built for King Ludwig II of Bavaria.

Web Addresses

www.castlesontheweb.com
This site offers an extensive database of links to castle-related things, including sites such as castles for kids, with free software for building a castle of your own and online heraldry games involving roleplay.

www.nationalgeographic.com/features/97/castles/enter.html
This is a charming, interactive site for younger children based around exploring a medieval castle and meeting all of its ghostly inhabitants, who even call you by your name.

kotn.ntu.ac.uk/castle
A fun, fictional, but historically accurate rendition of a castle based on Nottingham Castle in England, as it was around 1480. Move around the castle and learn what happened where—listen to music in the main hall, write recipes in the kitchen, and dress a knight in his outfit for a tournament.

library.thinkquest.org/10949
The ThinkQuest Library is a collection of more than 5,500 educational web sites designed by participants in the ThinkQuest competitions. This is an informative site touching on a variety of related medieval topics, including fortifications, war and buildings, society, and how people lived.

www.castlewales.com/life
www.medieval-castles.net
Useful web sites describing all aspects of a medieval castle, including its design, defenses, and domestic life.

www.castles-of-britain.com
This site is dedicated to the study and promotion of British castles and offers lots of information on all aspects of castle life, including everyday topics such as bathing and washing.

www.tower-of-london.com
This is the official site for the Tower of London—home and prison to many of England's medieval monarchs. Play games, take a virtual tour, and read about its history, ghosts, traditions, and ceremonies.

tayci.tripod.com/boy2knight.html
Among other things, this web site explains how a young boy may have become a knight in medieval times.

www.stemnet.nf.ca/CITE/medieval_castles.htm
This is a useful site containing a list of castle-related web sites for both children and adults.

score.rims.k12.ca.us/activity/castle_builder
Find out why castles were such an important part of medieval life and learn how they were built and who lived in them. This interesting site offers class research projects covering all kinds of medieval topics such as feudalism, food and feasting, monks, nuns, knights, and weapons.

www.yourchildlearns.com/heraldry.htm
Download free software and make your own coat of arms. Here you can also learn about the Middle Ages, feudalism, knights, and chivalry.

www.castles.org/kids
This site offers a simple, well-illustrated, straightforward story about King Edward and his castle and is suitable for younger children.

Quick-fire Quiz ANSWERS

1,000
QUESTIONS
& ANSWERS
FACTFILE
INVENTIONS

Contents

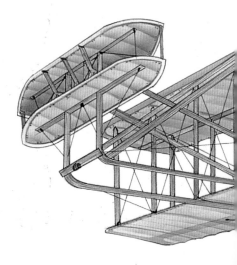

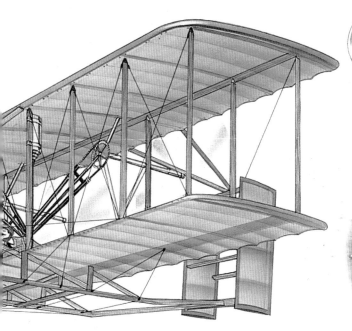

Writing and Printing

The first real writing system was invented by the Sumerians over 5,000 years ago. They used pictures called pictograms to stand for objects, ideas, and sounds. Today, the written or printed word is central to human communication.

Who invented printing?

Block printing was invented by the Chinese nearly 2,000 years ago. They carved characters on wooden blocks, covered them in ink, and stamped them onto paper. Modern printing, with movable metal type, began in the 1440s when Johannes Gutenberg from Germany developed the printing press.

When were periods and commas first used?

Medieval monks and scribes produced handwritten, beautifully decorated, illuminated manuscripts. To make the manuscripts easier to read, the scribes separated words with spaces, used capital and lowercase letters, and introduced a system of punctuation, including periods and commas.

Why did typewriters make you crazy?

People are often scared of new inventions—when the first typewriter went on sale in 1874, some doctors said that using one could make you go insane! However, the typewriter was a huge success for its American inventor, Christopher Latham Sholes. The first successful portable typewriter appeared in the early 1900s, and electric typewriters whirred into action in 1901.

Who invented the paper clip?

The paper clip is so simple and useful, it is surprising that it is such a recent invention. It first appeared in 1900, invented by Johan Vaalar, a young scientist who worked for an invention office in Norway. Before the paper clip, people used straight pins or ribbons tied through holes in the corner of the pages to fasten papers together temporarily.

How do ballpoint pens work?

Ladislao Biro, a Hungarian journalist, invented the ballpoint pen in 1938. It contained a tube of quick-drying ink, which rolled evenly onto the paper thanks to a tiny, movable ball at the tip.

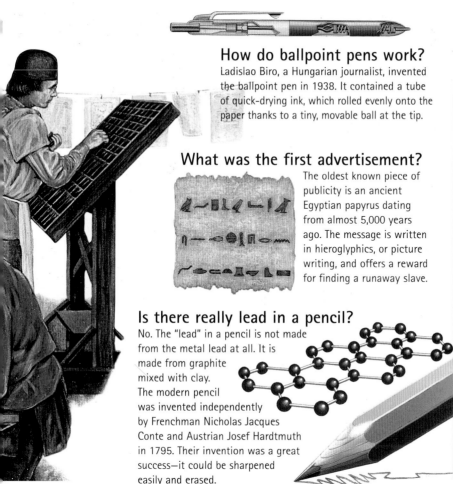

What was the first advertisement?

The oldest known piece of publicity is an ancient Egyptian papyrus dating from almost 5,000 years ago. The message is written in hieroglyphics, or picture writing, and offers a reward for finding a runaway slave.

Is there really lead in a pencil?

No. The "lead" in a pencil is not made from the metal lead at all. It is made from graphite mixed with clay. The modern pencil was invented independently by Frenchman Nicholas Jacques Conte and Austrian Josef Hardtmuth in 1795. Their invention was a great success—it could be sharpened easily and erased.

How does a mouse draw?

A computer mouse allows the user to move the cursor around the screen to give the computer commands. Using a mouse, designers can draw new details on a picture. The computer mouse was invented in the United States in 1964 by Douglas Englehart. He also invented a foot-controlled "rat," but it never caught on.

Why were felt-tip pens invented?

The Japanese inventor hoped that the pen's soft tip would make people's handwriting more graceful—like the brushstrokes in Japanese writing. The first felt-tips went on sale in Japan in 1962.

Medicine

Doctors in the ancient world used herbs, surgery, and "magic" to treat illnesses. Scientific medicine began in the 1600s with the invention of the microscope and an understanding of anatomy. Technical advances in the 1900s led to modern medicine.

Who were the first doctors?

The earliest doctors were physicians in ancient Egypt and China. In Egypt, physicians used drugs and potions. Surgeons treated injuries, while priests dealt with evil spirits. The first known physician was an Egyptian named Imhotep, who lived about 4,600 years ago.

When were bacteria discovered?

The Dutch instrument-maker Anton van Leeuwenhoek made the first high-powered microscope. It could magnify an object up to 200 times. In 1683, he published drawings of bacteria— tiny living things that can cause disease. He was building on the work of English scientist Robert Hooke, who had discovered 20 years earlier that living things were made up of small cells.

Modern microscope

Who discovered how blood flows?

In 1628, an English doctor, William Harvey, found that the heart pumps blood into the arteries. He showed that it circulates all around the body and returns to the heart along the veins.

What are medicines made from?

Most modern medicines are made from chemicals, but many were once made from plants. The heart medicine digitalis comes from foxgloves, quinine from the cinchona tree is used to treat malaria, and aspirin is made from willow tree bark.

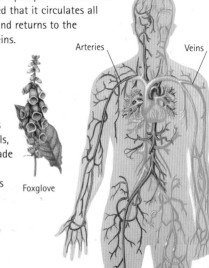

Arteries

Veins

Foxglove

Can artificial limbs move?

Back in the Middle Ages, the French surgeon Amboise Paré used springs and cogs to move artificial arms and legs. Today, whole legs and arms can be replaced with computer-controlled, plastic or metal limbs. In some cases, nerve endings in the patient's limb send messages to motors in the artificial limb to make it move.

Artificial arm and hand

Prosthetic hook

How can we see our bones?

We can see the bones in our bodies by taking X rays of them. In 1895, the German scientist Wilhelm Röntgen discovered that X rays could pass through paper, wood, and flesh, but not through metal or bone. Within months, doctors were using X rays to photograph bones in the body.

What is a body scan?

In 1972, British scientist Godfrey Hounsfield developed a Computerized Tomography (CT) scanner to take pictures of the inside of the body. CT scanners take thousands of X rays of the brain and body and build them up into a three-dimensional picture for doctors to use.

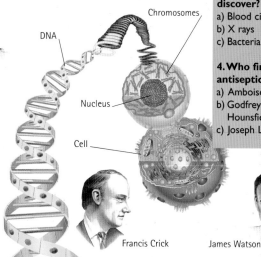

Chromosomes
DNA
Nucleus
Cell

Francis Crick

James Watson

Who made surgery safer?

In 1865, the Scottish surgeon Joseph Lister was the first doctor to use antiseptics during surgery to prevent patients from dying from infections. He sprayed carbolic acid around the operating room and soaked dressings in it to kill germs.

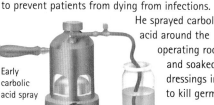

Early carbolic acid spray

Quick-fire Quiz

1. What is digitalis made from?
a) Willow tree
b) Cinchona tree
c) Foxglove

2. Which of these can X rays not pass through?
a) Wood
b) Bone
c) Flesh

3. What did William Harvey discover?
a) Blood circulation
b) X rays
c) Bacteria

4. Who first used antiseptics?
a) Amboise Paré
b) Godfrey Hounsfield
c) Joseph Lister

What is the double helix?

DNA (deoxyribonucleic acid) is the chemical that controls how cells behave and reproduce. In 1953, two scientists, Francis Crick from England and James Watson from the United States, figured out that DNA was made up of a twisted spiral—a double helix.

Buildings

The first permanent buildings were put up about 10,000 years ago. At first, people used natural materials like wood and stone, and most of the work was done by hand with simple tools. Today, high-tech machines and materials are used to build huge skyscrapers.

What is a Gothic building?

The Gothic style of building began in the mid-1100s in western Europe. It was mainly used for churches and cathedrals, which often had tall spires and towers, pointed arches, carved stonework, and fancy windows. The workers had to scramble up and down wooden scaffolding that was held up with rope, as there were no cranes to help them.

What was Stonehenge for?

Stonehenge, in England, was built about 5,000 years ago. The standing megaliths (big stones) were arranged to mark the midsummer sunrise and the midwinter moonrise. It may have been a religious meeting place or a huge outdoor calendar used to study the movement of the sun.

Can bridges carry water?

Bridges for carrying water were first built by the Assyrians around 700 B.C. Three hundred years later, the Romans improved the technique, building huge stone aqueducts to supply their cities with running water. Many Roman aqueducts still stand today.

Who designed a saillike roof?

One of the most distinctive modern buildings is the Opera House in Sydney Harbour, Australia. The architect, Jorn Utzon from Denmark, designed it to look like wind-filled sails. The main roof is made from concrete segments covered with thousands of ceramic tiles. The Opera House took 15 years to build and was finished in 1973.

How are suspension bridges built?

The towers are built first. Steel ropes are suspended from the towers, and special machines spin these into strong steel cables. Long steel cables called hangers are attached to the suspending cables. Finally, sections of the deck are lifted into place and fixed to the hangers.

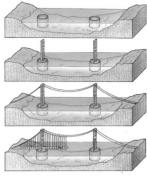

How old are the pyramids?

The first true pyramid was built in Egypt in about 2575 B.C. Each of these huge tombs for the dead pharaohs took about 20 years to build. Thousands of workers dragged the huge stones up ramps and levered them into place with wooden poles.

Are there wire bridges?

In 1883, the Brooklyn Bridge in New York was the first suspension bridge built using steel cables, which can carry huge loads. Its designer, John Roebling, used over 1,175 miles of wire anchored with around 90,000 tons of masonry.

Do buildings have skeletons?

In the 1880s, architects began to use a skeleton of steel and concrete columns to support the roof, walls, and floors of buildings. They fixed the outer walls to this framework. This allowed them to build very tall buildings. The first skyscraper, built in Chicago, was ten stories tall. Today many tower over 1,300 feet high.

Food and Agriculture

F arming probably began about 10,000 years ago in the Middle East. Early farmers harvested wild wheat and barley and sowed some of the seeds to grow new crops. Gradually, farmers developed tools, and after the 1700s, farms began to be mechanized.

Who invented the milking machine?

In 1860, American Lee Colvin invented the milking machine, which sped up milking. Hoses linked rubber caps on the cow's udder to a bucket and bellows. Pumping the bellows milked the cow. Modern milking machines use a similar idea. Today, many milking parlors are computer-controlled.

Cups attached to a cow's udder

Did early farmers use plows?

Wooden plows evolved from digging sticks used in Mesopotamia over 5,500 years ago. At first, people pulled plows, but then oxen were used. Plows with iron blades to break up heavy soil were made about 4,000 years later. More land could be cultivated with these, so farms grew larger.

Who first used windmills?

Windmills were first used in Persia over 1,200 years ago. By the 1200s, they were being used in Europe, mainly to grind grain. During the 1700s and 1800s, thousands were built to grind grain, power saws, raise materials from mines, and pump water.

What is organic farming?

Artificial fertilizers were first made commercially by Sir John Bennet Lawes in England in 1842. Now many farmers use them to increase their crop. In the 1970s, some farmers, worried about the effects of these fertilizers, returned to organic farming, in which only natural fertilizers are used.

What is a combine harvester?

A combine harvester reaps, threshes, loads grain onto trailers, and bales the leftover straw. The first one, built by American Hyram Moore in the late 1830s, was pulled by horses. Later, tractors were used. By the 1930s, they were diesel-powered.

Why are crops sprayed?

Crops are sprayed with pesticides to kill unwanted pests that could destroy the crop. The first synthetic insecticide, DDT, was isolated in 1874 by Othmar Zeidler from Germany. It was first made commercially in 1939, when a German chemist, Paul Muller, found it could kill insects, including the mosquitoes that carry disease.

Quick-fire Quiz

1. Who first used windmills?
a) The Chinese
b) The Persians
c) The Sumerians

2. When was the seed drill invented?
a) 1501
b) 1601
c) 1701

3. Who invented the milking machine?
a) Lee Colvin
b) Jethro Tull
c) Hyram Moore

4. What is DDT?
a) A fertilizer
b) An insecticide
c) A machine

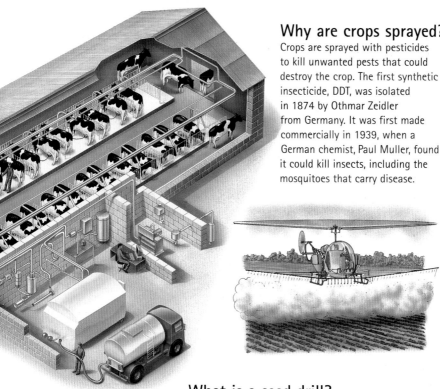

What is a seed drill?

Seed used to be scattered on the fields by hand. Then, in 1701, English farmer Jethro Tull developed a machine that could drill and sow seeds in straight lines. His machine, called a seed drill, fed seeds at an even rate into a furrow made by a coulter, or blade.

Can farm animals be cloned?

Scientists can make clones (identical copies) of living things by growing a new organism from a cell taken from the "parent." In February 1997, Dolly the sheep made history—she was a clone of her mother. She was grown from one of her mother's cells instead of from an egg. A year later, a cow was produced in the same way.

213

At Home

The first homes were caves and simple huts. Slowly, people developed new skills to build better homes, preserve food, and make their lives more comfortable. Modern homes have electricity, gas, plumbing, and household goods and furniture.

Prehistoric home

Well

Waste dump

Open fire

Preserved fish

Central heating radiator

Sewage pipe

Water pipe

Who invented furniture?

Simple wooden furniture has probably been used since people began to build permanent homes. In Egypt, beautiful, carved furniture was being made over 3,500 years ago. These luxurious articles were found in a tomb for a dead pharaoh to use in the afterlife.

Have homes changed?

In prehistoric times (and still in some parts of the world today) people lived in homes built from mud or stones, cooked on open fires, and got water from wells. Modern homes are stronger and more comfortable. From the 1880s, homes were wired with electricity, giving light and power at the flick of a switch.

When was the iron invented?

American Henry Seely made the first working electric iron in 1882, and it went on sale in 1885. Before that, people used flat irons. These were solid metal irons that had to be heated on a fire before they could be used to press clothes.

How was food kept cool?

Over 4,000 years ago, people stored food in ice pits to keep it cool. Early domestic refrigerators—insulated cabinets for holding ice—first appeared in the United States around 1850. The first mechanical one, powered by a steam pump, was invented by German engineer Karl von Linde in 1879. Within 12 years he had sold 12,000 in Germany and the United States. The first electric refrigerator, developed by Swedish engineers von Platen and Munters, went on sale in 1925.

How old is the flushing toilet?

The ancient Mesopotamians had special seats with holes and water running underneath to take away waste. This idea was developed further by John Harington, who designed the earliest flushing toilet with a cistern in 1596. The first practical flushing toilet was made by Alexander Cumming in the 1770s. Before toilets became popular, people used chamber pots instead.

Flushing toilet

Chamber pot

Television antenna   Modern home

Television satellite dish

Electrical power

Quick-fire Quiz

1. What powered Karl von Linde's refrigerator?
a) Electricity
b) Microwaves
c) Steam

2. When did light bulbs go on sale?
a) 1780
b) 1880
c) 1980

3. Who made the first working electric iron?
a) Henry Seely
b) Joseph Swan
c) Thomas Edison

4. Who invented home heating?
a) The Egyptians
b) The Romans
c) The Greeks

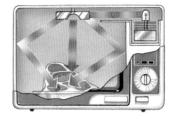

Which waves can melt chocolate?

American Percy Spencer discovered microwave cooking by accident. He had been working on ways of using invisible microwaves to detect aircraft. When he found that these waves had melted a chocolate bar in his pocket, he realized they could be used to cook food, too. In 1946, the first microwave oven was developed, and in 1955, commercial ones appeared.

Who lit up homes?

In 1878, Briton Joseph Swan demonstrated his electric light bulb. A year later, the American inventor Thomas Edison made a long-lasting light bulb with a carbon filament, which went on sale in 1880. The two men eventually set up a joint company to make light bulbs.

How old is home heating?

The ancient Romans first developed a system of heating their houses with hot air, called a hypocaust, nearly 2,000 years ago. Warm air, heated by burning fuel in a furnace, flowed through tiled flues in the walls into the spaces beneath the floor, heating the rooms above.

215

Clothes and Fabrics

Early people wore animal skins to keep themselves warm, but about 10,000 years ago, people learned how to make cloth. They used a spindle to spin wool, cotton, flax, or hemp into thread, which could be woven into fabric. These fabrics were then made into clothes.

How old are needles?

Bone needles over 20,000 years old were found in Stone Age caves in France. They were probably used to stitch animal skins together. Modern metal needles were developed in the 1400s.

How do zippers work?

Zippers have two rows of teeth joined together by a sliding "key," which locks the teeth together or pulls them apart. American Whitcomb Judson invented the first zipper in the 1890s. In 1913, Gideon Sundback patented the interlocking zipper.

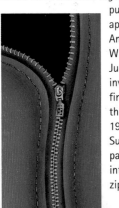

Who wore safety pins?

Ancient Egyptians first invented safety pin-type clasps, which they wore like brooches. The modern safety pin was "reinvented" by American Walter Hunt in 1849. He didn't make any money from his invention—he gave the patent away to repay a $15 debt!

Linen weaving in ancient Egypt

Who invented the loom?

Simple looms were used in Turkey almost 7,000 years ago. These early weavers made cloth much as we do today, by interlacing (or weaving) threads together at right angles to one another. Cloth was handwoven until mechanical and power-driven looms were invented in the mid-1700s.

How are shoes made?

Shoes have been worn for thousands of years, and until the mid-1800s, they were all handmade. These Native American moccasins were made by hand from soft deerskin and adorned with colored porcupine quills. This took many hours. Today a pair of shoes can be made in minutes by a machine in a factory.

Who tanned leather?

Leather clothing, footwear, and household goods were used over 5,000 years ago in Mesopotamia. In the past, people tanned leather by rubbing the hides with the juices of bark and roots that contain the chemical tannin. (This is where tanning gets its name.) Sometimes skins were soaked in salt and the chemical alum to preserve them.

Quick-fire Quiz

1. When were zippers invented?
   a) 1690s
   b) 1790s
   c) 1890s

2. Who first made silk?
   a) The Romans
   b) Native Americans
   c) The Chinese

3. Who invented the spinning jenny?
   a) Whitcomb Judson
   b) Elias Howe
   c) James Hargreaves

4. What did George de Mestral invent?
   a) Velcro
   b) Lock-stitch sewing machine
   c) Safety pin

Which machine was destroyed?

French tailor Barthélemy Thimonnier developed a sewing machine in 1829. Other tailors destroyed it, fearing it would put them out of work. In the United States, a lock-stitch machine was invented by Walter Hunt in 1833, and Elias Howe made a better machine in 1845. Sewing machines became widely available in the late 1850s.

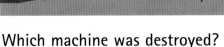

Early sewing machine

What was a spinning jenny?

In 1764, Englishman James Hargreaves invented an automatic spinning machine called the spinning jenny. It could spin eight reels of thread at once, compared with the one reel made by an ordinary spinning wheel.

What is Velcro?

Swiss engineer George de Mestral spent eight years developing Velcro. It is made from two nylon strips—one covered with tiny loops, the other with tiny hooks. The strips stick to each other when pressed together, but can easily be ripped apart. Velcro went on sale in the mid-1960s.

What was China's best-kept secret?

Silk was first discovered by the Chinese over 4,600 years ago. They set up farms to breed silkworms about 3,500 years ago, but kept the method a secret for another 2,000 years. Silk was so valuable that the Chinese traded it for gold and silver.

Useful Materials

Once, people used only natural materials such as wood or cotton to make things. Later, they discovered how to extract metals from ore found in the ground. Today, synthetic materials such as nylon, plastic, and fiberglass are used to make many goods, from cars to clothes.

Pottery-making in ancient China

Is glass made from sand?

Glass is made by heating silica (sand), limestone, and soda ash to very high temperatures. It can then be colored and shaped. Many churches have windows made of stained glass, like this one. The oldest surviving window, in Augsberg Cathedral, Germany, dates from 1065.

Why do cars rust?

Iron and steel objects rust in damp air because the iron changes into a red-brown iron oxide, a mixture of iron and oxygen. In 1913, Briton Harry Brearley added the metal chromium to steel to make the first successful, rust-resistant stainless steel.

What is steel?

Steel, a strong metal made from iron, was first developed over 3,000 years ago. In 1856, the British inventor Henry Bessemer devised an inexpensive way of producing steel. Molten iron was poured into a converter, and hot air or oxygen was blown over it. Most of the carbon in the iron was burned, turning it into steel.

Steel-making

Where was china made?

Pottery goods have been made for about 9,000 years, but fine china, or porcelain, was only invented about 1,200 years ago in China. The art remained a secret until just over 300 years ago, when fine porcelain goods were taken to the West.

Who first used plants to make materials?

People have made useful materials from plant fibers for thousands of years, and many are still used today. About 5,000 years ago, cotton plants were first cultivated in India, and the Chinese used the fibrous stems of hemp to make rope. The ancient Egyptians made fine linen fabric from flax stems.

Quick-fire Quiz

1. What was made from hemp?
a) China
b) Rope
c) Plastic

2. When was polyethylene discovered?
a) 1739
b) 1839
c) 1939

3. Where was rubber discovered?
a) China
b) Brazil
c) India

4. Who made steel cheap?
a) Henry Bessemer
b) Harry Brearley
c) Wallace Carothers

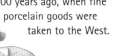

Are plastics oily?

All plastics, such as polyvinylchloride (PVC), polyethylene, nylon, and some paints, are made from chemicals found in oil, natural gas, or coal. Polyethylene was first discovered by accident in 1939 by chemists working at ICI in Great Britain. Two years later, nylon was made by Wallace Carothers in the United States.

Is fiberglass strong?

Fiberglass material is made by mixing glass fibers and plastic. It was developed in the United States in the 1930s. It is flame-resistant, does not rust, and is tough enough to make car bodies or boats. It is also used to insulate buildings.

Fiberglass canoe

Bakelite radio

What was Bakelite?

In 1909, a Belgian-American chemist named Leo Hendrik Baekeland made the world's first artificial plastic—Bakelite. As it did not conduct heat or electricity, it was ideal for making electrical goods.

Bakelite radio

Is rubber liquid?

Natural rubber is made from latex, the thick, runny sap of rubber trees. The latex is collected, strained, mixed with acid to solidify it, and rolled into sheets. Wild rubber was discovered in Brazil in the early 1800s and was first used for waterproofing. Today we mostly use synthetic rubber, developed over 60 years ago.

Energy

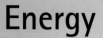

People use energy for all kinds of activities, from powering cars to lighting their homes. Most of the energy we use is made by burning fossil fuels such as coal, gas, and oil. Renewable energy sources like solar, water, and wind power can be used to generate electricity.

Arkwright's mill

Did water power run factories?
Watermills have been used for over 2,000 years to grind corn. In 1771, Richard Arkwright turned a watermill into a cloth-making factory, using the waterwheel to power his new spinning machines.

What is a wind farm?
Modern windmills are used to turn machines called turbines, which generate, or make, electricity. These wind turbines are grouped together in wind farms. The first large wind generator was built by the American Palmer Putnam in 1940.

Who made engines steam?
An English blacksmith, Thomas Newcomen, built the first practical steam engine in 1712. Scotsman James Watt came up with an improved design, and in 1782, his double-action steam engine was used to power factory machinery.

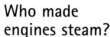

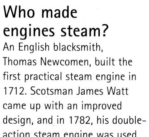

Crane raises and
lowers equipment
to the seabed

Derrick

Drill bit

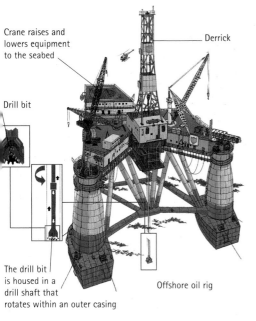

The drill bit
is housed in a
drill shaft that
rotates within an outer casing

Offshore oil rig

Is oil found beneath the sea?
In the 1970s, large oil deposits were found under
the North Sea. Oil wells were drilled 650 feet into
the seabed. Offshore oil rigs were built to pump
the oil to the surface. These rigs are supported
on steel or concrete structures sunk
deep into the seabed.

What is a hydrodam?
Hydroelectric power plants are often built inside
dams called hydrodams. Water from a lake behind
the dam gushes down pipes, turning turbines that
drive generators and make electricity. The world's
first major hydroelectric power plant opened
in 1895 at Niagara Falls.

Can the sun heat a home?
A few modern homes have solar panels
in the roof. Some use the sun's energy
to heat water. Others contain electronic
devices called photovoltaic (solar) cells
that change sunlight into electricity.
Solar power can run machines. The
first practical solar-powered machine,
a steam engine, was developed by
Frenchman Augustin Mouchet in 1861.

Who split the atom?
In 1932, British scientists John
Cockroft and Ernest Walton first
split the atom, releasing huge
amounts of energy. In the United
States, in 1942, Italian-born Enrico
Fermi and his team built the first
successful nuclear reactor to
control this energy. In 1954, the
first nuclear power plant was
opened in the Soviet Union.

What are
fossil fuels?
Coal, oil, and gas
are called fossil fuels.
Coal is the remains
of ancient plants
that lived and died
in prehistoric forests.
Oil and gas are made
from the dead bodies
of tiny sea creatures.

The first coal-fired power plant to
generate electricity opened in 1882.

Calculations

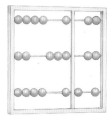
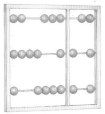

When people first began to count, they could use only their fingers and toes. But soon they invented tally sticks and number systems to record and calculate measurements. Numbers are the basis of all calculations. Today, most people use a modern version of numbers invented in Arabia (0 to 10).

Who invented the abacus?
A simple Mesopotamian abacus dates back 5,000 years. The Chinese abacus, designed about 1,700 years ago, is a rapid tool for adding, subtracting, multiplying, and dividing. It is made up of rows of beads representing ones, tens, hundreds, and thousands.

What was an astrolabe?
The astrolabe was originally a circular map of the heavens that astronomers used to measure the height of stars and planets. In the early Middle Ages, Arab scholars adapted the astrolabe to measure latitude and help them navigate at sea.

Astrolabe

Moroccan students in the Middle Ages

What was the earliest money?
Long ago, people traded goods for the things they wanted. The people of ancient Lydia (now Turkey) were the first to make coins, about 2,700 years ago. They used electrum, a mixture of gold and silver. The Chinese invented paper money about 1,200 years ago.

Who first used weights?
The first known standard weights and scales were used by the Babylonians about 4,600 years ago. The ancient Egyptians also used sensitive scales and weights to weigh precious stones and gold over 5,000 years ago.

The Babylonians used three standard weights

Who made the first mechanical calculator?

The first mechanical calculator was made by Frenchman Blaise Pascal in 1642, when he was aged only 19. It had a row of toothed wheels with numbers around them. Numbers to be added or subtracted were dialed in, and the answer appeared behind holes at the top. Modern electronic pocket calculators went on sale in 1971. They can do complicated calculations in seconds.

What was a handspan?

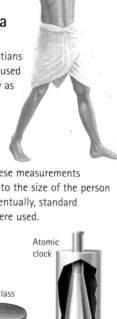

The ancient Egyptians and the Romans used parts of the body as measuring units. They used the size of the hand, foot, and arm to calculate distances, but these measurements varied according to the size of the person making them. Eventually, standard measurements were used.

Quick-fire Quiz

1. What does a sundial measure?
a) Distance
b) Time
c) Weight

2. Where were coins invented?
a) Egypt
b) China
c) Turkey

3. What did Blaise Pascal build?
a) An abacus
b) A calculator
c) A clock

4. When was the mercury thermometer invented?
a) 1614
b) 1714
c) 1814

What were the first clocks?

Sundials and shadow clocks, which use the sun's position in the sky to measure time, were first used in ancient Egypt. The Babylonians divided the sundial's circle into 360 parts, or degrees, and divided it into 12 hours. In the Middle Ages, the hourglass or sandglass was a popular clock. Atomic clocks were first developed in 1969 and are accurate to one second in 1.6 million years!

Atomic clock

Sandglass

Sundial

How do we measure temperature?

The first practical sealed alcohol thermometers, in which liquid rose up a tube as it was heated, were made around 1660. In 1714, German Gabriel Fahrenheit made a more accurate thermometer using mercury.

Alcohol thermometer

Who was Einstein?

Albert Einstein was a brilliant German scientist who studied many things, including energy and time. In 1915, he developed the special theory of relativity, which says that if you could travel almost as fast as the speed of light, time would slow down and your mass would increase.

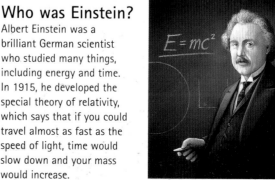

$E = mc^2$

223

Computers

Modern computers—electronic machines that can store and process huge amounts of information—were first designed in the 1940s. Computers can do billions of calculations a second. We use them for many tasks, from predicting the weather to making other machines.

Why were computers as big as a room?

Americans John Mauchly and J. Prosper Eckert, Jr., built the first automatic computer, ENIAC, in 1945. It filled two rooms and weighed as much as five elephants. It was so large because it used 19,000 valves, each as big as a hand, to control the switches that made it work. Computers grew smaller in the 1950s, when tiny transistors replaced valves.

What are microchips?

In the 1960s, scientists came up with a new way to run computers. They used a tiny slice, or chip, of a material called silicon to make the electronic "brain" that controls a computer. Today, a tiny microchip contains up to 250,000 parts that tell it how to work. A computer uses different microchips to do different jobs.

Who developed personal computers?

The first successful personal computer was developed by Steve Jobs and Steve Wozniak in 1978. At first only a few people could afford them, but today personal computers are found in schools, offices, and homes all over the world.

Who was Mr. Babbage?

In 1834, the British mathematician Charles Babbage designed the first mechanical computer that could be programmed, but he did not have the money or technology to build it. His machine was finally made in 1991—and it worked!

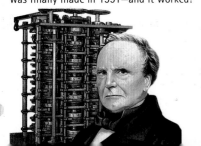

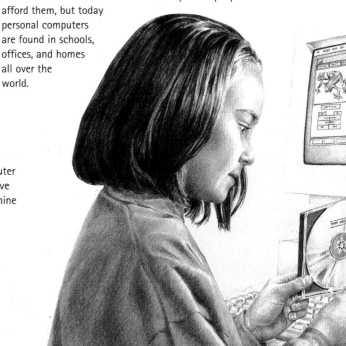

How do computers work?

All computers change the information they handle into numbers, which are stored as electrical signals. In modern computers, these signals are either "on," represented by 1, or "off," represented by 0. All numbers, letters, and pictures are turned into a sequence of 1s and 0s (called binary code). A computer does rapid calculations using these numbers, which are then changed into words and pictures that you can understand.

Do computers have disks?

The information used to run computer programs is usually stored as electrical pulses on magnetic disks. Plastic "floppy disks" were created by the company IBM in 1970. In 1983, compact discs (CDs), plastic-coated metal discs read by laser, went on sale. CDs used by computers can store vast amounts of information.

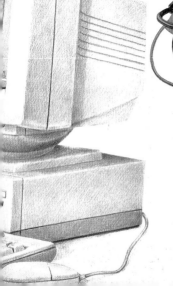

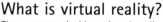

Can robots see?

The first industrial robot— a computer-controlled machine that carries out tasks—was made in the United States in 1962. In 1980, the first robot that could "see" using electronic eyes was developed in America. Today, some robots have laser vision systems and can both see and hear.

What is virtual reality?

The computer inside a virtual reality headset creates scenes and sounds that seem real to the wearer. This system was pioneered by Ivan Sutherland in 1965 but was not fully developed until the 1990s. Virtual reality headsets are used for games and for learning different skills.

What is the Net?

Computers anywhere in the world can be linked via a telephone line and a gadget called a modem. This network, called the Internet (or Net for short), is used by over 40 million people. The Internet was first developed in the late 1960s by the U.S. government as a safe way to communicate in wartime.

Communications

Before the printing press was invented in the 1450s, people could only share information by word of mouth or by writing letters. Today we use books, newspapers, radio, television, telephone, and e-mail to spread news and views.

Who first recorded sound?

In 1877, the famous American inventor Thomas Edison built a machine to record sound. The sounds were stored as patterns of indented lines on a tin-foil cylinder. The first words to be recorded clearly were "Mary had a little lamb."

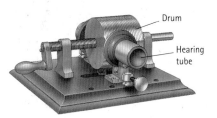

Drum

Hearing tube

Who made the first telephone?

In 1875, the Scottish-American inventor Alexander Graham Bell discovered a way to send the human voice along wires. A year later he built the first working telephone, and within months, hundreds of telephone bells were ringing all over America.

Can glass fibers talk?

Optical fibers are strands of glass twisted into a cable that can transmit light. In 1976, Charles Kao and George Hockham had the idea of using them to carry telephone calls at the speed of light. The first fiber-optic telephone link was set up in America in 1977.

Who invented the radio?

Italian Guglielmo Marconi built the first set that sent messages using radio waves in 1895. His machine produced radio waves by making a strong electric spark. The system was known as the wireless because the signals were sent through the air, not along a wire. Marconi sent the first signal across the Atlantic in 1901, and public radio broadcasts began about 20 years later.

Who said, "Number, please"?

The first telephone exchange, set up in America in 1878, was manual and served 21 customers. An operator answered your call, took the number you wanted, and plugged in your line to complete the electrical circuit and connect your call. The first automatic exchange was installed in America in 1892.

The Morse Code

a	•—	s	•••
b	—•••	t	—
c	—•—•	u	••—
d	—••	v	•••—
e	•	w	•——
f	••—•	x	—••—
g	——•	y	—•——
h	••••	z	——••
i	••	0	—————
j	•———	1	•————
k	—•—	2	••———
l	•—••	3	•••——
m	——	4	••••—
n	—•	5	•••••
o	———	6	—••••
p	•——•	7	——•••
q	——•—	8	———••
r	•—•	9	————•

Early telegraph machine

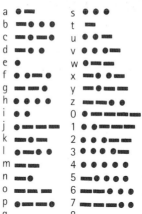

When did phones become portable?

In the early 1980s, computers allowed the telephone to lose its wires and become portable. A system of low-powered radio stations link the moving telephone to a computer network that keeps track of the caller.

What is Morse Code?

Before the telephone was invented, people sent messages by telegraph. It used a coded series of short and long electrical signals, known as "dots" and "dashes." The code was invented by the American Samuel Morse.

How do telephone calls travel around the world?

Communication satellites orbiting the earth pick up signals and send them on to a receiver thousands of miles away. The first one, *Telstar*, went into orbit in 1962. It could relay 12 telephone calls or one television channel. Satellites today carry thousands of calls and several channels at once.

On Film

Before cameras were developed, people could only record images by drawing or painting them. Photography was invented in the early 1800s. At first it was a slow process, and all pictures were in black and white. Now we have film and video cameras to record people and places all over the world.

Who first said, "Smile, please"?

Frenchman Joseph Niépce took the first permanent photograph in about 1827. The photo, a view from Niépce's window, took eight hours to develop. In the late 1800s, taking photos took so long that people needed a backrest to help them sit still!

What is a Polaroid®?

The Polaroid® camera, invented by American Edwin Land in 1947, produces "instant" photos. It uses slim plastic envelopes instead of a roll of film. Inside is a sheet of film and a packet of processing chemicals, which bursts as the photo is ejected. The picture develops in about 60 seconds.

Did early cameras use rolls of film?

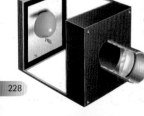

Early box cameras used a lens to focus the light rays onto a metal or glass photographic plate at the back of the camera. The light changed the chemicals on the plate, and the picture developed in a few minutes. Rolls of film were first introduced in 1888 by American George Eastman.

When did movie stars first talk?

Early movies were silent—actors had to be good mime artists. Words were shown on screen to explain the action, and an organist played music to liven up the film. The first full-length movie with sound was *The Jazz Singer*, shown in the United States in 1927. It was so popular that silent movies soon lost their appeal, and "talkies" (talking pictures) took over.

Who invented television?

The Scottish inventor John Logie Baird first demonstrated the television in public in 1926. His original machine was made from an old box, knitting needles, a cake pan, and a bicycle lamp! The first picture of a human face was a blurry image of 15-year-old William Taynton.

Rotating disc

Baird's camera had a mechanical scanner with a rotating disc. This was soon replaced by the electronic scanner developed by Russian-American Vladimir Zworykin in 1923.

Baird's television, 1930

How do color television cameras work?

The first color televisions went on sale in the 1950s. Color television cameras split the light from the filmed scene into three images—one red, one green, and one blue. The light from each image is turned into an electrical signal, which is recorded with the sound signal on film or tape. A color television converts these signals back into the colored picture.

Quick-fire Quiz

1. When was the first talkie shown?
a) 1917
b) 1927
c) 1937

2. Who invented television?
a) Thomas Edison
b) George Eastman
c) John Logie Baird

3. What did Edwin Land invent?
a) Polaroid® camera
b) Color television
c) Movies

4. Who was the first photographer?
a) Louis Lumière
b) Auguste Lumière
c) Joseph Niépce

Who made the first movie?

American Thomas Edison was the first person to film moving pictures, but French brothers Auguste and Louis Lumière were the first to show a "movie" to an audience. The brothers made 10 films in 1895 and built a machine to show them on screen to audiences in Paris clubs and cafés.

When did home videos arrive?

Videotape was invented in 1956; the first camcorder, or video camera-recorder, was developed in the 1960s. Modern, lightweight camcorders went on sale in the 1980s. A camcorder uses magnetic tapes instead of photographic film to record the images and sound.

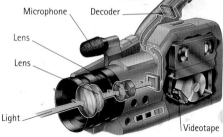

Lens
Microphone   Decoder
Lens
Lens
Light
Videotape

Travel on Land

Prehistoric people had to walk everywhere, carrying their goods or dragging them on sleds. By 3000 B.C., people had developed wheeled vehicles pulled by animals. In the late 1800s, the invention of the steam engine and the gasoline engine changed land travel completely.

What is a TGV?

The French TGV (*Train à Grande Vitesse*) first went into service in 1981. These speedy electric trains can travel at over 185 miles per hour on special tracks. The first electric train was demonstrated at an exhibition in Germany in 1879.

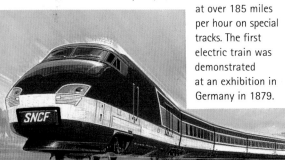

Did cars run on steam?

The first cars ran on steam, but they were noisy and often broke down. Early cars were not allowed to travel faster than walking pace, and in some countries a man with a red flag had to walk in front to warn people they were coming!

When was the bicycle invented?

The first bicycle, invented in the 1790s in France, had no pedals—riders had to push their feet along the ground! A German, Baron von Drais, made a bike with a steerable front wheel in 1817. The first bike with pedals and cranks to turn the back wheel was designed by Scotsman Kirkpatrick Macmillan in 1839.

Who invented the wheel?

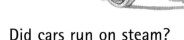

The wheel was invented around 6,000 years ago in the Middle East. Laid on its side, it was used to make pottery. Around 500 years later, the Sumerians living in the same region turned wheels upright and used them on horse-drawn chariots. The first wheels were solid, made from three planks of wood pegged together and cut to shape. The plank wheel turned on a fixed axle.

Can the sun power cars?

Engineers are experimenting with a new form of energy to power car engines—energy from the sun. Several prototypes run on solar-powered batteries. A few of these solar cars have reached speeds of 90 miles per hour in races across Australia.

What is a maglev?

"Maglevs," or magnetic levitation trains, hover above the track, supported by magnetic fields. They are driven by linear motors with no moving parts. The trains are still being developed—but, once in use, they may reach speeds of over 400 miles per hour.

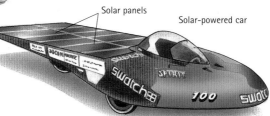

Solar panels

Solar-powered car

Who was Mr. Benz?

In 1885, the German engineer Karl Benz built the first vehicle to be powered by a gasoline engine. The first four-wheeled car was developed in 1886 by another German, Gottlieb Daimler.

Which train was a winner?

In 1829, Englishman George Stevenson and his son Robert entered a contest to find the fastest steam train. Their winning engine, the *Rocket*, could pull a train at 29 miles per hour—twice as fast as their rivals. The first steam locomotive was developed by the English engineer Richard Trevithick in 1803.

What was a Tin Lizzie?

Hand-built early cars were too expensive for most people. But in 1908 in America, Henry Ford had the idea of mass-producing cars on his other invention—

the assembly line. In the next 20 years, he sold 15 million Model T cars, also known as Tin Lizzies.

On the Sea

Early people traveled over water using rafts and dugout canoes. About 5,000 years ago, the Sumerians and Egyptians built ships with sails and oars. In the 1800s, steam engines took over from sails and steel replaced wood. A hundred years later, ships with gasoline engines took to the waves.

What was a trireme?

Triremes were fast ships powered by three rows of oarsmen on each side. The Greeks first built triremes in about 650 B.C. Later triremes were up to 130 feet long, with a pointed ram at the front to smash into enemy ships.

When were paddle steamers first used?

The Frenchman Jouffroy d'Abbans built the first working steamboat in 1783. Within 20 years, paddle steamers were being used to ferry people and goods up and down rivers and across the sea.

How did sailors find their way?

In the mid-1700s, two British inventions helped sailors fix their position at sea. The sextant, invented by John Campbell, determined latitude by measuring the angle of the sun or stars above the horizon. John Harrison's chronometer— a kind of clock—helped measure longitude.

Sextant

How do divers swim under water?

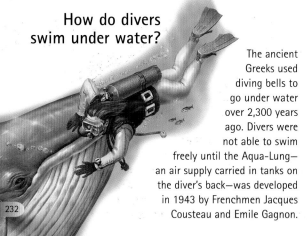

The ancient Greeks used diving bells to go under water over 2,300 years ago. Divers were not able to swim freely until the Aqua-Lung— an air supply carried in tanks on the diver's back—was developed in 1943 by Frenchmen Jacques Cousteau and Emile Gagnon.

Why were clippers fast?

The super-fast clipper of the mid-1800s had a new shape of hull and a combination of square and triangular sails, with which it could catch and use even the slightest breeze. Clippers could maintain speeds of 23 miles per hour.

Quick-fire Quiz

1. When was the first steamboat trip?
   a) 1683
   b) 1783
   c) 1883

2. Who designed the hovercraft?
   a) John Campbell
   b) Christopher Cockerel
   c) Emile Gagnon

3. What was the *Turtle*?
   a) A steamship
   b) An aircraft carrier
   c) A submarine

4. Who first built triremes?
   a) The Romans
   b) The Egyptians
   c) The Greeks

When were submarines invented?

In 1620, Dutchman Cornelius Drebbel's wooden submarine, rowed by 12 oarsmen, traveled several miles up the Thames River in London, England. The *Turtle*, the first submarine that could rise and sink, was designed by American David Bushnell in 1776. It was used in the American Revolution.

The *Turtle*

What craft floats on air?

Hovercraft can skim over land or water on a cushion of air blown down by fans and trapped inside a flexible rubber skirt. The hovercraft was designed by the British engineer Christopher Cockerel in the 1950s and made its first test run in 1959.

How do jet aircraft land on ships?

The first carrier for jet aircraft, USS *Forrestal*, was completed in 1955. Aircraft can take off and land on the deck in mid-ocean. During takeoff, the aircraft is propelled forward by a device called a catapult. When it lands, the aircraft is slowed down by huge arrester wires stretched across the deck.

Over 2,000 years ago, the Chinese flew war kites to firebomb their enemies, but they did not travel in them. Air transportation did not begin until the 1780s, when hot-air balloons took to the skies. Just over 100 years later, powered flight got off to a bumpy start.

How do hang gliders fly?

Hang gliders depend on the wind and rising warm air to fly. In 1853, British engineer George Cayley was the first to design a suitably shaped wing. Nearly 100 years later, in the 1940s, American Francis Rogallo developed a triangular kite that gave rise to modern hang gliders.

When was the first flight?

The first flight was made in a hot-air balloon on November 21, 1783, by François de Rozier and the Marquis d'Arlandes. The balloon, made by the French Montgolfier brothers, had a basket for passengers slung under the huge paper balloon.

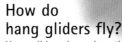

Who was the first hang glider?

Otto Lilienthal, a German engineer, designed and flew over 15 different hang gliders. He made the first flight in which the pilot controlled the machine. Lilienthal died in 1896 when his hang glider crashed.

Who were the Wright brothers?

American brothers Orville and Wilbur Wright had the idea of fitting a gasoline engine and propeller to their glider. On December 17, 1903, Orville made the world's first powered flight. *Flyer 1* flew for 12 seconds and covered 120 feet—less than the length of a jumbo jet!

How do helicopters rise vertically?

Helicopters have one or two large rotors made up of long, thin wings. When the rotors spin around, they lift the aircraft and drive it along. Helicopters can fly forward, backward, and sideways. The first single-blade helicopter was built by Russian-American Igor Sikorsky in 1939.

Can airplanes land by themselves?

Modern jet liners are controlled from a high-tech flight deck. They even have computer-controlled autopilot systems to land planes in bad weather when the pilot cannot see the runway clearly. The first autopilot landing of a scheduled airliner was in 1965 at Heathrow Airport in England.

What were zeppelins?

Zeppelins (named after their German inventor, Ferdinand von Zeppelin) were giant airships up to 800 feet long. They were powered by gasoline engines and a propeller, and were filled with hydrogen gas, which is lighter than air but very flammable. The first zeppelin flight was in 1900.

Are helicopters really 500 years old?

The Italian artist and inventor Leonardo da Vinci sketched a simple helicopter (see above) over 500 years ago, but it was never built. The French inventor Paul Cornu built the first helicopter in 1907—it rose one foot off the ground and hovered there for 20 seconds. Cornu's helicopter was very difficult to control, and it was not until the 1930s that helicopters became a practical means of flying.

Jet power—when and where?

Gloster
E28/39 jet

In the 1930s, both Great Britain and Germany were working on a new form of power for aircraft—the jet engine. The British engineer Frank Whittle came up with the idea in 1929, and prototypes were built by Whittle in Great Britain and by Hans von Ohain in Germany. The first jet aircraft, built by German Ernst Heinkel, took to the air in 1939. Two years later, Whittle's engine powered the Gloster E28/39 jet. Jet engines allow planes to travel much faster—some military jets can zoom along at 2,000 miles per hour!

Quick-fire Quiz

1. Name the Wright brothers' first plane:
a) Gloster
b) Flyer I
c) Orville

2. Who was the first hang glider pilot?
a) Ferdinand von Zeppelin
b) Frank Whittle
c) Otto Lilienthal

3. Which gas was used in zeppelins?
a) Oxygen
b) Helium
c) Hydrogen

4. Who sketched the first helicopter?
a) George Cayley
b) Igor Sikorsky
c) Leonardo da Vinci

Into Space

From the early 1950s, the United States and the Soviet Union raced to be first in space. In 1957, the U.S.S.R. launched the first satellite, *Sputnik I*. Four years later, Soviet cosmonaut Yuri Gagarin blasted into orbit in *Vostok I*. His trip around the world lasted under 2 hours, but manned space flight was launched.

Who first saw stars?

In 1609, the Italian scientist Galileo was the first person to look at the stars through a telescope. His studies led him to suggest that the earth moved around the sun and was not at the center of the universe, as people then thought.

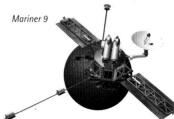

Mariner 9

Which telescopes detect radio waves?

Stars and other objects in space give out radio waves as well as light. Radio telescopes have huge, dish-shaped antennae to pick up these radio waves. Radio telescopes have discovered exploding galaxies, radiation from distant galaxies, and spinning neutron stars called pulsars.

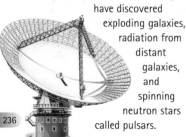

Is there life on other planets?

The other planets in our solar system are probably not able to support life, but scientists are looking farther away. In 1974, astronomers beamed a radio message into space from a huge radio telescope in Puerto Rico. They aimed it at a dense star cluster called M13, over 25,000 light years away. The message is traveling at the speed of light, so we will have to wait 50,000 years for a reply!

What is a space probe?

Space probes are unmanned spacecraft that travel into space. Several have been sent to other planets in the solar system. *Mariner 9*, launched in 1971, visited Mars. *Mariner 10*, launched in 1973, was the first probe to visit two planets. It flew by Venus and visited Mercury three times, where it found that the daytime temperatures were hot enough to melt lead.

Who was the first man on the moon?

American Neil Armstrong was the first man to set foot on the moon in July 1969. He and fellow astronaut Edwin "Buzz" Aldrin put up the American flag and a plaque saying, "We come in peace for all mankind."

When did people first walk in space?

In 1965, the Soviet cosmonaut Aleksei Leonov made the first space walk, but he had to remain attached to the spacecraft. In the early 1980s, scientists developed the MMU (manned maneuvering unit), which let astronauts walk freely in space. The first free spacewalk took place from the American *Challenger* in 1984.

What is the space shuttle?

Early spacecraft used rocket power to blast them into space. Then American scientists came up with the idea of building a reusable spacecraft. The space shuttle still needs rocket power to take off, but it lands like an airplane and can be reused. In 1981, the first space shuttle, *Columbia*, took off.

What is a space station?

Space stations are large spacecraft that spend several years orbiting the earth. The first space station was the Soviet *Salyut I*, which was launched in 1971. Modern space stations like the Soviet *Mir* use solar panels to power the station while it is in orbit. The crew can stay in space for many months, carrying out scientific experiments and repairing equipment.

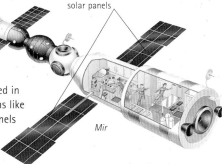

solar panels

Mir

Timeline

Hundreds of inventions and discoveries have marked human progress from the Stone Age to the Space Age. Some happened by accident; others took people years to perfect. Here are a few important milestones.

20,000 B.C. to 2000 B.C.

c.20,000 B.C. Bone needles used
c.8000 B.C. First permanent houses built
4000–3000 B.C. Earliest known writing (cuneiform, Sumeria)
3500 B.C. Simple plows pulled by people (Sumeria)
3200 B.C. About 300 years after the potter's wheel was invented, people made simple wheeled vehicles (Sumeria)
3000 B.C. Simple glass beads made (Egypt)
c.2800 B.C. Stonehenge built in England; first step pyramids built in Egypt
2350 B.C. First sit-down toilets (Mesopotamia)

1900 B.C. to 0

c.1900 B.C. Metalworkers began extracting iron from its ore; steel made c.1200 B.C.
1000–700 B.C. First shadow clocks (Egypt); by 700 B.C. divided sundial in use
c.690 B.C. First bridges (aqueducts) used to carry water (Assyria)
c.620 B.C. First coins made from electrum in Lydia (Asia Minor)
c.450 B.C. Decimal abacus invented (simpler stick and dust tray abacus invented in Mesopotamia c.2500 B.C.)
c.85 B.C. First water-powered mills used to grind flour (Greece)

A.D. 1 to 1400

105 Tsai Lun made paper from pulp (China)
600 Chess developed (India or China)
c.840 Camera obscura developed (China)
c.868 First printed book *Diamond Sutra* (China)
c.1000 Spinning wheel used (Asia)
c.1090 Magnetic compass invented (China, Arabia)
c.1300 First mechanical clocks with equal time periods developed (Europe)
c.1300 Astrolabe adapted for sea navigation (Arabia)

1401 to 1700

c.1440 Gutenberg developed printing press with movable type (Germany); first book printed c.1450
c.1590 Janssen made compound microscope (Netherlands)
c.1592 Galileo made first thermometer (Italy)
1608 Lippershey made working telescope (Netherlands)
1609 Galileo first person to look at stars through a telescope (Italy)
c.1620 Drebble built first submarine (England)
c.1642 Pascal built calculating machine (France)
c.1683 Leeuwenhoek made first high-power microscope (Netherlands)

1701 to 1800

1712 Newcomen built steam-powered engine (England)
1714 Fahrenheit developed mercury thermometer (Germany)
1752 Franklin developed lightning conductor (U.S.A.)
1757 Campbell built sextant (England)
1759 Harrison developed accurate chronometer (England)
1764 Hargreaves built spinning jenny (England)
1765 Watt built condensing steam engine (Scotland)
1769 Arkwright built powered spinning machine (England)
1783 Montgolfier brothers built first practical hot-air balloon (France)
1783 D'Abbans built first steamboat (France)
1785 Cartwright built power loom (England)

1801 to 1900

1803 Trevethick built steam train (England)
1821 Faraday made first electric motor (England)
c.1827 First photograph taken by Niépce (France)
1829 Stevenson's steam train *Rocket*
built (England)
1829 Sewing machine built by Thimonnier
(France)
1837 Telegraph developed by Morse
(U.S.A.) and Cooke and Wheatstone
(England)
1839 First practical bicycle built by
Macmillan (Scotland)
1852 Gifford built first working, steam-powered
airship (France)
1853 Cayley pioneered glider technology (England)
1856 Bessemer invented cheap steel-making
process (England)
1865 Lister first used antiseptics (England)
1867 Monier developed wire-reinforced
concrete (France)
1873 Sholes made first practical
commercial typewriter (U.S.A.)
1875 Bell invented
telephone (U.S.A.)
1877 Edison developed
the phonograph (U.S.A.)
1878/9 Swan (England) and
Edison (U.S.A.) made electric
light bulb
1882 First power plant opened
by Edison (U.S.A.)
1882 Seely built first practical electric
iron (U.S.A.)
1884 Daimler made first lightweight gasoline
engines (Germany)
1885 Benz made first gasoline-driven motor car
(Germany)
1893 Judson made the first zipper
(U.S.A.)
1895 Wilhelm Röntgen discovered
X rays (Germany)
1895 Marconi invented radio
communication (Italy)
1895 Lumière brothers first showed
a movie to an audience (France)

1901 to 2000

1903 Wright brothers flew first powered aircraft (U.S.A.)
1907 First helicopter built by Cornu (France)
1925 Baird invented television; he demonstrated
it in 1926 (Scotland)
1929 Whittle patented idea of the
jet engine (England)
1933 Polyethylene discovered at ICI
(England)
1935 Carothers made nylon (U.S.A.)
1936 Focke made first practical helicopter
(Germany)
1942 Fermi built first nuclear reactor (U.S.A.)
1945 Mauchly and Eckert developed first automatic
computer (U.S.A.)
1947 Land invented Polaroid® camera (U.S.A.)
1948 First atomic clock built (U.S.A.)
1953 DNA double helix discovered by Crick (England),
Watson (U.S.A.), and Wilkins (England)
1955 Cockerel invented hovercraft (England)
1957 First artificial satellite sent into orbit (U.S.S.R.)
1959 Integrated circuit (silicon chip) developed (U.S.A.)
1960 Maiman developed laser (U.S.A.)
1961 First manned space flight (U.S.S.R.)
1964 Computer mouse invented by Engelhart (U.S.A.)
1967 First heart transplant by Barnard (South Africa)
1969 First manned moon landing (U.S.A.)
1970 Floppy disk developed by IBM (U.S.A.)
1971 Microprocessor patented by Intel (U.S.A.)
1978 Personal computer developed by Jobs and
Wozniak (U.S.A.)
1979 Compact disc developed by Sony and Philips
1981 Space shuttle developed (U.S.A.)
1983 Satellite TV developed (U.S.A.)
1984 Genetic fingerprinting developed (Great Britain)
1989 Game Boy™ launched by Nintendo (Japan)
c.1992 Virtual reality helmets devised (U.S.A.)
1992 First map of human chromosome (France,
Great Britain, U.S.A.)
1995 First DNA database set up (Great Britain)
1997 First successful clone of a mammal
(Great Britain)
c.1997 Sikorsky developed robotic helicopter
(U.S.A.)
1997 Biorobotics pioneered by Shimoyama's
team (Japan)

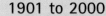

Web Addresses

www.s9.com/biography

A biographical dictionary site with basic information on more than 28,000 men and women who have shaped our world from ancient times to the present day. It also has book links to Barnes & Noble.

www.enchantedlearning.com/inventors

Visit Zoom Inventors and Inventions for a lively presentation of historical and technological facts.

www.howstuffworks.com

This is a site aimed at children and young adults explaining how things work. It covers a vast number of topics from cell phones, air conditioners, and inkjet printers to animals, insects, credit cards, movies, and guitars—an endless list.

www.bbc.co.uk/history/multimedia_zone

This is an enjoyable site with educational games and animations, including topics such as Stephenson's Rocket, blast furnaces, paddle steamships, spring mills, and winding gears.

www.uspto.gov/go/kids

This is the kids' site for the United States Patent and Trademark Office. Highly interactive, it offers games, information, and links, as well as resources for parents and teachers, including information on how to help a child make a patent application.

www.cbc.ca/kids/general/the-lab/history-of-invention/default.html

This offers an invention timeline that is constantly being updated. E-mail your suggestions for inventions you think are interesting.

www.brainpop.com

This is a science, technology, and health site for kids with lively graphics, quizzes, and movies on everything from assembly lines to lasers, photography, refrigerators, and televisions. Perform experiments in the company of Bob the Rat, and ask Tim and Moby, Tim's friendly robot, any science and technology questions that you have. There are lots of activities on this site and for each one, you can earn points and win prizes.

inventors.about.com/cs/younginventors

This kid's site is related to *inventors.about.com*, with areas aimed at a variety of ages and levels. Plenty of information on the history and stories behind different inventions, as well as explanations of how each thing works. Search by name, letter, or subject, such as famous inventors, famous inventions, women inventors, or wacky patents. There are many useful invention and inventing links, including a section for sites about children who have made and patented successful inventions.

www.build-it-yourself.com

This site is an inventor's club for kids aged 8–16 and is aimed at inspiring young people to build whimsical toys. Discover how to "build-it-yourself" and turn unwanted junk into trucks, boats, robots, and much more.

edtech.kennesaw.edu/web/inventor.html

This site offers a variety of invention and inventor-related links, from the history of inventions to invention games.

kids.patentcafe.com

This is a great site with lively graphics and plenty of activities. Learn about famous inventors and then try your hand at developing and creating your own inventions.

Quick-fire Quiz ANSWERS

Page 207 Writing and Printing
1. a   2. c   3. c   4. b

Page 209 Medicine
1. c   2. b   3. a   4. c

Page 211 Buildings
1. c   2. b   3. b   4. c

Page 213 Food and Agriculture
1. b   2. c   3. a   4. b

Page 215 At Home
1. c   2. b   3. a   4. b

Page 217 Clothes and Fabric
1. c   2. c   3. c   4. a

Page 219 Useful Materials
1. b   2. c   3. b   4. a

Page 221 Energy
1. b   2. c   3. a   4. b

Page 223 Calculations
1. b   2. c   3. b   4. b

Page 225 Computers
1. b   2. c   3. a   4. c

Page 227 Communications
1. b   2. c   3. b   4. b

Page 229 On Film
1. b   2. c   3. a   4. c

Page 231 Travel on Land
1. b   2. b   3. c   4. b

Page 233 On the Sea
1. b   2. b   3. c   4. c

Page 235 By Air
1. b   2. c   3. c   4. c

Page 237 Into Space
1. c   2. b   3. c   4. b

1,000 QUESTIONS & ANSWERS FACTFILE
TRANSPORTATION

Contents

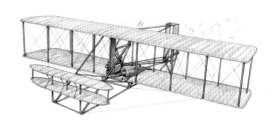

Early Transportation

Before the invention of the wheel around 5,000 years ago, few people traveled far from home; when they did, they went on foot. Gradually people learned to tame and ride animals such as horses and camels, but it was the wheel that enabled people to transport large loads with ease, especially after good roads were built.

How did early people transport heavy loads?

Many structures of the ancient world, such as the pyramids in Egypt, were built with huge stones that could weigh several tons each. We do not know for sure how people moved these stones to the construction sites. They may have dragged the stones over wooden poles laid on the ground (above) or made sleds mounted on wooden runners. They even may have laid wooden paths to help the sleds move more smoothly.

What was the "ship of the desert"?

The camel was called the "ship of the desert" because it was used in the deserts of Asia and northern Africa to carry both people and goods. Camels were prized for their stamina—they could survive long periods with little food or water. One-humped dromedaries and two-humped Bactrian camels were both in use by 1500 B.C. Camels are still used today for transportation.

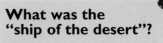

Ceramic rider from China, around 80 B.C.

What is a travois?

Native Americans were often on the move, hunting and gathering food. The Plains Indians used a travois—a simple sled—to transport their goods. They tied two teepee poles to the harness of a trained dog and strung their belongings between the poles.

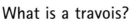

How did people travel before the invention of the wheel?

In some countries, wealthy people were carried on litters—platforms held up by parallel poles (left). Heavy loads were carried by pack animals—mules or donkeys in Europe, llamas in South America.

How did horse collars help transport heavy loads?

In the past horses wore throat harnesses when dragging loads, but the harnesses put great pressure on their windpipes, making breathing difficult. The Chinese solved this problem with a padded collar that fit around a horse's shoulders and neck, away from the windpipe. This collar enables a horse to pull up to four times as much weight as it could with a harness.

Can you ride without stirrups?

Yes. Early riders were very skilled at controlling horses with their legs and knees. Stirrups were probably invented in India around 200 B.C., and they made horses even easier to control. Horses began to be used more in warfare because riders could perform the twists and turns needed in battle. Also, soldiers needed their hands less for controlling the horses, so they could use weapons more easily.

How were the first wheels made?

The first wheels were made by nailing together planks of wood to form solid disks (above). They were strong but very heavy and were used for carts and war chariots.

What were wheelbarrows first used for?

The Chinese invented the first wheelbarrows, which were simple, wooden vehicles that were pushed along to carry people. Modern wheelbarrows are similar in design. They have one wheel at the front and two support legs at the back, but they are used to carry small loads—not people!

Cars

In just 100 years, cars have changed the world, bringing easy, convenient transportation within the reach of ordinary people for the first time. There are now motor vehicles for every imaginable purpose, from ambulances and race cars to buses and jeeps. However, gas-powered vehicles cause problems, polluting the air and draining valuable oil reserves, so designers are working on cars that use less energy and keep our air cleaner.

How long are limousines?

People who want to make a big impression often choose big cars—and cars do not get much bigger than a 100-foot (30-m)-long stretch limousine (above). Stretch limousines are usually about 26 feet (8m) long. Their length can make them difficult to drive—especially around corners!

What was the first car?

The first real motorcar was a three-wheeler built by German engineer Carl Benz in 1885. It had a small gasoline engine underneath the passenger seat that drove the back wheels to a top speed of about 9 miles per hour (15km/h). Benz went on to build many more cars, becoming the world's first automobile manufacturer.

Can there be a low-energy car?

Manufacturers are trying to design cars that use less energy. They have designed lightweight cars that use less gas, as well as electric cars. But coal and oil must be used to generate electricity for electric cars, so these vehicles are not as low-energy as they seem. One day we might ride around in solar-powered cars that are covered with light-sensitive panels (left).

What are crumple zones?

Modern cars are designed to protect passengers in a crash. The passenger compartments are surrounded by metal bars to shield those inside. But the front and rear of cars are designed to crumple in a crash, absorbing some of the impact shock. These parts are called crumple zones.

How fast can cars go?

By attaching jet engines to specially designed, streamlined cars, Englishman Richard Noble has built faster cars than anyone else. His most recent car, *Thrust SSC* (right), set a new record in 1997, powering to an amazing 756.93 miles per hour (1220.86km/h)—faster than the speed of sound.

Thrust SSC

How does the engine drive the wheels?

Most modern cars have front-wheel drive, which means the front wheels both drive the car and steer it. Power travels from the engine to the wheels through a short bar called a half shaft. Between the engine and the half shaft is a gearbox, which allows the driver to select a slower but more powerful gear for accelerating, or a higher, more economical gear for cruising at high speed.

What stops cars from skidding?

In wet conditions cars are more likely to skid. This is why car tires have a pattern of grooves called a tread. Water from the road gathers in the tread, then is pushed back onto the road, away from the tire's path. Modern tires are relatively wide to further reduce the risk of skidding.

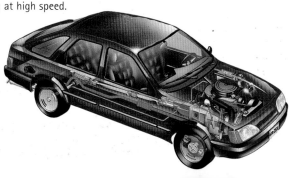

Race Cars

In the early 1900s cars began to be designed
for speed, and special tracks were built for racing.
Today automobile racing is still popular—Formula
One and Indy car racing are multimillion-dollar
sports with amazing, high-tech cars, skilled
drivers, and huge support teams.

What is pole position?

Pole position is the first place on the grid from
which a race starts. The driver in pole position has
an advantage over the other drivers. The position of the
cars is determined during the previous qualifying laps,
when the cars are timed as they drive the course.
The driver with the fastest lap wins pole position,
and the others line up behind
in the order of their
qualifying times.

How do race cars stick to the track?

Formula One cars are lower and more streamlined than any other type of vehicle.
The shape of the car is important in two ways. First, the streamlining
enables air to flow easily over the vehicle, cutting down drag
(air resistance) and allowing the car to go faster.
Second, the air flow, aided by specially
shaped wings on the front and
rear, pushes the car down
onto the track, holding it
close to the road.

Air flow

How do race-car drivers choose their tires?

If the weather is dry, racing drivers will choose tires called slicks. Slicks are wide tires with no tread. They grip well on dry tracks and get sticky as they warm up, helping the cars grip the road. In wet weather, slicks do not grip well, and drivers usually switch to tires with treads.

How powerful are car engines?

Most family cars have six-cylinder engines that are designed to travel comfortably at or near the maximum road speed limit. Race cars are designed for much higher speeds. Formula One cars can reach speeds of 200 miles per hour (322km/h) and have very powerful, 12-cylinder engines.

Why do racing drivers remove steering wheels?

To keep a race car light, streamlined, and efficient, everything is as small as possible. The cockpit, where the driver sits, is very cramped, and the driver's legs nestle under the steering wheel in the front, or nose, of the car. To squeeze their legs into the narrow nose, drivers must first remove the steering wheel.

Quick-fire Quiz

1. Which most affects how a car holds on to the road?
   a) The car's shape
   b) The car's material
   c) The car's size

2. Which tires are used in dry conditions?
   a) Tires with treads
   b) Slicks
   c) Narrow tires

3. Why are qualifying laps important?
   a) Points are scored
   b) Grid position is determined
   c) Drivers are eliminated

4. What is the front of a race car called?
   a) The bumper
   b) The beak
   c) The nose

What happens in the pit?

A Formula One car enters the pit—the service area at the side of the track—at least once during a race to refuel. Using special equipment, the highly skilled pit mechanics fill gas tanks and change tires in a matter of seconds. The mechanics can usually fix any mechanical problems very quickly in the pit.

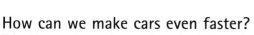

How can we make cars even faster?

Using bigger engines makes cars faster, but it also makes them heavier, which slows them down. Because of this, race-car designers concentrate on making the vehicles more streamlined, and they aim to use new materials that are very strong but also very lightweight, such as carbon fiber. Designers use computers to try out new ideas in theory before testing them on working cars.

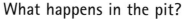

Trucks

Early trucks were small, but as engines got larger, designers made larger trucks that could transport almost anything. Long-distance trucks have big engines, but there is still room in the cabs to make drivers comfortable—some even have beds!

How many cars can you drive at a time?

You can only really drive one car at a time—but a modern car transporter can carry as many as nine. The upper deck of the transporter lowers at the rear so that cars can drive onto it. Then the deck is raised so that more cars can be driven onto the lower deck. Wedges and straps keep the cars from moving while the transporter is in motion.

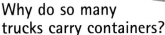

Why do so many trucks carry containers?

Containers are large, metal boxes that come in two standard sizes. Tractor-semitrailers can be standardized to carry both sizes, and cranes are also standardized to load the containers on to ships (below).

How does a dump truck dump?

To lift and dump a heavy load, a dump truck uses a powerful hydraulic system. Pressure is applied to a liquid, which pushes up a piston connected to the bottom of the dump truck's container. When the pressure is released, the container lowers.

How are liquids transported?

Gasoline, chemicals, milk, and other liquids are transported in huge tankers that can hold thousands of gallons (right). The inside of each tank is divided into sections to prevent the liquids from moving around, which would make driving difficult. Each section has its own inlet on the top for filling and a nozzle at the bottom for emptying.

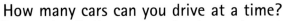

How do you drive a road train?

A road train looks like a normal truck from the front— it is only when the long train of trailers winds into view that it is clear where this impressive vehicle got its name. It is driven like a normal truck, but to turn corners the driver has to swing out in the opposite direction to the bend, so that the trailers follow in the right line. Road trains are often seen in countries that have long stretches of straight roads, like Australia.

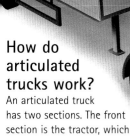

What can trucks carry?

Trucks can be adapted to carry virtually any type of load. Tankers carry liquids, special trailers carry animals, and garbage trucks have crushing machinery. Low-loaders (above) have long, low platforms to transport other vehicles or awkward cargo, like logs.

How much can a truck carry?

The trucks used on construction sites are some of the world's biggest vehicles. Many trucks can carry more than 100 tons, but a "monster" truck will take up to 330 tons—the weight of a jumbo jet!

How do articulated trucks work?

An articulated truck has two sections. The front section is the tractor, which contains the engine and the driver; the rear section is the trailer, which carries the load. A joint links the two sections, allowing the truck to turn with more flexibility than a one-section vehicle of the same length. Cables connect the trailer's brakes and lights to the tractor, giving the driver full control.

Quick-fire Quiz

1. Where are road trains especially hard to drive?
a) On straight roads
b) In the country
c) Around corners

2. How many standard sizes of containers are there?
a) One
b) Two
c) Three

3. What kind of dumping system do trucks use?
a) Hydraulic
b) Spring
c) Manual

4. What is the front section of an articulated truck called?
a) The trailer
b) The tractor
c) The engine

Special Vehicles

Motor vehicles are the most adaptable form of transportation. They can be used to rescue people in an emergency, to harvest crops on a farm, or to build towering structures. Manufacturers start with the same basic machinery found on cars—wheels, gears, brakes, and engines—and add the specialized equipment needed to create the best machine for the job.

Why do tractors have such big wheels?

The big rear wheels of a tractor spread out the vehicle's weight so that it does not sink into soft or muddy ground. The large wheels have thick tires with chunky treads to provide plenty of grip on the ground. Many tractors have a connection at the rear that can provide power for other farm machinery.

What vehicles do police use?

Police forces use motorcycles to pass through busy traffic quickly. They also use heavily armored vans to control riots. Police cars have flashing lights and sirens as warning signals, and they carry all kinds of equipment in their trunks. Police drivers are trained to drive safely at high speeds.

What are the special features of ambulances?

Ambulances are ordinary vans or cars that carry medical equipment to give emergency treatment to sick or injured people as they are driven to the hospital. Ambulances must be seen and heard easily—they have sirens and flashing lights, and the word "ambulance" is often written in reverse on the front so that other drivers can read it the right way around in their rear-view mirrors.

How do machines tunnel underground?

Special tunnel-boring machines are used to dig tunnels, with conveyor belts to remove the rubble. If the rock is very hard, machines drill small holes and fill them with explosives to blast away the rock. Tunnels are usually lined with both steel and concrete for extra reinforcement.

How does a fire engine save lives?

There are several types of fire engines. Some have platforms or ladders that extend to over 100 feet (30m) high so that firefighters can rescue people trapped in burning buildings. Some fire engines have pumps powerful enough to deliver up to 738 gallons (2,840l) of water in one minute.

When were tanks first used?

Tanks made their first major appearance in 1916, during World War I. They were heavily armored to withstand machine-gun fire and explosions, and their "caterpillar" tracks could easily plow through barbed wire and trenches. Tanks can have many different features—gun turrets, ammunition stores, periscopes, and armored plating.

How does a streetcar work?

A streetcar looks like an ordinary bus, but instead of using a diesel engine, it runs on electricity. On the top of the streetcar are two arms with wheels at the ends. These wheels connect to two overhead wires that supply the power. A streetcar can only travel along the routes laid out by the power wires.

Quick-fire Quiz

1. Why does a tractor have large wheels?
a) To help it go faster
b) To spread out its weight over soft ground
c) To drive through water easily

2. What powers a streetcar?
a) Diesel
b) Electricity
c) Gas

3. How far can some fire engines' ladders reach?
a) 10 feet
b) 50 feet
c) 100 feet

4. What prevents a JCB from toppling over?
a) The backhoe
b) Hydraulics
c) The wheels and steel props

Which digger is the best?

The JCB is the most versatile machine for digging. It has both a big scoop for picking up material from the surface and a backhoe for digging holes, carrying rubble, and other uses. The JCB's sturdy wheels and strong, steel props prevent it from toppling over when performing complicated maneuvers with heavy loads. Both the shovel and the props are powered by hydraulics, which means that the driver can move them easily in any direction just by flicking a series of levers in the cab.

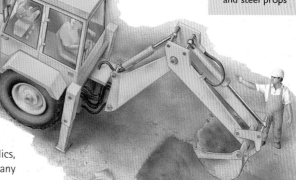

Trains

The first railroad networks appeared in England during the 1800s, and soon railroads were being built all over the world. They changed people's lives, allowing them to travel farther and faster than ever before. Railroads also made it possible to transport large loads of heavy goods over land for the first time.

Were there trains before steam power?

Yes. As early as 1550, mine owners in Germany were hauling stone, coal, and iron ore out of mines using trucks on tracks. The trucks were pulled by horses (above) or pushed along by the miners themselves. Most of these early railroads were very short.

What were Big Boys?

Big Boys were the largest steam locomotive trains ever built. They ran on the Union Pacific Railroad in the 1940s, hauling heavy goods up the Rocky Mountains. The engines were 130 feet (40m) long and could reach speeds of up to 80 miles per hour (130km/h).

How can trains run on electricity?

Many trains are attached to overhead electric cables that supply electricity to motors that turn the wheels. The trains are linked to the cables by special connectors that use adjustable springs to take up any slack when the trains are traveling uphill.

How fast are bullet trains?

The Japanese bullet train is built for speed—the most recent model has reached speeds of up to 223 miles per hour (360km/h). It runs on special tracks without sharp bends, which would slow down the train. The French TGV (*Train à Grande Vitesse*) can travel at a similar speed.

Which trains hover in the air?

Maglev (magnetic levitation) trains are held just above the track by magnetic force. When they move, the trains do not touch the track, so there is no friction to slow them down. Scientists believe that one day it will be possible to travel at speeds of up to 435 miles per hour (700km/h) in maglev trains.

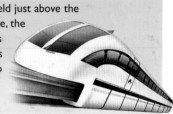

What was special about the *Rocket*?

The *Rocket* was a famous locomotive designed by British engineer George Stephenson. It was built in 1829, when a competition was held to find the best engine for the new Liverpool-to-Manchester railroad. The *Rocket* was the winner, reaching a top speed of 29 miles per hour (47km/h).

What were the "Flying Hamburgers"?

In 1933 new diesel express trains (left) were built to run between Berlin and Hamburg in Germany. They were sleek, streamlined, and very fast for the time, reaching 109 miles per hour (175km/h). They became known as the "Flying Hamburgers." The trains were so successful that they were used throughout Germany until the 1960s.

What are cowcatchers?

The first American railroads were not protected by fences, so cattle often wandered onto the lines. Special guards called cowcatchers were attached to the front of steam locomotives (right) to nudge the cows to safety, away from the wheels. The first locomotive to have a cowcatcher was the *John Bull*, which was built in 1831.

Quick-fire Quiz

1. How fast could the *Rocket* travel?
a) 9 miles per hour
b) 29 miles per hour
c) 92 miles per hour

2. What do maglev trains avoid?
a) Delay
b) Friction
c) Engines

3. Where were the earliest trains used?
a) In mines
b) In cities
c) On the coast

4. Why can a bullet train travel so fast?
a) Its tracks have no sharp curves
b) It does not stop at stations
c) It carries few passengers

Bicycles

Cycling is a cheap, healthy, and fun way to travel. The modern bicycle, with its diamond-shaped frame and equal-sized wheels, appeared just over 100 years ago. Since then manufacturers have made bikes for every kind of activity, from lightweight cycles for racing to BMX bikes for tricks. There are even folding bicycles that fit into the trunk of a car!

What was the first bicycle?

A machine called the draisienne (right) appeared in the early 1800s. It had a seat, two wheels, and handlebars, just like a modern bike. But it was not a true bicycle, because it had no pedals— riders had to stride along the ground while the seat took most of their weight. Draisiennes were uncomfortable and hard to ride, so they did not catch on.

Were penny-farthings safe?

With its giant front wheel and tiny rear wheel, the 1870 penny-farthing was not easy to ride. Many people needed steps to climb onto it, and once on the seat, it was very easy to fall off. Even so, many people bought penny-farthings. They liked the idea that, unlike a horse, the bicycle did not need feeding or looking after!

Why are racing bikes so light?

The lighter its frame, the less effort it takes to pedal a racing bike, so the faster you go. Designers make racing-bike frames with very light metals, such as aluminum alloys. Narrow, treadless tires reduce friction between the wheels and the road to make the bikes go faster.

How do you ride a unicycle?

A unicycle has a seat and two pedals, but only one wheel. Unicyclists let the seat take their weight, then rock the pedals back and forth to balance. Beginners usually ask two friends to support them as they pedal, but after a couple of hours riders can usually balance on their own. Skilled riders can learn to play basketball, hockey, and tag on unicyles.

What makes mountain bikes special?

Mountain bikes need to be extra-strong for cross-country riding. They have tough, metal frames, tires with deep treads to provide plenty of grip, and many gears to make cycling up and down hills easy.

Quick-fire Quiz

1. What was unusual about the draisienne?
a) It had no seat
b) It had no pedals
c) It had no handlebars

2. How did people get onto a penny-farthing?
a) By jumping
b) With steps
c) With a mechanical lifting device

3. How many people could ride the *Décuplette*?
a) Two
b) Five
c) Ten

4. Which tires do racing bikes have?
a) Narrow, treadless tires
b) Thick, rugged tires
c) Solid tires

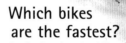

Which bikes are the fastest?

Professional racing bikes (left), which are the fastest bicycles, need to be very streamlined. The frame, wheels, and handlebars are all designed to reduce drag (air resistance). High-tech materials that are strong and light, such as carbon fiber, are used. Even the cyclist is streamlined, wearing a special helmet to reduce drag.

What can bicycles carry?

In many parts of Asia few people can afford a car, and three-wheeled bikes are popular alternatives. These vehicles often have platforms for carrying goods (right), and many riders earn money by making deliveries. Trishaws—tricycles with small seats at the rear—also provide income for riders who ferry passengers around.

How many people can ride on one bike?

Some people like riding tandems, or bicycles built for two (above), but at the end of the 1800s, some bikes were built for even more people. A number of four-seaters appeared, and there was even one French bicycle, the *Décuplette*, that carried ten people!

Motorcycles

The very first motorcyle was built in 1868 and was powered by a small steam engine! But ever since Daimler made his first machine in 1885 (below), motorcycles have had gasoline engines. There are all kinds of different motorcycles, from slow, economical scooters to powerful, expensive bikes that give exhilarating rides on open roads.

Why was Daimler's first motorcycle made of wood?

When German engineer Gottlieb Daimler made his first gasoline engine, he tested it by attaching it to a homemade wooden bicycle, creating the first-ever gasoline-powered motorcycle. He probably used wood because many vehicles were wooden in those days, but he may have regretted his choice when the bike was destroyed by fire in 1903!

How are motorcycles built for speed?

Motorcycles, especially those designed for racing, have large, powerful engines and streamlined frames to reduce drag. The seats are set back and the handlebars are low so that the rider's head and shoulders stay down. This helps cut drag even more, enabling the rider to gain valuable seconds.

What is special about dirt bikes?

Dirt bikes are designed to be raced over muddy, bumpy courses at high speed. They have sturdy frames, thick tires with deep treads, and big mudguards to protect the rider from the mud and stones that the wheels kick up. Good suspension helps absorb some of the shock, but riders must still expect a rough ride!

How do you corner fast?

Motorcyclists go around bends, or "corner," by leaning into the curve. On fast bends, racing riders lean so far that it looks as if they will topple over! Professional riders know just how far to lean to give them the best route around the curve at the fastest possible speed.

When is a bike not a bike?

When it's a trike! Three-wheeled tricycles, like this all-terrain vehicle (ATV), are more stable than ordinary bikes because of the support from the extra wheel. This means that ATVs can be used off-road over bumpy ground. They are also used for racing.

What is a chopper?

A chopper is a motorcycle with a low seat, raised handlebars, and a long fork that supports the front wheel. Most choppers do not start out like this—they are ordinary bikes that have been altered, or customized, by their owners. The biker has to chop up the original bike, alter it, and then put it back together. The result is a unique chopper.

Which motorcycles are best in the city?

Many people think that mopeds, or scooters, are ideal in the city. Mopeds first appeared in Italy in the 1940s, but they are still very popular today. They are not too expensive and are easy to ride. Mopeds' engines are small but suitable for busy city streets, where you cannot go too fast. Often the engines are covered to keep noise to a minimum.

Why were sidecars invented?

Sidecars were originally made to enable motorcyclists to carry extra passengers in comfort. But it was not long before another class of motor sports developed—racing motorcycles with special, flattened sidecars attached! During races, the sidecar passengers must move around, shifting their weight into the best positions to keep the machines stable at high speed.

Boats

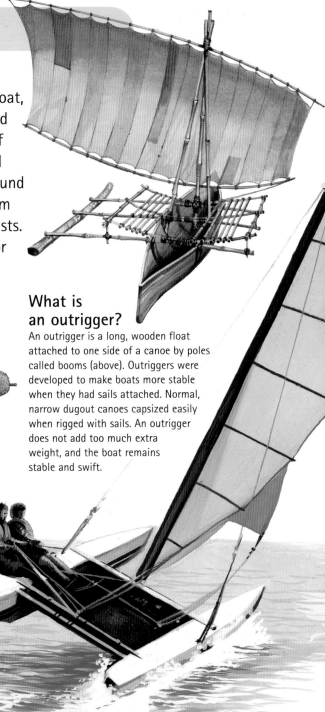

From the simplest canoe to the most powerful modern speedboat, there are now boats for every need and for conditions in every part of the world. In the past people used small boats simply for getting around or for jobs like fishing, sailing them up and down rivers and along coasts. Many of today's boats are built for pleasure—either for racing or for cruising.

What is an outrigger?

An outrigger is a long, wooden float attached to one side of a canoe by poles called booms (above). Outriggers were developed to make boats more stable when they had sails attached. Normal, narrow dugout canoes capsized easily when rigged with sails. An outrigger does not add too much extra weight, and the boat remains stable and swift.

What were early boats like?

The first boats were made from simple materials that were easy to find and work with. Reeds were bound tightly together to form strong, watertight boats (above). Dugout canoes were another early type of watercraft, built by prehistoric people thousands of years ago and still used today in some parts of the world. They were made from tree trunks, which were hollowed out in the middle either with stone tools or by small fires that burned away the excess wood.

Are two hulls better than one?

The hull is the main body of a boat or ship. Boats with twin hulls are called catamarans (left). They are very wide and can accommodate large sails, which means that the boat can sail fast. Catamarans were developed thousands of years ago on islands in the Pacific Ocean. They are now popular for both racing and recreation.

Which boat can you carry on your back?

The coracle is a tiny, lightweight boat that has been around for thousands of years and is still used today in some parts of England and Wales. It is made from leather, which is stretched over the wooden framework, and is just big enough to carry one fisherman. When the fisherman returns to shore, he lifts out the boat, hoists it onto his shoulders, and walks home.

Which boats are best for racing?

People race all kinds of boats, from tiny dinghies to large yachts. Races are organized in different classes so that boats of the same type race against each other. Most racing boats have sleek hulls made of strong, lightweight materials. Large sails are vital for speed.

Which are the fastest boats?

The fastest boats are speedboats, which combine powerful engines with sleek, pointed hulls. Swiftest of all is the hydroplane (above), which rises up out of the water as it speeds along. The world water speed record is 316.89 miles per hour (511.11km/h), achieved by Ken Warby of Australia in a hydroplane.

Can boats sail uphill?

Yes, with help from locks—sections of a canal or river that can be closed off by gates. Lock-keepers open the lower gates, allowing the boat in, and the lock fills with water until it is the same level as the water upstream. Then the upper gates open, and the boat sails out. To sail downstream, the process works in reverse.

Boat sails through lower gates of lock

Gates close and water enters lock

Upper gates open

Quick-fire Quiz

1. How many hulls does a catamaran have?
a) One
b) Two
c) Three

2. What are dugout canoes made from?
a) Reeds
b) Tree trunks
c) Planks of wood

3. Why do people use outriggers?
a) To stabilize canoes being used with sails
b) To carry more passengers
c) To look good

4. Which type of boats are the fastest?
a) Dinghies
b) Coracles
c) Hydroplanes

Ships

Ships have been used for thousands of years because it was often easier to sail along a river or coast than to build a road. Over time bigger and better boats were built, from the small, wooden sailing vessels of early times to the huge liners and tankers of today, which can sail around the world. Ships with engines were introduced in the 1800s, so they no longer had to depend on a good wind to get them moving.

What were the first sailing boats like?

The world's first sailing ships probably sailed about 5,000 years ago in the Mediterranean Sea and along the Nile River in Egypt. They had solitary, square sails on tall, wooden masts (above). Their hulls were made of wood, and they were steered by a large, wooden oar at the stern, or back, of the boat.

How did clippers race across the oceans?

Clippers were the fastest sailing ships of the 1800s. They often carried tea from China to Europe. Clippers had sleek, streamlined hulls and many large sails, which enabled them to skim through the water quickly. One clipper sailed from Melbourne, Australia, to London, England, in just 85 days.

Which ships are the biggest?

The world's biggest ships are supertankers. These enormous vessels weigh up to 500,000 tons and are around 1,500 feet (450m) long. It would be possible to build even bigger tankers—up to one million tons—but no port in the world would be large enough to handle such huge ships.

Why did early steamships have sails?

There were several reasons for keeping a set of sails on a steamer. By using sail power when the wind was favorable, ship-owners could travel farther on a load of coal, saving money. It also meant that less coal needed to be carried, allowing more room for cargo.

Why are oil slicks dangerous?

When a tanker spills oil, the oil floats on the surface of the water in a thin layer called a slick. The slick from a large tanker can spread out for many miles, causing damage to the environment. Oil sticks to the feathers of seabirds, often killing them. Oil-polluted beaches can take months to clear.

Which ship is the most luxurious?

Perhaps the most luxurious ship is the cruise liner *Grand Princess* (right). Its 12 decks offer 2,600 passengers everything they could expect in the best hotel, and more—a casino, a theater, a virtual-reality center, and many different restaurants. The swimming pool even has a movable roof to protect it in bad weather.

Grand Princess

Submarines

Submarines add a new dimension to warfare, enabling forces to creep up on enemy ships and launch surprise attacks. These powerful craft played an important role in both world wars. But underwater vessels also have peaceful uses—they can be used to explore the deep, dark trenches of the oceans, discovering new species of marine life.

Turtle

What were early submarines like?

Early submarines were small, wooden vessels that could hold only one person. They were operated by handles and foot pedals that moved two propellers—one to dive and ascend, and one to travel forward. The *Turtle* (above), a famous early submarine, was built during the Revolutionary War in 1776 to plant explosives below British ships.

Air out

Compressed-air tanks

Compressed air in

Water in— submarine dives

Ballast tanks

Water out— submarine rises

How do submarines dive?

The hull of a submarine has two walls with large containers called ballast tanks between them. When the tanks contain air, the submarine floats on the surface like a normal ship. When the captain wants to dive, the tanks are gradually filled with water. This makes the vessel heavier, so it dives toward the bottom of the ocean. When it is time to surface, compressed air is released into the ballast tanks to force the water out.

Why do submarines have "wings"?

Submarines have small "wings" called hydroplanes. These can be moved up and down to help submarines climb and dive. The hydroplanes can also tilt submarines sideways to change direction.

How are nuclear submarines useful?

The submarine below is powered by an onboard nuclear reactor. The advantage of this form of power is that the vessel can sail an almost unlimited distance without the need to refuel. This is useful in wartime, when submarines may have to travel thousands of miles from port. The drawback is that nuclear submarines are difficult and costly to maintain, and they produce hazardous waste that needs to be treated with great caution.

Do submarines have weapons?

Most submarines are military machines used for patrolling the oceans. Submarines may have to fire at enemy craft, so they are equipped with special missiles called torpedoes. Torpedoes propel themselves through the water, often over very great distances.

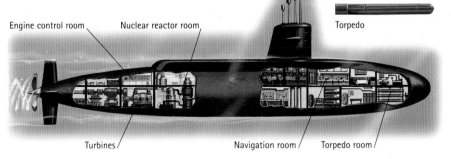

Engine control room   Nuclear reactor room

Torpedo

Turbines   Navigation room   Torpedo room

Why are submarine hulls so strong?

The deeper underwater a submarine dives, the greater the pressure applied to it from the water. In 1960, when two scientists dived 35,788 feet (10,911m) into the Marianas Trench—the deepest underwater gorge known on earth—their vessel, the *Trieste* (right), had to be heavily reinforced to avoid being crushed.

Trieste

How can crews see above the surface?

Submarine crews use a device called a periscope to see what is happening on the surface. A periscope is a long tube with an angled mirror at each end. The submariner looks at the lower mirror and sees the reflected image of what is above. When the vessel dives deep, the periscope tube is lowered into the body of the submarine.

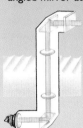

What is a submersible?

A submersible is a small submarine used for a variety of underwater jobs—exploration, marine biology, repairs to oil rigs, and laying pipelines. Some are remote-controlled. *Deepstar IV* (left) can operate at depths of more than 3,935 feet (1,200m).

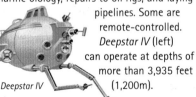

Deepstar IV

Quick-fire Quiz

1. What are the "wings" of a submarine called?
a) Hydroplanes
b) Hydrofoils
c) Hydroponics

2. What happens to a submarine when it dives?
a) Water empties out of the ballast tanks
b) Oil flows through the ballast tanks
c) Water flows into the ballast tanks

3. What weapons do submarines sometimes use?
a) Torpedoes
b) Heat seekers
c) Submersibles

4. What is the deepest known place on earth?
a) The Dead Sea
b) The Marianas Trench
c) The South Pacific

Hovercraft and Hydrofoils

There are several types of craft that work by skimming over the surface of the water. The most common are hovercraft and hydrofoils, which use two very different designs to keep their hulls out of the water. Hovercraft and hydrofoils are some of the fastest and most efficient craft afloat, but they tend to be uncomfortable, and even unstable. Because of this, they are not used as much now as they were in the past.

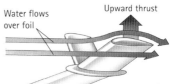

Is this ship taking off?

No, it's a hydrofoil! It has a set of foils that lift the hull out of the water as it moves. The less contact the hydrofoil has with the water, the less drag it experiences, and the faster it can go. This reduces the amount of fuel the vessel uses and makes it very efficient.

Water flows over foil

Upward thrust

How do foils work?

As the hydrofoil speeds along, water flows over the foils, which are specially curved to provide an upward thrust. The faster the vessel travels, the greater the lift produced by the foils.

Fully submerged hydrofoil

Surface-piercing hydrofoil

What are foils?

Foils are the underwater fins or wings beneath hydrofoils. There are two main types—those that stay submerged and those that pierce the surface of the water. Submerged foils are popular because they allow high speeds and operate well in rough seas when used with an automatic control system. Surface-piercing foils are useful when boats tip to one side, because more of the foil on that side is pulled underwater, creating forces that pull the boat upright again.

How does a hovercraft hover?

A huge fan pumps air into the area under a hovercraft (below). This creates a cushion of air on which the craft rides, or hovers. Because air escapes from around the edge of the vehicle, the fan has to keep working whenever the craft is in motion to keep it from sinking into the sea.

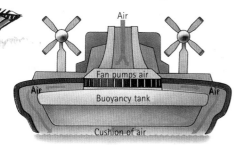

Air
Fan pumps air
Air
Air
Buoyancy tank
Cushion of air

Can hovercraft travel over both land and sea?

Hovercraft are amphibious —in other words, they can move over both land and water. Because they have no wheels, they can even travel over bumpy terrain and marshland, where it is difficult for wheeled vehicles to go. Surfaces such as ice, mud, and even quicksand pose no problems for hovercraft.

What are hovercraft used for?

Hovercraft are normally used for ferrying passengers. They are ideal for this type of job because they can cover short journeys at high speeds. Sometimes armed forces use hovercraft to travel over different terrains.

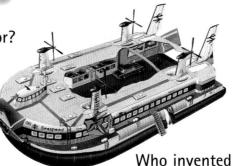

Who invented the hovercraft?

Hovercraft, or Air-Cushion Vehicles (ACVs), were invented by British engineer Christopher Cockerell in the 1950s. Cockerell tested his designs with a hairdryer and two tin cans.

What is a hovercraft's skirt?

Most hovercraft have a length of flexible rubber that goes all the way around the underside of the vehicles. This is called the skirt. The skirt raises the hovercraft higher and is very flexible. This helps the craft ride easily and smoothly over the waves. The skirt also helps keep in the cushion of air underneath the hovercraft.

GH-2005

Airplanes

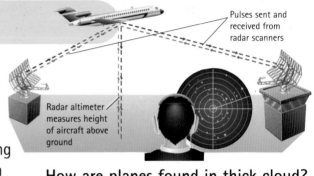

Pulses sent and received from radar scanners

Radar altimeter measures height of aircraft above ground

American brothers Wilbur and Orville Wright built the first airplane (below) in 1903 and flew it for only 12 seconds. Today jet airliners can fly for hours, carrying hundreds of people vast distances in comfort. It is even possible to fly faster than the speed of sound.

How are planes found in thick cloud?

Air-traffic controllers need to keep track of hundreds of aircraft in the sky to prevent collisions. They are not able to see most aircraft with the naked eye because of darkness, poor weather conditions, and long distances. This is why air-traffic controllers use radar, which bounces radio waves off of objects, to find out their position. The airplanes appear as dots on the radar screens in the airport control tower.

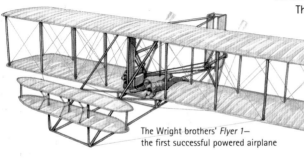

The Wright brothers' *Flyer 1*—the first successful powered airplane

Why do airplanes need instruments?

A modern airplane is a complicated piece of machinery that uses many different systems such as engines, hydraulics, and control surfaces. The pilot needs to know how all these are functioning, and the instruments in the cockpit give the answers. Also, navigational instruments indicate how high the plane is flying, how fast it is going, and in what direction.

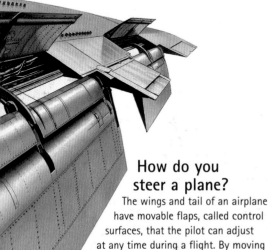

How do you steer a plane?

The wings and tail of an airplane have movable flaps, called control surfaces, that the pilot can adjust at any time during a flight. By moving controls in the cockpit, the pilot can change the control surfaces to make the plane climb or dive and turn left or right.

Quick-fire Quiz

1. Who flew the first airplane?
a) The Wright brothers
b) The Montgolfier brothers
c) The Marx brothers

2. What is the nickname for the Harrier aircraft?
a) Lightning jet
b) Jumbo jet
c) Jump jet

3. What is forced out of the back of a jet engine?
a) Exhaust gases
b) Hot water
c) Hot air

4. What do air-traffic controllers use?
a) Sonar
b) Radar
c) Metal detectors

How do planes fly so fast?

The fastest planes normally have jet engines, which create a force much like when air is let out of a balloon. The engine burns fuel and forces the exhaust gases out of the back of the engine at high speed. This creates a huge backward force, and the reaction against this force pushes the aircraft forward.

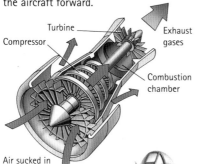

Turbine

Compressor

Exhaust gases

Combustion chamber

Air sucked in

Why did Concorde's nose droop?

Concorde's long, pointed nose made it sleek and helped it fly faster than any other airliner. But the nose obstructed the pilot's line of vision during takeoff and landing, so a special mechanism was used to lower it out of sight.

Flight position

Takeoff and landing position

How can a jet jump?

Vertical Takeoff and Landing (VTOL) aircraft are useful in places where there are no runways. The first airplane able to take off vertically was the British Hawker Siddeley Harrier, known as the jump jet. The nozzles of its jet engines, which point backward in normal flight, swivel toward the ground to give the vertical force needed for takeoff.

A Harrier jump jet

Which are the largest airliners?

The biggest passenger-carriers are the wide-bodied super jets. The first and best-known is the Boeing 747, often called the jumbo jet. About 230 feet (70m) long, it can carry almost 500 passengers and cruises at around 620 miles per hour (1,000km/h).

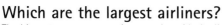

Gliders

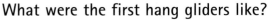

Gliders are simple, lightweight aircraft with no engines. They are cheaper to run than powered airplanes and have been popular with flying enthusiasts for years. Hang gliders give an even greater feeling of freedom in the skies. Both types of aircraft are simple, but they require special skills and training to fly.

What were the first hang gliders like?

The first hang gliders aimed to copy the flight of birds (above), but failed because they focused more on flapping than gliding. German inventor Otto Lilienthal experimented with fixed-wing gliders and made important notes about control surfaces. He crashed to his death in 1896 while flying one of his inventions.

How does the pilot control a hang glider?

The first hang gliders were steered by the pilot shifting his or her weight toward the desired direction. More modern hang gliders have tails with movable surfaces, similar to those on full-size airplanes, that can be adjusted using hand controls.

How do you launch a glider?

A glider has no engine, so it is pulled along to gain the speed needed for lift. Usually a powerful car or an ordinary airplane tows the glider. When there is enough lift, the glider pilot releases the tow rope and is able to glide smoothly away.

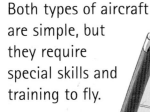

Lift

Airfoil

What is an airfoil?

An airfoil is the cross-section of a wing that is shaped to produce an upward motion, or lift, with little drag. Airfoils are curved on the top to force air to flow over them quickly, creating lift. The faster the air flows over the wings, the more lift is created, so gliders must fly at a certain speed to stay airborne.

What are microlights?

Microlights are tiny airplanes with small engines. They carry one or two people and are made of the lightest possible materials—often aluminum alloy frameworks and plastic body shells. Some microlights have solid, fixed wings, but most have flexible, fabric wings, as hang gliders do. Ultralights are smaller and lighter microlights.

Can you control where gliders land?

Like powered airplanes, gliders have control surfaces on their wings and tails so the pilot can steer an accurate course. In addition they have air brakes that stick out from the wings to provide a steep and speedy descent when it is time to land.

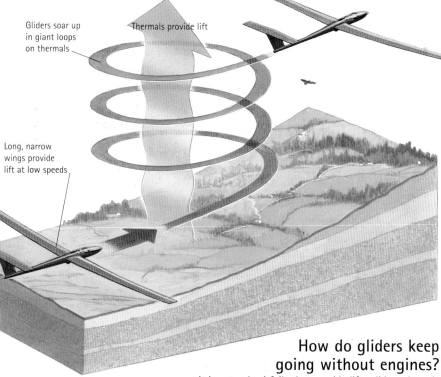

Gliders soar up in giant loops on thermals

Thermals provide lift

Long, narrow wings provide lift at low speeds

How do gliders keep going without engines?

It is not only airfoils that provide lift—gliders also rely on thermals (currents of warm air) to keep going without engines. Like birds, pilots search for the thermals, which swirl up into the atmosphere and provide lift. Experienced pilots can stay aloft for hours soaring on thermals.

Quick-fire Quiz

1. Why are gliders towed?
a) Because they have no engines
b) Because they have no pilots to fly them
c) Because their gas tanks cannot carry enough fuel

2. What are currents of warm air called?
a) Thermos
b) Winds
c) Thermals

3. What are the wings of most microlights made of?
a) Metal
b) Fabric
c) Wood

4. How were the first hang gliders steered?
a) By the pilot shifting weight
b) By using control surfaces
c) By using steering wheels

Helicopters

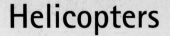

Helicopters are the most versatile of all aircraft. They can take off and land vertically and can hover in midair. Helicopters are built in all sizes, from small craft used for business travel to huge craft used to transport goods. Helicopters are also used by emergency services to get to the scene of an accident quickly and easily.

What keeps helicopters in the sky?

Instead of wings, helicopters have at least one set of whirring blades, called rotor blades or rotors. The rotors spin around at high speed, acting like huge propellers to pull helicopters up into the air. This lift effect is reduced by speed, so helicopters usually cruise at only 81 to 149 miles per hour (130 to 240km/h), much slower than most airplanes.

Why do helicopters have extra rotors on their tails?

Without tail rotors, helicopters would spin around in circles. The turning of the tail rotors creates forces that are opposite to the ones created by the main rotor blades, preventing the spinning. The tail rotors are also used for steering—changing the angle, or pitch, of the blades alters the direction the helicopter flies in.

Why are helicopters ideal for rescue work?

Helicopters are the most maneuverable of all aircraft. In the hands of skilled pilots, helicopters can fly very slowly, change direction easily, and even hover directly over one spot, allowing people to be winched on board from below. Helicopters can also land in very confined spaces, so they can access awkward rescue sites.

What is an autogiro?

An autogiro (right) is an aircraft that has a normal propeller at the front to drive it forward, as well as a set of horizontal rotors. Unlike a helicopter, an autogiro's rotors are not powered, but spin freely as the aircraft moves to provide lift for takeoff. Autogiros, invented by engineer Juan de la Cierva, were popular in the 1930s.

How are helicopters used in warfare?

In warfare, helicopters are used to transport troops and equipment. This is because they can land and take off quickly in very confined or awkward spaces near battlefields. In fact, helicopters can remain almost motionless when they hover in the air, so sometimes they do not need to land at all. Some military helicopters are large enough to carry vehicles such as armored cars or troop carriers.

Forward flight—
rotor blades tilted forward

Backward flight—
rotor blades tilted backward

Hovering—
rotor blades at same pitch

Who invented the helicopter?

It is thought that many centuries ago the Chinese made tiny helicopters as toys, but the first serious design for a helicopter as a means of transportation was made by Leonardo da Vinci, the Italian artist. His design had one screw-shaped propeller that aimed to provide lift by winding itself up into the air.

How is a helicopter controlled?

The pilot of a helicopter controls the aircraft by altering the angle, or pitch, of the rotor blades. In the cockpit there are two controls—the collective pitch and the cyclic pitch. These allow the pilot to adjust the blades to the appropriate position for climbing, descending, hovering, or even flying backward.

Spacecraft

In 1957 the Soviet Union sent the first satellite, *Sputnik I*, into orbit around Earth—the space age had begun. Since then astronauts have visited the moon, and scientists regularly work on board space stations. At first astronauts traveled in tiny capsules, sent into space by single-use rockets. Now they use space shuttles—spacecraft that can be used again and again, just like airplanes.

How are space shuttles launched?

Space shuttles are launched by being blasted into the sky by a pair of rockets, which are fueled from a huge tank that sits between them. When the shuttle has left Earth's atmosphere, the rockets parachute back to Earth, where they are collected and recycled. The fuel tank has to be discarded.

What is escape velocity?

Earth has a strong gravitational pull, so a lot of power is needed to get away from the planet and into space. Spacecraft use rockets—the only devices with the power to fly at the speed required to escape Earth's gravity. This speed, known as escape velocity ("velocity" means "speed"), is about 7 miles per second (11km/sec). Because of the pull of gravity, shuttles do not need the rockets when they return to Earth.

What can space shuttles carry?

Space shuttles are large craft that carry astronauts as well as scientific equipment, which is used to conduct experiments once the shuttle is in orbit. Shuttles also carry satellites, which are released into Earth's orbit. The satellites are used for communications or for sending back information about the weather.

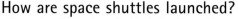

What was the first creature in space?

The first creature in space was a dog named Laika (right), who spent a week in orbit on board the Soviet *Sputnik 2* in 1957. The first human in space was Soviet astronaut Yuri Gagarin, who left Earth in *Vostok I* on April 12, 1961.

Where do space stations get power?

Space stations run mainly on solar power. They have huge panels of solar cells, called solar arrays. The arrays gather sunlight, which is converted into electricity. This means that space stations do not need to carry fossil fuels like coal or oil.

Solar panels

Mir space station

Can astronauts travel outside their spacecraft?

Astronauts may need to go outside their spacecraft in order to perform external repairs. Astronauts wear extravehicular mobility units (EMUs) and must either remain attached to the spacecraft or operate manned maneuvering units (MMUs). MMUs are special backpacks with rocket thrusters that control direction and movement (left).

What are probes?

Space probes are crewless spacecraft that collect data. They are able to send beautiful images back to Earth from outer space. Fly-by probes gather information as they pass different planets. Orbiters fly toward a target planet, go into orbit around it, and observe it over a long period. Landing probes send craft down to a planet's surface. Probes use the gravitational pull from planets to travel.

A Viking probe orbits Mars

Can you drive a car in space?

Special cars called moon buggies or lunar rovers (right) have been driven on the surface of the moon. In 1997 a small rover traveled over the rocky surface of Mars as part of the Mars Pathfinder project. This rover, called *Sojourner*, was remote-controlled and could journey only a short distance.

Unusual Transportation

Some forms of transportation cannot be categorized as cars, trains, boats, or airplanes. New vehicles have been invented because of the need to travel in difficult conditions, such as snow, ice, or steep ground. Other machines have developed because people keep inventing new forms of transportation to carry us in ways that are faster, easier, or just more fun!

How can people speed through snow?

In the frozen regions of Canada, getting around quickly can be a problem. Canadian inventor Joseph Armand-Bombardier came up with the answer in the 1930s—a vehicle with tracks powered by a gasoline engine at the back, with steerable, skilike runners at the front. These first snowmobiles were used by the army as troop carriers, but today's vehicles are smaller, designed for one person to ride like a motorcycle (below).

How do people build a railroad where there is not enough room?

They build a monorail. A monorail is a railroad that runs on a single rail. There are two main types—those that run on rails on the ground and those that run along overhead rails (above). In some cities, the overhead rail system has been used to save space on the ground.

Which type of transportation is the most fun?

Simple, cheap devices like skateboards, rollerblades, and ice skates allow people to speed around and have a lot of fun. It is even possible to play sports and perform tricks while using them—with a little practice!

When is drag useful?

Drag—resistance from the air—is a problem for many forms of transportation because it slows them down. Parachutists, however, rely on drag for a safe landing. The large canopy of a parachute is the opposite of streamlined— it is large and rounded to trap as much air as possible to slow descent.

Canopy

Steering lines

Quick-fire Quiz

1. What type of engine is used to power a jetski?
a) A diesel engine
b) A water-jet engine
c) A steam-jet engine

2. Which part of a snowmobile can be steered?
a) The runners
b) The tracks
c) The wheels

3. What do parachutes rely on?
a) Heat
b) Streamlining
c) Drag

4. What is the rail that is laid between railroad tracks in a mountainous area called?
a) The rack rail
b) The pinion rail
c) The cog rail

What is a personal watercraft?

A personal watercraft is a small vessel like a watergoing motorcycle, also known as a jetski. Jetskis carry one or two people quickly through the waves. They are powered by water-jet engines, which force water out of the crafts' sterns, creating forces like the ones from jet engines on aircraft.

How can people travel up steep mountains?

In mountainous areas a third rail, called a rack rail, is laid between the two normal train tracks. The rack rail is toothed and connects to cog wheels, or pinion wheels, under the carriages of the train. This locks the train tight to the track. Cable cars, which travel along cables strung between high towers, are also used, because they avoid contact with the ground altogether.

Web Addresses

www.brainpop.com

This kids' science, technology, and health site offers lively graphics, quizzes, and movies. Perform experiments in the company of Bob the Rat, and ask Tim and Moby, Tim's friendly robot, any science and technology questions that you have. There are lots of activities on this site, and for each one you can earn points and win prizes.

www.enchantedlearning.com

Visit Zoom Inventor and Inventions on this site to find out about many different types of transportation and navigation, from the airplane, Aqua-Lung, and astrolabe to traffic lights and windshield wipers.

travel.howstuffworks.com

This is a very useful site for children and young adults that covers topics such as cars, engines, aviation, space travel, jets, GPS, Concorde, roller coasters, hot-air balloons, air-traffic control, and even how time travel *could* work!

www.bbc.co.uk/education/dynamo/history/show.htm

This site offers fun animations and games for younger children, showing how types of transportation, such as trains and planes, have changed over the years.

www.ltmuseum.co.uk

This site for the Transport Museum in London, England, is a resource for teachers, parents, and other adults and offers information on the museum and events, as well as access to other resources. A kids' site called The Wheelies offers facts, figures, and quizzes, and Busabout gives a history of London's buses.

www.nasm.si.edu/wrightbrothers/

The Smithsonian National Air and Space Museum online, with an introduction to Wilbur and Orville Wright, a history of flight and flying machines, the restoration of the Wright Flyer, plus interactive experiments and classroom activities.

www.faa.gov/education/kidcornr.cfm

A fun site from the Federal Aviation Authority, separated into age groupings, aimed at kids from five years to teenagers. It offers plenty of activities, from coloring books to crosswords and easy experiments to do at home, including how to make styrofoam gliders and paper helicopters.

www.kidgrid.com/kgmachines.htm

This site lists many useful links to transportation, inventions, and technology web sites.

www.transport-pf.or.jp/english

This is a superb web site for kids, covering all aspects of transportation, from its history to the future. Follow the Tran family on travel adventures and play transportation games.

inventors.about.com/library/inventors/blrailroad.htm

The history of the railroad. Includes links to information about other types of transportation.

inventors.about.com/library/inventors/blcar.htm

The history of the development of the motor car.

Quick-fire Quiz
ANSWERS

Page 245 Early Transportation
1. b 2. a 3. a 4. c

Page 247 Cars
1. b 2. c 3. a 4. c

Page 249 Race Cars
1. a 2. b 3. b 4. c

Page 251 Trucks
1. c 2. b 3. a 4. b

Page 253 Special Vehicles
1. b 2. b 3. b 4. c

Page 255 Trains
1. c 2. b 3. a 4. a

Page 257 Bicycles
1. b 2. b 3. c 4. a

Page 259 Motorcycles
1. b 2. a 3. b 4. b

Page 261 Boats
1. b 2. b 3. a 4. c

Page 263 Ships
1. b 2. c 3. a 4. b

Page 265 Submarines
1. a 2. c 3. a 4. b

Page 267 Hovercraft and Hydrofoils
1. c 2. b 3. a 4. a

Page 269 Airplanes
1. a 2. c 3. a 4. b

Page 371 Gliders
1. a 2. c 3. b 4. a

Page 273 Helicopters
1. a 2. b 3. a 4. b

Page 275 Spacecraft
1. c 2. c 3. a 4. b

Page 277 Unusual Transportation
1. b 2. a 3. c 4. a

1,000 QUESTIONS & ANSWERS FACTFILE

INDEX